HOPEFUL

OMID DJALILI

D1390497

headline

First published in 2014
by HEADLINE PUBLISHING GROUP

First published in paperback in 2015
by HEADLINE PUBLISHING GROUP

2

Cataloguing in Publication Data is available from the British Library

ISBN 978 1 4722 1866 7

Typeset in Life by Palimpsest Book Production Ltd, Falkirk, Stirlingshire
Printed and bound in Great Britain by Clays Ltd, St Ives plc

Headline's policy is to use papers that are natural, renewable and
recyclable products and made from wood grown in sustainable forests.
The logging and manufacturing processes are expected to conform to
the environmental regulations of the country of origin.

MIX
Paper from
responsible sources
FSC® C104740

HEADLINE PUBLISHING GROUP
An Hachette UK Company
338 Euston Road
London NW1 3BH

www.headline.co.uk
www.hachette.co.uk

For Isabella, Louis, and Daniel

'Be thou not hopeless under any circumstances, but rather be firm in thy hope.'

Bahá'í writings

CHAPTER ONE

The Bearcat

'For myself I am an optimist – it does not seem to be much use to be anything else.'

Winston Churchill

Bearcat Comedy Club in Twickenham, 9 March 1996

It sounds like it should possess an edgy glamour, but in reality, the Bearcat is a scout hut in Whitton. I was one of two 'open spots' performing that night; the other was an extremely good-looking, long-haired, half-Indian bloke. I'd done the Edinburgh Festival the summer before and, fuelled by an alarming off-the-Richter-scale supply of self-belief, I wrote to all the comedy clubs in London listed in *Time Out*:

Hello, my name is Omid. You might have heard of me as the 'Short Fat Kebab-Shop Owner's Son', having just stormed the Edinburgh Festival ('a stand-up caught between cultural icons like Ayatollah Khomeini and Dickie Davies' – the Independent). I'm writing now to say I would be willing to come to your comedy club establishment to perform comedy. I can offer a

1 hour, 45-min or a 25-min set. Finance is negotiable. Get back to me ASAP.

Several weeks later, nothing. Then a lone phone call from a bloke called Grahame:

'Hello, is that Kebab?'

'Yes.'

'Got your letter. Come down and do five. If you're good you can come back and do a paid ten. If you're not, try again next year.'

I arrived at a dark and smoky function room connected to the Turk's Head pub, and was greeted by Grahame, a tall man with an impressive moustache, who ushered me towards a 'backstage area' with no door that provided the audience with candid scenes of performers preparing to go on stage. Already weird. There I was welcomed by James, another tall man who ran the club with Grahame. They both had day jobs as school teachers. James even did his introductions holding a black folder, rather like a headmaster at a rather more interesting than usual school assembly.

On this auspicious occasion, James introduced me with a sense of wry mystery: 'And now, something from Iran.' Remarkably, my five minutes went down well. I had a few crowd-pleasing gags which I felt a little ashamed about, but my shame lessened having followed the half-Indian bloke, whose disastrous five minutes included repeating the line 'Trust me, I'm a doctor', his signature catchphrase, to general apathy and bemusement. His set ended in a flame of heckles and chants of 'Off! Off! Off!' After the gig I learned that he had been doing comedy for three years and insisted positively that this gig had 'been quite good, actually'. I was surprised to find out that he also worked as a promoter and even more surprised when he promptly offered me £50 to come to Wimbledon and do his comedy night. This was on top of getting booked for a further ten-minute slot at the Bearcat. The ball was well and truly rolling.

The next week I turned up at the venue in Wimbledon (now the Polka Children's Theatre). I'd been worrying excessively about how to begin my act, having been listening to bootleg tapes of Lenny Bruce. I had somehow convinced myself that I had to replace funny with 'important issues' and social commentary. I had practised in front of the mirror (a technique well honed in fringe theatre) – speaking first in a droll manner then shouting ideas cultivated to challenge preconceptions and make the audience think as well as laugh. I had my heart set on a strong current-affairs opening with a statement about Mad Cow Disease, which had featured heavily in the news that day. I was armed and ready.

As I waited anxiously backstage I observed the act before me, a comic performing 'alternative ventriloquism'; i.e. purposefully low level and appalling. The synch of the man's speech with his puppet was all wrong, like a badly dubbed Chinese kung fu movie, and it was getting big laughs. He even had a finale that involved drinking beer and trying to talk at the same time. Clearly unable to achieve this proficiently, his puppet opened its mouth and all the audience could hear were noises of the comedian garbling into his pint glass. Mind-bogglingly raucous laughter ensued. I knew I had to be on top of my game to follow that.

I'd already decided that when I was introduced I would come bounding ironically on to the stage like a Shakespearean actor. Unfortunately the introduction I received was less than inspiring – 'Please will you welcome Omar Darjeeling!' (it took a full year before anyone got my name right on the comedy circuit) – nevertheless I pranced onto the stage regardless, hoping to fill the space with the most expansive presence I could muster.

Unaware of the location of the recent beer spillage, I headed nimbly straight into a puddle, slipped and fell hard. For a moment it seemed that my body was flying horizontally mid-air. The audience hooted with delight. As I picked myself up and clambered to the microphone, still trying to figure out what had happened, I realised that the microphone was firmly attached to its stand and refused to budge. As I struggled to pull it out, the audience started to titter again. A slow but steady comedy instinct pulsed within me, and told me to keep up the physical struggling, as this seemed to be getting laughs. At one point it must have looked like I was wrestling with the microphone stand, as the mic stubbornly resisted my attempts to remove it from its base. When it finally popped out (unexpectedly), it banged into my head violently and with such force that a three-inch cut appeared across my brow. I shouted 'Ow!' in genuine pain. By this time the audience were clapping.

Trying to soldier on from this series of unfortunate events, I started speaking but realised that I was barely audible. I'd pulled the mic so hard that the cord had also disconnected. My rather formal opening pleasantries were met with shouts of: 'The lead's come out, you twat!' (one heckle amongst other obscenities). As I looked down, I took a step forward to pick up the cord but didn't register how close I was to the edge of the stage. The white tape they use to define the edge nowadays was not compulsory then – and I fell head-first off the platform. I remember looking up at the ceiling from the floor and noticing the pretty wooden panels under the roof. In a brief snatched moment of relaxation I marvelled at how the reflected beams from the theatre lights gave the place an almost Gothic aesthetic. I even wondered if Dracula's castle in Transylvania looked a bit like that?

Presumably I was still in a daze from the fall, but I slowly came to, and was helped back up by punters who were telling me: 'Brilliant, mate. You can't stop now, keep going.' I tried to pull myself up swiftly, but realised the stage was rather too high for me to do anything with elegance, let alone athleticism. That ship had sailed. I was left with no choice other than to heave my left leg up and, stomach first, 'walrus' back into the spotlight. Sadly, as I lifted my leg, I stretched a little too ambitiously and my black trousers ripped on cue, suddenly revealing a patch of bright, white underwear. Again the audience laughed and clapped their appreciation. As I shuffled chest-first on to the stage, my grey shirt soaked up all the remaining spilled beer.

I slowly rose and gathered myself before my audience. I was sweaty, concussed, wet-shirted and bleeding heavily from a large vertical cut on my forehead, but still determined to complete my five-minute set. Catching my breath I waited for the noise to die down and simply said, in all sincerity, as no one could have predicted this particular sequence of disasters:

'Sorry . . . can I start again?'

CHAPTER TWO

Beginnings

'Don't be satisfied with stories, how things have gone with others. Unfold your own myth.'

Rumi, thirteenth-century Persian poet

I was born one sunny afternoon at St Mary Abbots Hospital off the Marloes Road in Kensington at 3.52 p.m. on Thursday 30 September 1965, the youngest child of Ahmad and Parvaneh Djalili. My parents had come from Tehran to London in 1958, the year my brother Javid was born. My sister Roxana followed in 1961 after which I, according to my mother, 'popped out with unusual ease'. It seems they finally got it right third time round. Actually, my parents never said this, but I always thought they should have done.

Before leaving Iran my father was a photographer, manager and chief salesman of a photographic shop called 'Photo Cinemayi'. Not many people possessed cameras in Iran in the 1950s so the only way to preserve memories from special events was to invite the most important guest – the person who owned the camera. It was also considered the height of fashion to dress up in your best clothes and visit Photo Cinemayi for group family tableaux. Not all his commissions were quite so congenial. He also covered the odd public hanging. He once told me how he even 'admired' the courage of one Turkish criminal who shouted at the jeering onlookers: 'You lot can all kiss my behind!', making the crowd surge towards him in anger. The man's final words were: 'One by one, if you don't mind.'

Interestingly, my father first laid eyes on my mother at the wedding of his good friend Ata Samii. Ata was marrying my mother's older sister Baraz, and my father was invited as both close friend and photographer. Although my mother Parvaneh was only fifteen at the time, my father became instantly smitten – and began a long and patient wait during the ten years it took until she agreed to marry him. In fact many of the photos from Ata and Baraz's wedding that day are shots of my mother, some in soft focus, unashamedly showing his obvious fixation.

Parvaneh was beautiful, extrovert and vivacious, no doubt appealing to my father's more reticent temperament. She came from Shemiran, a wealthy suburb to the north of Tehran, where the air was cleaner and the houses grander with large gardens and grounds. My mother attended the Noorbakhsh high school for girls in Tehran, a progressive institution where the girls, reminiscent of Communist China, would do morning exercises in unison before first lesson. The school specialised in churning out an impressive array of female scientists. My mother, however, chose to pursue domestic science, with a particular emphasis on dressmaking skills.

After school she became a confident and creative dressmaker, with the capacity to recreate her favourite 1940s and '50s styles just from observing them closely in her favourite British and American movies. Her love of dressmaking continued after she moved to London and for a while she assisted the famous Iranian singer Googoosh who stayed with us sometimes, and sought fashion tips from my mother. Apparently my mother also gave her advice on how to manage quick costume changes during live shows. I remember them laughing hysterically together in a practice dry run as Googoosh struggled, trapped within vast folds of sequined material because a button from her dress had caught in one of her complicated hair ornaments. Not being able to see where she was going, she keeled over and crashed into the tea table. I remember feeling in awe of their hilarity.

My parents eventually married in 1957 and in 1958 they decided to leave Iran and move to London for a short while. My mother, being eight years younger than my father, wanted travel and adventure. She joked that 'take me to London' was her prerequisite to accepting my father's proposal. As an aspiring dress designer, she was keen to experience the culture and excitement of Europe and the opportunities afforded in the West. My father was only too happy to oblige.

When they arrived in London, my father became a 'local liaison officer' at the Imperial Iranian Embassy. Much of his work involved helping fellow Iranians who had come over for medical assistance. In addition, he continued his role as photographer, taking copious professional photos at Embassy functions and parties, which would appear in the Iranian newspaper, *Kayhan*.

Although my parents were excited to be in London, they always assumed they would return home to Iran at some point. The Islamic Revolution in 1979 put an abrupt halt to that plan. But they showed a great degree of foresight and tenacity in building up a sideline business to support themselves after the Iranian Embassy changed hands. A business that would shape my entire life.

My parents started taking in lodgers almost as soon as they arrived in London. This part of their work began gradually. It grew out of a Persian custom – when you went overseas you would stay with 'friends of friends', and pay a little something to your host for costs and expenses. This slowly turned into the main family income. During this period, my mother embraced a new role as capable tour guide and gained great expertise in taking sprawling and talkative groups of Iranians around the London sights. As well as standard photo opportunities by famous landmarks (once nearly getting arrested for trying to remove a Queen's Guard's hat in Whitehall just to get a reaction, having heard they are trained never to react to anything), my mother's 'tours' also included visits to the Lyceum Ballroom in the Strand, the Hammersmith Palais and the Empire Leicester Square. She also introduced bewildered Iranians to her favourite shows, *Oh! Calcutta!*, *Hair* and the mildly outrageous *The Romans in Britain*. Whereas the nudity in these shows outraged London's West End, most of the Iranian guests took it in their stride, assuming it was a theatrical representation of a factual documentary.

I've often wondered whether, if she were born into a different culture or era, my mother might have been a fashion designer or even a rather excellent comedienne. She certainly 'loved a joke', as they say, and I often heard her on the phone to Iran laughing hysterically at some new gag that was doing the rounds (like the way they do on social media these days) and then rushing to tell my dad. She was a well-known heckler at Iranian functions, her interjections always getting a laugh or a clap – her most popular, in response to long unwieldy talks by overly verbose Iranian speakers, being '*de begoo digheh!*' (get on with it!).

When I was three it was decided that I should attend the local nursery school. Unfortunately my nursery career ended on the first day when I threw up and was promptly dispatched home. This incident provided an unfortunate metaphor that could also be applied to my later relationship with formal education. However, in my defence, on this particular occasion I had become increasingly terrified because the language I heard, understood and spoke at home did not correspond to the language I was hearing for the first time. In fact, I felt out of synch with my environment in every conceivable way. They played, I watched. They lay down contentedly for a nap, I remained rigidly awake on a crumb-infested and milk-stained pink corduroy bean-bag. Why my father had insisted I take this pink corduroy bean-bag with me to the nursery is still a mystery but at least it gave me somewhere to sit awake and stare at the other children as they slept.

Adrenaline was coursing through my veins and at one point I presumed I'd been kidnapped. This anxiety drove me to the refuge of the toilet whereupon I vomited with a great violence. Before I knew it, I was perched on my favourite window seat back home, minding my own business, playing with the occasional toy car, but mostly staring blankly at the street below. If only they'd left me alone in the first place, everyone would have been spared the hassle. I vowed to be master of my own destiny thereafter.

Luckily, when I turned four, I found a playmate called Sarah. She lived in the flat directly above us and had short dark hair, rosy cheeks and red patterned dresses that made her look like a Russian matryoshka doll. My friendship with Sarah spanned almost a year, and her home became my unofficial kindergarten.

Her flat was considerably larger and tidier than mine. It was 1969 and the design was 'open plan' – light, minimalist and airy with modern décor, which gave it a futuristic science-fiction movie vibe. Though completely opposite to what I was used to, I felt comfortable and grew attached to the place. I don't remember much about my interactions with Sarah beyond a blurry recollection of us quietly exchanging coloured bricks back and forth. However I did enjoy the high-quality healthy snacks provided by her mother, and particularly remember homemade popcorn as a rare delicacy. I also appreciated the light jazz music buzzing in the background. What you'd call 'vibey'.

Being so used to my own company I was unusually relaxed playing with Sarah and don't remember any conflict. Once, out of the blue, she told me I was her best friend. I wasn't sure what 'best friend' actually meant because Sarah was, to date, my only friend. If anything this declaration alarmed me as I hadn't considered the existence of Sarah having any other friends either.

After my first few visits to Sarah's flat, rather than asking to be taken there, I habitually began to make my own way upstairs, even packing a few cars as my personal contribution to our play session. Leaving the shadowy world of adults to rage on without me, I would climb one flight of stairs, and knock on Sarah's door three times. On seeing me she would calmly fetch the bricks and off we went, happily occupied for the next couple of hours. It was a good arrangement. After a while Sarah's mother produced some plastic farm animals and a round yellow wheel that made animal sounds when a cord was pulled. We honed our burgeoning cognitive and linguistic skills by providing voices for pigs, sheep and chickens. The animals usually conversed in polite American accents, as we were heavily influenced by Sarah's experience of *Sesame Street* on a recent US holiday. Sadly Sarah never visited me downstairs. My mother was grateful that I was occupied but – perhaps due to so much responsibility with our guests – didn't feel confident enough to return the compliment. Possibly Sarah's mother also preferred our friendship to take place under her supervision. It was a given that my home was too destabilising for a British four-year-old.

One day I ran up the stairs and knocked as usual, but was confused to find a strange older lady instead of Sarah's mother.

'I'm sorry, little chap, Sarah doesn't live here any more. She's gone away.'

I felt a sharp, sad feeling in my throat and a lurching sensation in my stomach. For a brief, deluded moment I chose to assume 'away' meant an actual place. I asked when she was coming back.

'She's not coming back. They've moved.'

Some important lessons were learned that day:

1) No one tells me anything.
2) Girls could not be trusted.
3) Life is unpredictable and full of unbearable shocks.
4) A pink corduroy bean-bag is no substitute for a best friend.
5) I'm going to have abandonment issues when I'm older.

CHAPTER THREE

The Unfortunate Coconut Incident

'A fool thinks himself to be wise, but a wise man knows himself to be a fool.'

William Shakespeare

By the time I started primary school I was ready for company, having recovered from the memory of that dreadful day at nursery school, and then the shock of Sarah's departure. I had spent a long time staring out of the window as I listened to Persian radio and observed the various guests go about their business. It was a pleasant surprise to realise that I could share some of the day with peers my own age, and even run around outside. So I was glad to take my place at St Mary Abbots C of E infant school, tucked away in a discreet corner at the bottom of Church Street off High Street Kensington in west London. Unfortunately, it was never without angst.

1971, Show and Tell

A teacher in a stylish pink trouser suit stood at the front of a small hall with two coconut shells, one in each hand. I was six years old, sitting on the floor in the back row. Most days I wore a white polo-necked jumper and sported wild untamed curls. My eyes were already shadowed with dark circles due to excess TV and anxious preoccupations regarding life on other planets.

Miss Staples was in her late twenties, and possessed that mix of cuteness and respectability that seems to be character- istic of so many primary school teachers. I remember her showing us these strange objects and, not recognising them, my mind began to wander. Perhaps Miss Staples might go shopping later? Or meet her fiancé? He was a man called Steve who sometimes collected her from school in his Morris Minor. He wore heavy sideburns and had feathery hair like David Cassidy. I once saw them in Kensington Gardens, pouring cups of tea from a tartan-patterned flask and sharing an apple, passing it back and forth between them and taking turns to bite. They also had a packet of Kit-Kats lying next to them on the rug. It seemed like the height of romantic bliss. On another occasion I saw them holding hands outside a newsagent. It was electri- fying.

'Does anyone know what these are?'

A few swotty types raised their hands.

'Coconuts!'

'Yes, well done. Lovely, aren't they?'

The children who knew went 'hmmmm'.

I knew about apples, oranges and bananas. I even knew about pomegranates. I'd never heard the word 'coconut'. I wondered if I'd ever get the chance to taste one. I listened intently.

'Coconuts are a fruit. They have hard shells but at the centre there's delicious coconut water, and white bits that are chewy and crunchy.'

Miss Staples had a way with words. I imagined the taste of whipped cream flecked with pieces of ginger biscuits, and licked my lips.

'These are coconut *shells*. Do you know what sound they make if you bang them together?'

A hushed silence fell in the hall. It was a good question. If I had them in my possession, I'd definitely do something with those shells. My brain went into overdrive. 'Stick the shells together and use it as a football?' was the best I had, but I guessed Miss Staples wouldn't respond to that idea, so I kept quiet.

She asked again. 'There must be someone who knows?'

There wasn't.

'Well, if you hit the shells together, gently, it makes a "clopping" sound, like a horse trotting. Can you hear it?'

The assemblage looked on in amazement. The perfect sound of a horse trotting filled the hall. Some children looked startled and twisted around to see if Black Beauty had appeared.

'Does anyone want to come up and have a go?'

I shot my arm up immediately. Miss Staples looked around the room to see who was capable. She pointed at a girl in the front row.

'Ruth Stevens.'

I was gutted but I understood why Ruth was chosen. All she ever did at break times was pretend to be a horse. Her commitment to horses was not in question. Ruth took the coconut shells, banged them in a rather perfunctory manner, but received a well-deserved round of applause.

'Well done, Ruth! Anyone else like to have a go?'

I threw my hand up, whispering passionately *'please! please!'* but this time she chose a boy with glasses who didn't even look like he cared. He banged the coconut shells, with very little heart in my opinion, though he also received encouraging applause and a beaming smile from Miss Staples. This felt wholly undeserved and my stomach churned in the face of the injustice.

'We might have time for one more . . .'

My arm went up. This time I decided to make eye contact with Miss Staples, trying to fix her gaze and show sincerity by impressing her with my cool and silent dignity.

'Anyone else?'

'ME!' I screamed from the back. 'ME! *PLEASE!*'

'Well, Omid, seeing as you seem to really want to . . .'

I remember wincing at this remark, knowing that it was slightly sarcastic and disrespectful. I let it go; as a six-year-old I'd learned to develop a thick skin to avoid chronic emotional breakdown. Besides, I was easily pleased. I was going to bang the shells in front of everyone and couldn't wait. In truth, I was elated. I tried to conceal my irrepressible excitement, but I could feel my face heat up, as I walked past all the children on the floor and took centre stage.

'Here you are.' She handed over the shells, and I received them ceremoniously. I looked at the crowd, savouring the moment. I clopped the shells together and waited for the applause. *My* applause.

But instead of applause, a roar came from my classmates. Laughter. I was horrified. Huge peals of laughter, children falling backwards and pointing. Confused, I looked up at Miss Staples for validation, for reassurance . . . but even she seemed to be restraining herself from laughing.

I had no idea what had just happened. I sat back down, humiliated. I felt like an alien. Worse, I thought I'd done something terribly wrong. Why did the others get applause but everyone laughed at me? Had I misunderstood what I was supposed to do? Had I missed some crucial nuance that was critical to mastering this simple task?

It's strange to think that, although I enjoyed being in the spotlight from a young age, I hated laughter as a child. Here it was aimed at me, towards me, and I was crushed. I sat down, hyperventilating and in a state of complete psychological disarray.

I have no memory of what I actually did to provoke such hilarity. Perhaps it was a combination of the off-kilter rhythm of my clopping, the awkward horse movements, or the ecstatic glee on my face that provoked the uproar. It could also be that it was 'just funny'.

Sometimes funny is inexplicable.

Sometimes funny is just funny.

CHAPTER FOUR

'Iran, Ancestral Homeland' – The Motherland

'Ghorboonet beram.'

Iranian saying

I have heard this phrase repeated throughout my life. Its literal meaning translates as: 'May my life be a sacrifice to yours.' It may sound over-dramatic or even sentimental, but there is something so pure and unbridled in the Iranian psyche that whenever it is said, I have never truly doubted that it is meant wholeheartedly. Admittedly *'ghorboonet beram'* is uttered across the whole gamut of social interactions – from heartbreaking airport farewells to expressing thanks for a cup of tea. But for me the ubiquitous usage of the phrase enhances rather than diminishes the levels of sincerity, and sums up the vitality of the Persian spirit.

Iran currently seems to have the grisly distinction of boasting the most horrendous human rights record on the planet. My wish for the people of Iran is that they might reclaim in the eyes of the world their reputation for warmth, humanity, playfulness, generosity and a raucous sense of humour. All of which and more I encountered on my childhood visits to my ancestral homeland.

When I returned from my first visit to Iran, aged two and a half, there was apparently a momentous scene when I spoke to my dad for the very first time. I had left London too young to be able to speak but had come back fluent in Farsi. I greeted my father at Heathrow with: *'Daddy, man farsi yad gereftam'* (Daddy, I learned Farsi). My father was so overjoyed by this statement, and my perfect Tehran accent, that he repeated this anecdote indiscriminately for the next four decades as an example of my linguistic and cultural prowess. *'Een rooza, zeeyad na'* (nowadays, not so much). My dad has a unique gift of stating the obvious with breathtaking tactlessness. I sat next to him as an adult during one of his many retellings of this incident, highlighting my cuteness as a child. He finished by pointing to my head and stomach, saying, *'Chaghi o kachali kharabesh kard'* (fatness and baldness ruined him), followed by, *'Az baski meekhoreh'* (it's because he eats so much), then, *'Maraze'* (it's an illness).

When we set out on this first trip to the land of my ancestors I was voted unanimously the 'life and soul of the party'. I've struggled ever since to regain that status. I probably peaked too early. We were in Iran for my Uncle Parviz's wedding. He was my mother's youngest and best-looking brother, and his bride, Simine, was the archetypal Persian princess beauty. At one point during the wedding ceremony, apparently mesmerised by the bride and groom, I ran to the front of the room where they were about to exchange their vows. The golden couple beamed such a smile of film-star radiance that it stopped me in my tracks. The crowd murmured its delight, as Simine beckoned me to join her saying, *'Beeya aziz'* (come here, darling). Family legend states that I laughed, fell over backwards in true slapstick style, jumped up hastily to rearrange my sailor suit and flew back to my seat on a wave of rapturous applause. My mother added the embellishment that I waved from my chair to acknowledge the crowd. In fact, I think it was her who did that.

It's fair to say, though, that despite being a fairly quiet child I craved the limelight from an early age. There is a picture of me somewhere, aged no more than about nine months old, smiling radiantly at the camera while everyone else is glued to the TV, gripped by the news that the Americans' attempt at a soft landing on the moon by the spacecraft *Surveyor 1* had been successful. I've been aware of the camera pretty much since I was six months old and yet I did my first Hollywood blockbuster when I was thirty-two. Go figure.

Most people's childhood photos portray a simply smaller yet still recognisable version of their current selves. In my case I'm not sure what went wrong. As a small child I was fair-skinned, curly haired and, dare I say it, impossibly cute. So much in fact that I was constantly cuddled, smothered, thrown around, bear-hugged and had my face pulled and twisted into all manner of contortions. Old home movies show me looking tense in the clutches of animated chatting adults, blissfully unaware of my desperate struggles to wrestle free.

Memories of Iran on my subsequent trip there, three years later, are more detailed and tremendously vivid. The trip lasted three months and I went with my mother and siblings while my father stayed behind in London to work. In those days schools didn't seem to query the long absences of children with overseas connections.

After a flight during which the eager pilot alerted our attention to almost every European city we cruised over, I was yearning to disembark. Before I knew it, I found myself hurled into the air by my cousin Soheil. He was only twenty-two at the time, but already balding, burly and bespectacled. Soheil was in fact the eldest son of Ata and Baraz, at whose wedding my parents had first met. He had a manic smile and a frantic energy that left me breathless. With no baggage reclaim, the system for collecting suitcases was rather haphazard – exacerbated perhaps by friends and family surging onto the runway to help (you could do that in Iran in the seventies) while the plane taxied and came to a standstill. I remember feeling overwhelmed by the smell and atmosphere of this new country. Soheil greeted us with that semi-cry we call 'boghz' in Iran (smiling whilst being on the verge of hysterical crying). I think at one point he was actually hyperventilating in an attempt to control his joy. I do remember how uncomfortable it felt to conduct a 'getting to know you' chat while being held aloft.

'You're back! Do you remember me?!'

I didn't, but against my better judgement I nodded yes.

Feverish with excitement, he shrieked: 'You do? What's my name?!'

Looking down at him from a great height, with the dim glow of the red sunset falling on the runway stretching out behind him and the sound of the plane's engines winding down in my ears, I said:

'Uncle Parviz?'

His face changed immediately.

'NO!'

My heart sank.

'Soheil! I'm Soheil!' He looked offended and devastated and for a second I thought he was going to drop me. In actual fact he didn't mind at all and it became apparent that my mother's family had a particularly keen sense of melodrama. The subtext of this vignette, I later deciphered, went something like this: 'If I didn't know you and love you I'd kill you for not remembering me. But as we're family I'll let you off.' He kept pretending to hit me then would start crying again in his state of 'boghz'. The whole family were in fact nutty and unpredictable, and I was often rendered speechless in their presence.

(I feel obliged to record that Soheil is now a highly respected knee surgeon living in California and is an extremely dignified and successful man, although he has never lost his infectious and volatile sense of *joie de vivre*. Having said that, I'm still a bit scared of him, mostly because of a genuine fear he might overwhelm me with his love and crush me to death by sitting on me.)

We arrived at my grandparents' house outside the city in a suburb of Tehran called Shemiran. Off the main road a short beaten track flanked by dense bushes led to a relatively small three-tiered house fronted by a huge garden. I'd heard about the garden. My heart pounded with excitement. It was actually the size of a football pitch with trees dotted about randomly, a pond in the middle, a large shed, and a massive open space where I imagined I could chase myself, shoot at myself and hide from myself. I often played alone. I wasn't lonely, I just couldn't cope with interruptions from my siblings when engaged in my personal fantasies. It disrupted the narrative. It was autumn and the trees gave off a reddish-brown hue, and the grass was thickly covered with fallen leaves. I saw dogs and shouted in English, 'Mummy, doggies!' She replied, '*Vahshee'an*' (they're wild), and sharply made me promise never to go near them.

As we approached the front door, a tiny little pixie woman rushed out with a stick to shoo the dogs away from the drive. My mother ran to her and there was more hysterical hugging and sobbing. This was Sakineh, the housekeeper who had helped raise my mother. I was hugged too but I was distracted. Looking back at the raggedy Alsatians, now loitering in the distance, staring sadly back as if jealous of human family connections and resigned to a bitter life of pointless roaming and loneliness, I made a mental note to relieve them of their torment.

My grandparents were happy to see me, but as grandchild no. 9 I instinctively knew I wasn't a huge priority in the great scheme of things and sloped off as soon as I could. My brother and sister joined me and we played games like 'Blind Man's Buff', 'Follow my Leader's Footsteps' and 'It'. We even walked around singing church songs we'd learned at school like 'Michael Row the Boat Ashore, Halleluya'. I didn't even know who this Michael was, but the song kept me connected to life in England, and I felt *this* was incredibly important. England was surrounded by water, after all, and rowing a boat ashore would make sense if our plane home had to make an emergency stop in France. Singing the song therefore became part of my personal discipline – a reminder to be on the alert for unexpected crises.

As the days rolled on we met other Iranian children who lived in the area. They joined us and we all used the garden as a kind of adventure playground. Knowing we were from Britain they were keen to learn English. Linking arms and roaming around the garden we taught them 1970s pop songs. There were varying degrees of enthusiasm for this activity, based on the catchiness of the songs, and how much we all understood of the lyrics.

The Jacksons always went down well. 'ABC, 1, 2, 3' was very easy to learn and appropriately educational. 'Raindrops Keep Fallin' on my Head' from the film *Butch Cassidy and the Sundance Kid* was another favourite. The film had miraculously made it to Iran, and Robert Redford and Paul Newman were perceived as benign blond demi-gods. But the song that really got everyone going was 'Kumbaya'. The kids thought 'Kumbaya' was a funny word and sang it enthusiastically in a faux-English haughty way. They even put special emphasis on the first syllable changing it to '*kun*' as it meant 'bottom' in Farsi. They also changed the 'baya' to '*beeya*', which in Farsi translates as 'here you are'. Many an uproarious hour was spent striding around my grandfather's garden with local Iranian kids all singing '*Kun-beeya* my Lord, *kun-beeya*', with hands outstretched as if offering a detached pair of buttocks to a king. Satirical comedy doesn't get much better than that.

Our British loyalties were keenly observed by the other children, never more noticeably than when we defied our elders by welcoming the wild dogs into the garden. In true British fashion we named them and they became our dear faithful friends. Rover and Snoopy were two of the regulars but Hamlet and Reza (he looked more Iranian for some reason) joined intermittently. Obviously we kept our new friendships quiet because we knew we'd get into trouble if the adults found out. Dogs were seldom domesticated in Iran, but we felt a sense of expertise because we'd handled pets at friends' houses in England. 'Give them love and they'll love you back' my sister would prounounce sagely, and the Iranian kids marvelled at our skills. We became dog whisperers, stroking them, giving them bits of leftover kebab, interpreting their tail wagging and barking rhythms. It was a miracle that we didn't get ripped to shreds. My brother even tried to place me on the back of one so I could imagine I was riding a horse. Hamlet put a stop to this by growling viciously. We all ran away in different directions, as did the dogs. Our mystic canine bubble had burst.

As the weather turned cooler we stayed inside more. I have a distinct memory of being fed crushed bananas while watching Disney cartoons dubbed into Farsi. I observed the women of the house, who were industriously engaged in dressmaking, handicrafts, complex emotional conversations and elaborate cooking. The men appeared to be less active and tended to recline on the comfortable sofas, satiated and mammalian, snoring after heavy meals.

We went to '*mehmoonis*' (house parties) and generally socialised with a vast array of family members and friends. Looking back, I think my mother needed to feel reconnected with her family and to give her children a sense of their cultural heritage. By and large this is what happened, although not always in ways she would have expected . . .

CHAPTER FIVE

The Incredible Snowball Fight

'Respond to every call that excites your spirit.'

Rumi

By the time December came, Tehran was hit with massive snow-falls. We were returning home from yet another lunch when we became stuck in a traffic jam caused by the snow. I was perched in the front seat with my mother, her arms perhaps holding me more tightly than usual because two nights earlier, I'd been fiddling unsupervised with one of the back doors, fascinated by the handle's complicated design. Unfortunately, during this fiddling, I pressed the handle down too hard, where-upon it flung open at 70 miles an hour. The momentum it took to push the door open meant that I also went swinging outwards (no one wore seatbelts in those days). Those micro moments whizzing above the motorway seemed to last forever, as I was suspended in the air, floating desperately between the door and the tarmac. Thankfully, quick as a flash my mother had grabbed me by the collar and yanked me back with the fury of a lioness with a recalcitrant cub. A *Keystone Cops*-like episode followed, with uncles shouting, gesticulating and struggling to tame the flapping door as we bowled along. I must have been in shock because I wasn't quite aware I was being told off. And it didn't seem to occur to anyone that I hadn't actually risked my life on purpose.

'Why were you playing with the door?'

'Dropping on the motorway, can you imagine?'

'You be dead . . . flat' – my uncle making a sign with his hand denoting flat – 'like Coyote in *Looney Tune*.'

I'd never heard an uncle say '*Looney Tunes*' before. I convulsed with laughter. Cartoons were my world, plus he forgot to pronounce the *s*. I didn't otherwise respond to the admonishments, so a tutting and head-shaking discussion broke out about children being far 'too curious', probably due to an English education.

After this incident, then, I accepted my current oppressive supervision in the front seat with my mother, despite feeling hot and uncomfortable in the steamed-up car. My mind began to wander. I imagined a massive snowball rolling along the street and gathering up all the stationary cars like a tornado. My brother tried to instigate an 'I spy' game but my uncles misunderstood and instead enacted scenes from French spy films they'd seen recently. This involved them raising their eyebrows, twirling their moustaches and reciting sentences in broken French, which my clever sister Roxana (who went on to become a bilingual French secretary) corrected, imperiously. This frustrated everyone, so it all ground to a halt. After some silence our attention turned to a young man who was sitting alone in an open-top jeep in the stationary line of cars nearby. He must have been about twenty-two and was shivering miserably. My mother said '*ay beechareh*' (poor thing) and we all stared at him for a moment, speculating that he would definitely suffer from rheumatism in later life.

Out of the blue, my brother Javid declared he was going to make a snowball and aim it at this young man. My mother protested *'beechareh kari nakardeh'* (the poor thing's done nothing). A hushed agreement descended in the car and we continued to sit in silence.

A minute later Javid shouted, *'Hala neegashkon!'* (look at him now!). We looked over and saw the man was, rather unfortunately, picking his nose in a most indelicate fashion. My uncles exclaimed, *'Behaya'* (shameless), *'Jeloyeh hameh!'* (in front of everyone!). By unanimous consent we agreed that my mother had been too hasty in curtailing my brother's unprovoked attack. 'PLEASE mum. Can I throw one?' With the air of a queen having now tired of the court jester, my mother coolly assented and my uncle chipped in with *'bezanesh'* (hit him). Javid immediately opened the window and started gathering snow from the roof.

'Vasta!' (wait!) my uncle exclaimed as we saw that the young man now appeared to be preening himself in the front mirror and examining his teeth. *'Sabr kon'* (wait for it). The tension was killing us. My uncle was watching like a hawk. *'Hala!'* (now!), he shouted, and Javid fired off his snowball. To our amazement it hit the guy smack between the ear and back of his head. The poor young man, now in shock, took a few seconds to process what had just happened. Feeling the snow trickle down his neck he looked back at us. We immediately snapped our heads forward, shunning culpability. Javid whispered: 'He's angry. He's making a snowball. What do we do, what do we do?'

My mother coolly instructed, *'Panjareho beband'* (close the window).

Bent on revenge the young man swung his arm back to lob a snowball at us. Suddenly, another snowball came flying in and hit him square in the face! The occupants of the car in front started laughing hysterically. A family, a bit like ours, had followed what was going on and decided to get in on the act.

The young man, now furious, threw his snowball back at them and missed. Suddenly he got pelted again from yet another car behind him, whereupon my brother, getting ready for the next round, received a massive snowball in the face from a different direction. Some other people two cars in front had decided to join the party and had decided that our car was now overdue for a pelting.

Shouting and scampering, people were now urgently getting out of their cars as a full-scale fight broke out. Rows upon rows of vehicles joined. The boy in the open-top jeep was getting smacked from all sides, snow exploding all around him like a white firework display. We, his original assailants, now feeling sorry for him, ardently fought back on his behalf. My mother, who had essentially started the whole thing, shouted out to *'velesh kon!'* (leave him alone!) and began lobbing snowballs to defend him. She even got out of the car at one point and, dodging the flying handfuls of snow, proceeded to give the young man a spare scarf she'd found in the back of our car. People started honking their horns as if it were a street celebration of Iran having qualified for the World Cup. Within minutes the snowball fight had spread across ten rows of cars. Then Javid shouted to me, 'Look!' and I beheld an image now printed in my mind forever: as far as the eye could see, on a road as long at the Champs Élysées in Paris, hundreds of people were out of their cars, men, women and children, in a full-on, manic, gleeful, ecstatic snowball battle. There was no hint of malice anywhere. It was a friendly but hard-fought battle; a battle *we had started*.

As the traffic finally moved on we carried on throwing snowballs at random cars hoping to start fresh skirmishes but the occupants, not having been involved in the original fight, were merely somewhat offended. As we travelled further away from the city, the sound of the odd snowball thudded against our car but soon tapered off. I went to bed quietly proud I belonged to this strange, random, spontaneous land. Could this have happened anywhere else in the world? I shut my eyes that night thinking 'no way', and imagined a life in Iran. I missed England but I began to think maybe I belonged here?

Over lunch the next day my grandfather announced that a temporary sewage problem had affected the house. Toilets could not be flushed for a few days so could we please use the chamber pots he had provided and dispose of their contents in the outdoor pit. Situated in the garden, I'd previously assumed this area was a pond. It was clearly an uncovered cesspit. Naturally, over the next days, the pit rose higher. One afternoon, just as we were all dressed up to go to a special lunch party (I wore a velvet jacket and cravat), my mother said she needed a few more minutes, which realistically meant another half an hour, so Javid and I went outside.

We took advantage of the freshly fallen snow to play 'Follow my Leader's Footsteps', a simple game where my brother walked around in the snow with me obediently following in the exact footprints he left. He swayed in random directions, making a figure of eight, explaining that pigeons walked this way because they had a brain the side of a peanut. He was always a mine of useful information. Inevitably, he walked up towards the cesspit. Like the grass, it too was covered in a thin blanket of snow, and because it was full, the pit was now parallel in height to the grass. Men were supposed to come the next day to empty it after weeks of accumulation.

From a distance my sister started shouting at me. She was far away so I couldn't understand why she was shouting. I heard her say something like: 'You're going in!'

I took this to mean 'come back, we're about to go' but I carried on the game regardless, putting a hand to my ear and shouting: 'I can't hear you!' I even remember how clear the sky was for a cold day and how much I was looking forward to lunch at the Oradpours', who always put on a fine spread. Would it be *Baghali polo* or *Zereshk polo*? I hoped it would be *Fesenjoon*, my favourite Iranian dish, I hadn't had it in a while, so tangy and tasty when made with the correct amount of pomegranates and crushed walnuts.

Then I fell. I didn't know where or how. It didn't hurt but I was definitely not walking any more. I was in a state of semi-flotation. I don't remember any smell, just a slow sinking feeling. I called out to my brother who turned around as if in slow motion. At first he didn't move. I called out again and he inched closer but I didn't understand why he was peering down at me with an expression of incredulity and disgust.

'Help me . . .'

Still, he didn't move, even when I pleaded again.

'I'm sinking!'

The cold excrement had now reached my neck. Sensing I was going under I instinctively doggie paddled (I'd had one swimming lesson at school) but I was sinking fast. I managed to get to the side of the pit and put my arm out to my brother, who was still staring at me with a frozen expression of outrage on his face that said: 'Who are you? I don't know you.' Luckily, he snapped out of it, and coming to his senses, he realised his little brother was going to disappear into excrement oblivion. He hastily offered an arm, as willingly and graciously as you possibly can for another arm thickly coated in human waste, and yanked me out. If he had acted seconds later, then I have no doubt that I would have sunk to the bottom and drowned. I flopped on to the grass like a baby seal born in brown amni-otic fluid. I was covered from chin to toe. My brother was staring incredulously at the filth on his own hand and arm while dry retching – possibly from the shock of my near-miss with death, as well as the cloying, rancid odour emanating from the pair of us. For a moment we had no words and just gazed at each other, panting. Javid came to his senses first: 'You better get inside before it cakes on you.'

My sister had obviously raised the alarm and as I walked zombie-like back to the house, a couple of uncles rushed out and looked at me in horror.

'*Chi shod?!*' (What happened?!)

'*Oftadam tu chaleh ann.*' (I fell in the poo pit.)

'*Tu chahleh goh chera bazieh mikardi?!*' (Why were you playing in the poo pit?!)

'*Vai, bachehayeh emrooz.*' (Bloody hell, the kids of today.)

My mother, not having been informed of this disaster, came bustling out the house looking glamorous and ready to set off for the party. '*Khob, berim. Hazerim?*' (So, let's go. Ready?) Sometimes she really dressed up like a movie star from Hollywood's Golden Age (occasionally a bit too much). And this was one of those occasions. '*Neegash kon,*' (look at him) said one of her brothers, weakly. It took a moment for her to register.

I'd seen American TV programmes where misfortune befalls a child, and the parents always reacted with deep sympathy. 'It's OK Jake, you're with Mommy now,' they would say, and they'd hug and cry together.

My mother exploded.

'*Pedar sageh naneh sag!* (Father dog mother dog!) *Chi kar kardi?!* (What have you done?!) *Vai khodayeh man!* (Oh my God!) *Meekoshamet!* (I'm going to kill you!)'

Sakineh ran ahead, laying down sheets for me to step into the house and up the stairs. I inched forwards, gingerly, amidst hysteria and commotion.

In the bath I was amazed at how rapidly and volcanically the brown stuff cascaded from my body. My mother held the shower head to my neck and started hosing me down, ripping off my clothes and berating me, her luck, my father, everyone, while stray particles flicked on to her beautiful dress.

'*Lebasam! Lebasam!*' (My clothes! My clothes!) she shouted, sobbing between words. '*Cheekar kardam ke be eenja reseedeh?* (What have I ever done to deserve this?) *Ogham gereft* (I'm gonna puke).'

I stood ashamed and impassive, waiting for the moment to pass. Mungo Jerry's 'In the Summertime' came into my mind and drowned my mother's shouting for a bit. I noticed a fleck of something on her necklace. I wondered if I should mention it, but decided to keep quiet.

An hour later my body was buzzing and I felt surprisingly invigorated from the sensation of having been scrubbed within an inch of my life. I kept mute though, as tensions were running high and my mother was still fighting back her exasperated tears. We drove to the lunch party in silence. As we got out the car, my brother whispered to my mother, '*Hanooz boo meedeh*' (he still smells). My mother said, '*Saket*' (quiet), but probably made a mental note to the tell the Oradpours, in case anyone brought it up, that I'd had an accident in my trousers on the way there. She sighed, '*Ay khodayeh man*' (oh God) and then rang the doorbell.

This incident indicates some philosophical implications, namely:

When you try to clean excrement off somebody else, chances are you'll get some on you.

CHAPTER SIX

'Iran, Ancestral Homeland' – The Fatherland

'You were born with wings, why prefer to crawl through life?'

Rumi

Since we were staying mostly with my mother's relatives, I saw less of my father's family. They had a rather different flavour, being somewhat more whimsical. They originated from Tabriz in the north of Iran and had lived at various points in Ishqabad, a city in Turkmenistan that possessed the first Bahá'í House of Worship. Many of my father's ancestors had been poets, musicians and teachers and were amongst some of the earliest Bahá'ís to be persecuted for their faith.*

---

*The Bahá'í Faith began in nineteenth-century Persia, and its adherents believe that all religions come from the same God and are in essence successive chapters of one faith. Bahá'u'lláh, the latest of these messengers, taught the Oneness of God, the Oneness of the human family and the Oneness of religion.

Since the 1979 Islamic Revolution in Iran, Bahá'ís have been systematically persecuted as a matter of government policy. This includes government-controlled propaganda and misrepresentation in the media as the regime continues to seek ways of manipulating the minds of Iranians by painting a prejudiced and inaccurate picture of the Bahá'í community and its teachings. During the first decade of this ongoing persecution more than 200 were tortured, executed or imprisoned and tens of thousands lost their jobs, education and other rights, solely because of religious beliefs. Government-led attacks have re-intensified over the last decade.

However, what has emerged recently is the extraordinary courage of prominent Iranian Muslims within Iran who have publicly defended the rights of the Bahá'ís.

One memory that stands out for me on that trip to Iran relates to my Uncle Ezzat, my father's youngest brother, and a fateful journey we made to Abadan in Southern Iran. It was a few days after the terrible 'pit' incident and my mother had decided to take me and my brother and sister away for the weekend. Waiting for our train, my mother informed us that Uncle Ezzat was going to join us during his lunch hour from work to help us load our suitcases on to the train, and possibly give us some *Pofak namaki* (a crisp snack not unlike Wotsits) for the journey. This filled me with excitement. Uncle Ezzat was sparkling and always effortlessly dapper in suit, glasses and shiny, sleek hair. He emanated an air of meek clerical obedience and a beguiling gentleness that endeared him to quieter children like myself. However, despite his punctiliousness and rectitude, Ezzat was also rather accident-prone and often seemed to fall victim to the unexpected. This weekend was to be no exception.

I was sitting on my suitcase when he arrived and noticed him from afar, waving enthusiastically before tripping over a crate at the other end of the platform. I was relieved to see him, not just because of the hysteria of recent days, but also because I was feeling emotionally drained from observing the explosive reunions and separations of Tehran's travellers. I wondered if people in Iran were not actually shouting, but simply had louder voices than British people – was it just an issue of genetics and vocal cord size? Uncle Ezzat with his softer voice was an interesting and welcome anomaly.

As we stood together watching the train pull in to the station, there was a crackle of excitement in the air due to my mother's thrilled announcements that we were to be the honoured guests of nightclub owners in Abadan. I didn't know what a nightclub was, and was already feeling beaten by my mother's elaborate packing for this trip, which seemed to have lasted several days in itself. Perhaps sensing my trepidation, Uncle Ezzat kept kissing us all goodbye and seemed genuinely sad that we were leaving. I found myself wishing that he could come too as I enjoyed his company, especially when he privately crooned Frank Sinatra songs and modestly shunned my lavish praise. He was definitely as good as Val Doonican, and much better than Engelbert Humperdink. 'Oh come on, they are gods!' he'd say bashfully.

Whether it was Ezzat's sadness or my secret yearning for his reassuring presence in such uncharted territory, my mother smelled weakness and pounced on him impulsively:

'Come with us! Maybe you'll meet someone – you never know, it's *cabaret*!'

Ezzat was a bachelor at the time and had been unlucky in affairs of the heart. My mother's favourite hobby was match-making. Laughing gently, he extricated himself from my mother's clutches, explaining that a six-hour train journey without prior planning was not going to be possible, what a shame but maybe next time.

My mother said there wasn't going to be a next time and '*toro khodah*' (for God's sake) just get on the train. As the altercation escalated, so did my own mounting panic. I was torn between my empathy for Ezzat's predicament and my genuine desire for him to jump on board. Similarly I was appalled by my mother's bullying manner, but dazzled by her energy and hilarious persistence.

As the train started to move, there was an almighty struggle. Ezzat, no longer in possession of his signature courtesy, was frantically pushing my mother away as she grappled with his jacket lapels, seized hold of his shirt and latched on, limpet-like. There were intense shouts of 'No!' and 'My boss will kill me!' but somehow, she yanked him on board as the train was moving. The door slammed shut; Ezzat was breathing rapidly, his hair tousled, glasses askew, with a look of genuine shock and distress on his face that morphed into a kind of defeated stupor for the remainder of the journey. We were all left in awe at the sheer force of my mother's will; it was frighteningly strong, almost superhuman, and reduced the whole carriage to respectful silence.

At the cabaret the following night, Ezzat was introduced to countless singers and glamorous artistes from Europe as well as Iran, sparkling and glittering in show clothes. My mother had befriended some of these performers with the aid of the nightclub owner's wife. Her well-intentioned but completely naïve and misguided purpose was to find a wife for Ezzat. The cabaret itself was spectacular, a massive theatre with an audience of 500 seated around enchanting candlelit tables. There was music, dance routines, magic acts and even a comedian. I was dazzled by the spectacle and allowed to stay up late, all the acts being relatively child-friendly. Feeling more than a little intimidated by all the attention, Ezzat retreated gratefully into the role of good uncle. He carried me to bed after I literally passed out with fatigue at midnight. Then he stoically kept vigil in the hotel, inwardly drafting nervous letters of explanation and apology to his boss.

I believe Ezzat was in fact fired from his job upon his return to Tehran. My mother, suitably chastened, never tried to match-make on his behalf again, although years later she loyally supported Ezzat's admiration for Anita Dobson from *EastEnders*, whom he lauded as 'the most beautiful and talented woman in the world'. Sadly his affections were never reciprocated.

He was and still is an immensely kind man with an open heart. As he grew older, he became even more sensitive and was personally affected by the injustices he saw in the world. He often wrote poems in response to the *Six O'Clock News* and was devastated by atrocities, terrorist attacks and world crises.

Many years ago, while Ezzat was visiting our home, we realised we had not seen him for several hours. We discovered him in bed, reeling from the revelations that had emerged during Martin Bashir's famous 1995 interview with Princess Diana the previous night. My father, in a bizarre act of 'tough love', tried to jolt him out of his malaise by pouring buckets of water over him. Apparently the origins of this technique can be traced back to their youth. Ezzat remained defiantly still beneath the covers, wet but resolute. He didn't move for the rest of the day. More in sorrow than in anger, he said he was not going to dignify or validate my father's bullish behaviour and he would get up when *he* was ready. This act of bravado seemed to be settling a score that had been waiting fifty years for resolution. When Ezzat finally emerged, dripping but triumphant, he had won my father's undying respect. Even in one's seventies, brotherly dynamics are a constant battle of wits.

CHAPTER SEVEN

The Joker

'This above all, to thine own self be true, and it must follow, as night follows day, thou canst not be false to any man.'
William Shakespeare

The summer of 1972 saw a huge family reunion. The Kensington Close Hotel in London was booked, and we all dressed up for a weekend of events, including a picnic in Hyde Park and a lunch in one of the banqueting rooms. Speeches, presentations, a photoshoot (organised of course by my father) – all exuded a B-movie glamour in keeping with 1970s garish fashions, the memory of which makes me view that time as though we were all actors in a US network mini-series starring Richard Chamberlain.

One evening in particular, I remember my four maternal uncles looking down at me like a collection of benevolent Mafia bosses and asking me that inevitable but highly pressurised question:

'What do you want to be when you're older?'

Questions from Iranian uncles required a pause of respectful rumination. By 1979, most of my extended family had left Iran for various parts of the Western world. They laid down roots in Austria, France, Germany, Denmark, Belgium and, in the US, Pennsylvania, Seattle and California. They were all successful as doctors, lawyers, carpet salesmen and officers in the military. Even if they did menial jobs they did them well, Iranians, by their nature, being generally tenacious and determined.

Uncle Parviz, for example, never bowed to pressure to have a 'profession' and had a series of so called 'menial' jobs that included security guard and petrol-pump attendant. But he landed on his feet working as a pizza chef, and gained a formidable reputation as the best pizza maker in Bellingham, probably in all Seattle state. People would travel from far away to watch his dough-spinning skills. Until his dying breath he never once had regrets concerning his various employments: 'You work, you get paid, the kids go to college, *va-asalam* (and that's it).'

His younger brother, my uncle Iraj, possessed a similar attitude. He was an actor, and therefore something of a pioneer amongst Iranians of that generation. He was seen as morally 'upstanding' so, whilst there was concern for his wellbeing, there was minimum discouragement of his artistic aspirations. I think this helped ease my path later, as Middle Eastern families were (with the exception of my mother) and still are, rather suspicious regarding the supposed 'looser morals' of artists and entertainers. Sadly, Uncle Iraj died aged forty-four while working – between acting jobs – at Kentucky Fried Chicken on Catalina Island off the coast of Los Angeles. I feel an affinity with him, as I see now we share physical and temperamental similarities in adulthood. He once appeared in a 1970s episode of *Starsky and Hutch* as a fruit seller, and probably could have forged a career doing ethnic bit parts. But he was proud (prouder than me, if that's possible) and saw himself as a serious actor. By all accounts his Othello was magnificent. The fact that his was in a production by a Mormon dramatic group in Salt Lake City was irrelevant; in my mother's eyes he was 'top Hallyvood acter'.

My third maternal uncle was Faramarz, the tallest member of the family who played for the Iranian national basketball team. He moved to the US at the age of twenty-five and had such a swagger about him that he was viewed proudly as the 'jock' of the family. He was a natural sportsman, who had an impressive quota of actual American friends and, most impressively, an authentic-sounding American accent. He was so integrated, 'you could almost pass him off as Italian' the family marvelled.

My fourth maternal uncle, Manouch, became an anaesthetist and moved to Villach, Austria, where he married Gisela, a Corinthian beauty with an outrageous sense of humour. She was a fine artist and brought a touch of bohemian cool to the family. Their three teenage children, Alex, Ramin and Sheida, spent happy summers and winters wearing black polo-neck jumpers and having philosophical conversations with their friends in a smoky coffee house called Café Nikolai, where everyone was called 'chazi' (darling) and I was accepted as a curiosity. Looking back, it was almost like an Austrian version of Friends where I had a recurring role as 'crazy cousin from London'. Unfortunately I broke someone's squash raquet one night in an open-air squash court and I was never invited back. I make it sound like I was playing too aggressively. Truth is I inadvertently sat on it.

So, rewinding, there I was, surrounded by these dark-suited and intimidating uncles.

'What do you want to be when you are older?'

I paused, remembering the awkwardness I'd felt at their question the day before. They'd already jokingly asked me, 'Are you a boy or a girl?'

I hadn't been sure if they were being playful or just genuinely confused by my long, curly, light-brown hair. I said 'boy'. Then there was the inevitable follow-up question: 'How do you *know* you're a boy?'

I felt proud of my resourcefulness when I assumed the simplest response was to display the contents of my trousers. I was genuinely surprised when they all took a sharp intake of breath and made assorted noises of shock and horror. If I hadn't been so young this could have been classed as 'indecent exposure'. My father, seeing my confusion, defended my actions, shouting: '*Barikalla!* (Well done!) He is presenting the evidence! *Ye roozi vakileh khoob meesheh!* (He'll be a good lawyer one day!)'

Everyone laughed. But I decided to lock myself in the bathroom. By the age of seven I was used to experiencing existential angst, and on that day I felt I had to review carefully the purpose and accomplishments of my short life to date.

'*The world is an illusion. These people have been created for the sole purpose of testing me.*' Young children are often raging narcissists and I was no exception.

It seemed to me that my only purpose in life now was to gather as much knowledge and power as I could, to gain my freedom. But until this liberation occurred, the only options of release to me were wild flights of fancy, courtesy of my relentless imagination. This was, after all, the psychedelic seventies.

Even iconic BBC children's programmes like *Play School* seemed to have psychedelic elements. *The Tomorrow People* and *Magpie* on ITV were also staples in our TV diet. Films like *2001: A Space Odyssey* and the 1950s space adventure *The Fantastic Planet* provided excellent fodder to stimulate my active dream life. The streets of my home turf became portals to fantastic new worlds while I was asleep: the roof of Cottesmore Court where we lived in Kensington was a runway and launch pad from which I would fly above the neighbourhood by airborne breast stroke. Or front crawl if I was in a hurry. Even now a song or a smell can throw me back to those days: Jethro Tull, Barclay James Harvest, Camel – I soaked up the hippie zeitgeist like a sponge. It was all about escape and fantasy worlds in those days. Who knows, maybe seventies Britain was so grim that everyone was going through their own flights of fancy as a kind of collective unconscious coping mechanism. It's no wonder I preferred to live within the haven of my own mind.

Around this time I also became fascinated with playing cards, the designs of which were also influenced by psychedelia. We had 'Kem' cards, made from durable plastic. The Kings, Queens and Jacks were especially fascinating because the images were so lifelike. Looking closely at the cards within each suit, I imagined a different kingdom in an alternate universe. Some had elaborate buildings with triangular flags blowing in the wind and others featured courtiers with shoulder-length hair, square hats and thin chin beards. It was all very *Shrek*.

The most intriguing figure in the deck of cards, and my personal favourite, was the Joker. Today, a lot of young people associate the Joker with Heath Ledger's *tour de force* in *Batman: The Dark Knight* – a brilliant portrayal of charismatic evil and madness. But in the Kem cards the Joker was a jolly fat man with a huge smile. Dressed as a court jester, wearing a hat with bells on, he had one eye shut and his index finger on his nose. He was somehow 'in the know', a sign of his mysterious access to power. And I wanted that knowledge. When I eventually learned to play cards it was explained that the Joker was 'wild'. Of course he was wild, I thought; he's the Joker, no one can keep him down, he's free as the wind, he does what he wants . . . he's invincible, indestructible.

I wanted to be the Joker.

So when my uncles asked me, 'What do you want to be when you're older?', I stared at them, about to reveal my secret.

I even put a finger to my nose, smiled that cheeky grin and slowly and deliberately said: 'I want to be a Joker.'

They erupted with laughter. 'Funny man! Ha ha! He wants to be a funny man! Omid is a JOKER!'

It took a few moments for me to realise that they thought I wanted to be a *comedian*. I couldn't think of anything worse. They seemed so excited by the thought. I don't know what comedians my uncles would have been exposed to at that time – *The Tonight Show* with Johnny Carson, Sammy Davis Jr, Don Rickles maybe? But clearly they had visions of themselves watching their little nephew doing sets at the Caesar's Palace one day in Vegas, followed by a Barry Manilow concert and a T-bone steak.

This could not be. I wasn't going to have people laughing at me again, not after that coconut incident at primary school. I knew at this moment I was going to have to work very hard. The task at hand was to figure out what on earth I had to do to be taken more seriously.

CHAPTER EIGHT

First Love

'Something opens our wings. Something makes boredom and hurt disappear.'

Rumi

I first became aware of football at primary school. I'd spent my first week in Class 1 silently observing the older boys kick a ball around at playtime. I remember feeling desperate to join in but was far too shy to impose. I often used to retrieve the ball for them, like a loyal dog. And like a dog, my enthusiasm was boundless. I 'fetched' their ball over and over again, hoping that my commitment would be acknowledged with an invitation to play. I did this every break and lunchtime for a week, only to conclude that these boys were selfish, crass and tragically unaware of sporting genius in their midst.

I became aware of a splinter group that played the game in a more subdued corner of the playground, the space inhabited by asthmatic kids and misfits. I was welcomed there, gleefully. But the apple core that doubled up for a ball got kicked to a pulp with surprising rapidity. Playing with a stem and a tiny slice of apple, whilst invaluable for developing new skills, was nevertheless demoralising. The others lost interest pretty quickly, but I insisted that we could continue with a pip. It seems ludicrous now, to have used an apple pip to play football, but at the time it seemed logical; you just had to make smaller goals. Keepy-ups were rather challenging, though. The highest number I achieved was two, but I persevered long after the whistle went. I remember the teacher booming: 'You, boy! What on *earth* are you doing? Get inside. NOW.' I'm convinced though, that this attention to detail, honed through training with apple pips, was what gave me a great first touch on the field of play in later years.

One day, I saw something that changed me forever. An older boy, in the year above, was wearing a royal blue Chelsea football top. He stood out like the child in the red coat in *Schindler's List*. He wore the top casually to school as if it were the most natural thing in the world. Football tops were not so easily available back then, very few outlets sold them. To wear it to school seemed unnecessarily brazen to me. It felt like he was flaunting his individuality. It was somehow inspiring and shocking at the same time. I wasn't even sure whether it was allowed, but the teachers didn't seem to bat an eyelid. Chelsea had won the FA Cup that summer and they were riding high.

Ian Spooner was after all very popular, being naturally talented at sports (later he became a gym instructor), so he was accustomed to kids staring. One break time I stood close to him in a gaggle of other boys, really just to get a proper look at the badge. Having said that, I often stood close to older boys in order to study them: their clothes, the way they did their hair, their mannerisms and speech patterns. I considered it important research in how to get ahead. I stood extra close to Ian Spooner, secretly wondering whether his charisma might rub off on me. I knew he was older and presumably light years ahead of me in wisdom, but for all I knew he could have been an idiot. The

Chelsea top was the clincher, though. It gave him primary school gravitas.

The colour itself was mesmerising: royal blue, deep and mystical. The crest of two stars, either side of a dragon holding a red staff, was a lodestone of wonder. The image, for some reason, conjured up an atmosphere of Middle Earth. I was never aware of J. R. R. Tolkien or *The Hobbit* or anything in popular culture that made children's imaginations run wild, but, as established, I needed very little stimulus to get my own mind fizzing and bubbling. The Chelsea football top represented escape. Chelsea FC, with the dragon and red staff, made absolute sense to me.

One rainy Wednesday, to my utter shock, Ian Spooner spoke to me. He could have addressed anyone, but he chose *me*. My heart pounded as I heard the words: 'What team do you support?' No doubt he may have been feeling uncomfortable because my nose was now nudging his left pectoral, hypnotised more than usual by the crest. 'You support Chelsea?' This was a question I'd never been asked before, and truthfully, I didn't even know what it meant. I felt it had something to do with a club of some sort, but I wasn't sure, so I just stared at him and said nothing. He lost interest and, as children are wont to do, he turned, with a sudden burst of speed, and ran away kicking a ball. I watched him, mute with awe.

I did later come to my senses after I wasted some money given to me as a gift, by taking Ian Spooner with me on a shopping spree to High Street Kensington. I foolishly spent it all on him to show my solidarity as a fellow Chelsea fan and to seek his approval. Teaching me a valuable lesson, he looked at me with all his gifts in his arms and instead of thanking me, he turned away, laughing and muttering, 'You mug!'

Yes, he was right.

Football was my first love. I wasn't even aware of loving

anything else at that time, other than certain items of 1970s British confectionery like Refreshers, Spangles and Opal Fruits ('*made to make your mouth water*') and possibly a Flake chocolate bar because the soft-focus adverts on TV seemed to promise a tranquil existence languishing with hippies in poppy fields.

So watching football live on TV for the first time was a major gamechanger. The FA Cup Final 1971 was also the day our family acquired a colour television.

Warm sunlight poured into our living room that Saturday afternoon in May. Eight or nine guests were dotted around the table eating a late lunch, and playing cards and the obligatory backgammon. No one was really paying attention to the TV as Liverpool and Arsenal made their entrances into the stadium. I cocked my head and understood that they seemed like important people, not least because 100,000 people were cheering. It was a bit like a scene from *Asterix the Gladiator*, which I was devouring at the time.

One guest, who I vaguely remember was called Mansuri, seemed to be getting very excited by the game. He kept looking at me saying '*neegah kon*' (watch), and '*bazieh khoobeh*' (it's a good game).

He beckoned me over: '*Besheen eenja*' (sit here). It was my first taste of football camaraderie. I zoned in and out of the action, playing idly on the floor with my Action Man and some Matchbox cars. No one had scored, so Mansuri's enthusiasm seemed disproportionate. He grabbed my attention at the final whistle when he slapped his hands and shouted, '*Vakhteh ezafeh!*' (extra time!) Suddenly everything seemed to change. Excitement started to bubble around the room.

'Extra time' seemed like an acknowledged special code phrase for 'stop what you are doing immediately'. In fact extra time was in those days a new and rarely used concept. Even my mother, who never watched football, took an interest. In fact she knew so little that when football rules were explained to her, she said, 'Why don't they just give each of them a ball so they don't all have to chase the *one* ball around? *Behtareh, nah?* (better, no?)'

Suddenly Steve Heighway scored and Mansuri yelled, *'Ajab goli!'* (what a goal!) The card games, the eating, the chatter, the backgammon: all stopped. My mother spontaneously started weeping with emotion. She looked at Steve Heighway adoringly and said, *'Ay khoda beyamorzesh'* (God bless him) as he ran away celebrating the goal. The Liverpool winger with the Mexican moustache was an Irish international but when one of the guests asked, *'Iranieh?'* (Is he Iranian?), there seemed to be a distinct possibility that indeed he was, despite the fact his name was Steve Heighway.

It was natural to start rooting for the red team because Mansuri seemed so enthusiastic about the goal: *'Che goleh ghashangee!'* (what a beautiful goal!) But then Arsenal equalised and Mansuri jumped up in excitement — *'Shance ovordan!'* (that was lucky!) and seemed overjoyed. On cue, I cheered obediently. We were apparently pro-Arsenal now. But as time went on, Mansuri became alternately more and more hyped up by both teams. It was quite unnerving.

Charlie George then hit his now-iconic winner and fell onto his back. Mansuri, practically frothing by this stage, went nuts, shouting: *'Gooool! Ajab goli!'* (what a goal!) His enthusiasm really bewildered me, as his allegiance had clearly switched from Liverpool to Arsenal mid-game. Liverpool were 2–1 down now; was he just supporting who ever *won?* That couldn't be right, I thought. Or could it? Maybe he was just a really nice man.

The fact was that, for Mansuri, it was not so much about supporting a particular team but about taking pleasure in the *drama* of the game. This is actually what true lovers of football do. I cried that day, especially when Arsenal lifted the Cup. My mum cried as well. She had no idea which team won, she was just so happy for them, and wept with euphoria as she cleared the plates away.

Eight years later when Arsenal played Man Utd in the 1979 FA Cup Final – one of the most dramatic finals in history – my mother cried again. This time she was moved by the sight of Alan Sunderland screaming with elation after he'd hit a last-minute winner for Arsenal to win 3–2. Even though Arsenal was in the exact same yellow strip from 1971, she had no idea it was the same team. In fact she didn't even recall the name Arsenal. She said all she remembered that day was feeling proud when the Iranian with the moustache 'shooted a goal'.

It was the first of a few rare occasions when our Persian guests showed an interest in football. In September of 1971 two middle-aged Iranian guys suddenly decided, on a whim, that since it was Saturday, they must see a live football match somewhere. They just didn't know where or when.

My dad, without even looking up from his backgammon game, suggested: 'Omid likes Chelsea. Take him with you. He can translate.'

Looking back, I am amazed by my father's unusual approach to hospitality. A six-year-old translator in charge of two foreign-looking blokes who didn't speak a word of English, in a climate of simmering, under-the-surface hooligan racist violence . . . there were so many reasons to stay at home and watch *Match of the Day*. And yet, strange as it may sound, it was probably my father's faith in my ability to handle challenging situations in childhood that has propelled me through my adult life. He might not have heaped lavish praise upon me, or known how to help me at school, but he entrusted me with tasks that he felt were important. In fact, his belief that I was equipped to carry out his strange requests was so strong that I rarely doubted myself either. Naturally this may have led to later delusion on my part, but the upside has always been a healthy confidence when faced with surreal situations.

So, on that day, I meandered distractedly through the back-streets of Kensington with my new mates until we spotted a cab. We jumped in and I said, 'Chelsea football.' Luckily the driver knew what I meant and drove us straight to Stamford Bridge, dropping us right outside the ground. The Iranian guys threw some paper money at the driver and we walked in the direction of the crowd noises. The second half was already under way and even the ticket touts had taken their coats off and were lounging in the September sunshine, counting their cash.

Six is perhaps slightly too young to negotiate with ticket touts in long black coats who talk out the side of their mouths, but I gave it my best shot. Confronted by two confused and moustached foreign gentlemen and a small child, the ticket touts snapped to attention.

'Looking to get in?' Quick as a flash I glanced over at a sign behind them that read 'Box Office'. I clocked the ticket prices above the sign – 80p, £1, £1.20 – and then spotted the 'closed' sign. I looked back at the touts and nodded. 'Is that three of ya?' I nodded again. 'Tell 'em it'll be £21. Game's sold out.' I translated and the touts made helpful number signs with their fingers. The Iranian gentlemen handed over their cash in another flurry of paper money that looked like far more than £21. The touts seemed overjoyed. I was happy, they were happy, we were all happy.

As we walked in, the empty seats around us made me query the touts' confidence that the game was in fact sold out. We took our places in the East Stand lower tier to a volley of shouting: 'Sit down!' and 'What time do you call this?!' This was embarrassing. *'Chi migan?'* (What are they saying?) I didn't answer. It was my first-ever football match. I kept my eyes fixed on the pitch, and noted that I felt simultaneously thrilled and desperate; thrilled by the sheer spectacle of it, the noise, the crowd, the colour of the blue of Chelsea and the claret of West Ham, but desperately uncomfortable that I was sharing this momentous experience with strange men whose names I didn't know, and who seemed ludicrously out of place at Chelsea. '*Chand chandan?*' (What's the score?) I politely asked an old man nearby. He swore profusely before informing me: 'Sorry, lad. We're 2–1 down.' I understood this to mean Chelsea 1 West Ham 2. It certainly explained the crowd's agitation. I recognised the West Ham captain Billy Bonds, mostly because Chelsea fans were shouting his name and hurling abuse. A cross came over and I saw Bonds rise like a salmon and head the ball in to make it 1–3. West Ham fans around us exploded into celebration.

After a bit more shouting and abuse, things got a little nastier so a few minutes before the end we got up and left, only to suffer another volley of abuse: 'Had enough already?! Go on, bugger off!' The Iranian men, satisfied they'd experienced a fantastic and thoroughly authentic live football experience, smiled broadly and waved to the fans. Inwardly I vowed to go to another match ASAP, if only to extinguish the memory of this unusually painful rite of passage.

In fact, I did go soon afterwards, and by the time I was ten Chelsea had become the focus of my life.

It seems amazing to me now that I used to go all alone to Chelsea matches as a small child. I usually had a little bit of money given to me by guests and I would spend it on trips to the lower East Stand at Stamford Bridge where I followed the games avidly. It was some years later I discovered that my parents, when hearing that I was off to 'watch the match at Chelsea', had presumed I was going to Kensington Gardens near our home, where I might loiter around and watch teenagers having a knockabout with jumpers for goal posts. They had no idea their young son was walking a mile and a half away to a stadium and spending time with some of the toughest blokes in west London. In general the worst it tended to get was frequent exposure to bad language. And I do remember thinking, 'This is good. It'll help me in later life not to be shocked by anyone or anything.'

I saw the odd snatches of unpleasant violence, sometimes, shockingly, between Chelsea fan and Chelsea fan in the upper tier where it was quite steep. I remember one occasion when it happened after a goal was scored. In this jubilant moment a fan lost his balance and fell on to the bloke sitting next to me who, whilst continuing to celebrate, instinctively reacted and punched the other guy three times in the face. It was a full minute later before everything calmed down. He turned round and apologised to the fan who was spluttering and rummaging for tissues. The victim, keeping his head up to stop the nose-bleed, waved his other arm to reassure his attacker, insisting, 'I'm fine, all right, no problem, mate.'

'Sorry didn't mean nothing, was just shocked.'

'Perfectly understandable, mate.'

The unspoken code was clear: it was 'nothing personal'.

I was even attacked once myself, on my way home after a memorial charity game in 1976 for the family of Peter Houseman, the famous Chelsea winger who scored at Wembley in the 1970 FA Cup Final. I was already quite far from the stadium at the upper end of Finborough Road near Earl's Court when, out of nowhere, an older boy started chasing me. Being a good six or seven years older he caught up with me quite rapidly, pushed me hard to the ground, ripped the blue and white Chelsea scarf from my neck and ran off.

I thought long and hard about this incident and deduced that, unlike me, this boy simply could not afford his own scarf.

'Nothing personal,' I decided.

Moreover, had he asked for it politely, I probably would have given it to him anyway.

I often fantasised about finding a way to get on to the Chelsea pitch. After some trial and error I realised that no one minded if you pretended to be a cleaner after the match had finished. In fact the staff appreciated the support. You didn't need a uniform or an identity card. You just needed to look vaguely beleaguered and keep your head down as you picked up bits of debris that floated around the stands. When most of it was done there was pretty much no one around and sometimes I would find myself alone in the stadium. I would walk carefully towards the pitch like a pilgrim and gingerly step on to the edge of the hallowed turf. I could never just walk on: that was tantamount to insolence.

Sometimes I would pretend to take a corner: left footed, in-swinger. When I was convinced no one was watching I'd pretend to go on a run from the halfway line. I was on a professional pitch surrounded in my head with all the top players chasing me down, so I raced on, beating players, riding tackles, looking up to see if I could make a pass, dummying the pass and running on to the penalty area. People were shouting 'Pass it!' and 'Back post!' but I knew I had the skill and capability to take it all the way on my own. With heart pounding I'd break into the penalty area, nip round the last defender, then get dramatically hacked down for a penalty. Of course, when touched you go down, but hearing Rodney Marsh on the subject once I took his advice and always snapped my head back as I fell to the ground. This was to convince the crowd and therefore the ref. 'Win the crowd and you will win your freedom' (Proximo, *Gladiator*). Maybe I shouldn't have screamed, 'Penalty, ref!' because up popped Ken Bates, the Chelsea chairman, from the stands shouting, *'Oi!!'* and I bolted like a horse. I was out of Stamford Bridge that night in less than twenty seconds.

But I didn't care. I'd just given myself the best thirtieth birthday present ever.

CHAPTER NINE

The Guesthouse

'This being human is a guesthouse. The dark thought, the shame, the malice, meet them at the door laughing and invite them in . . .'

Rumi

When I was a child, I thought our large family had an extremely wide and varied social circle. In reality, I was raised in a crazy and colourful guesthouse. Exposed to an unusual amount of 'life' during my formative years, the guesthouse was my cavalier parent: it fed me, chastised me, baffled, amused and confused me. And as I reached maturity it spewed me out into the world, jaded and street savvy, with the assumption that I was emotionally robust.

My mother had a saying: *'Tond o bad.'* Roughly translated from Farsi it means 'quick and bad'. In other words: 'Just get it over with, well or badly, who cares?' Protocols and social mores, especially British ones, were laughably dispensable to my mother. The very notion that it was *unusual* to have paying guests from Iran traipsing in and out of a quiet residential block in Kensington, was utterly alien to her: we were a family, and people lived with us, *'ze ki'* (so what). The threat of eviction, real or imagined, was always with me, lingering like a bad smell. My parents, ever optimistic, never worried. Their confidence was unshakeable. It came from an impressive delusion that they could keep passing off anyone who came to stay – about 2,000 people over twenty years – as 'cousins'. And they succeeded. This is in no small part down to the fact that their genuine (albeit overwhelming) warm-heartedness truly made no distinction between strangers and blood relatives.

By the mid-1970s our large apartment had become a major hub of activity in London W8. It was like living in the central location for an epic never-ending movie. Despite living there, I often felt that I was watching the film from the sidelines. The supporting cast were sick Iranians from all backgrounds, who had come to the UK for medical procedures: eye examinations, intestinal explorations, heart operations, cancer treatment, leg removals, skin disease, brain disease. Initially, these were referrals from the Iranian embassy where my father worked, but as the years went on, my parents established personal relationships with people who came back and who recommended others. Before long, our family became known in Iran and in England as a household who would take care of vulnerable individuals and those who were sometimes terminally ill. Due to these guests paying so much money for their medical treatment (never at any point did anyone exploit the NHS), my parents' roles as down-to-earth carers became even more meaningful. They provided a 'home from home' for Iranians, away from the formality of Harley Street where many of these patients went for consultations. In many ways, despite craving a more prominent role in their movie, I feel blessed to have borne witness to my parents' unflagging kindness and humanitarianism. No surprise, though, that I felt driven to seek external validation through showbiz.

There were so many guests that they tend to blur in my

memory, but I remember vividly a twenty-five-year-old young man called Yurosh. He had a growth disorder that left him in the body of a ten-year-old. Doctors were experimenting with growth hormone therapy at the time, and he participated in one of the first trials. I was ten years old, and considered Yurosh a friend. The fact that he behaved like an old man and just wanted to play Solitaire all the time was rather frustrating. He even smoked cigarettes, which I thought was hilarious because no one chastised him. Unfortunately the trials weren't successful and he returned to Iran, deeply disappointed. The sad news filtered back several years later that Yurosh had taken his own life. Severe depression had gone unnoticed and undiagnosed. Looking back, I can guess that many of the guests suffered from depression, and were battling it stoically. No one talked in psychotherapeutic terminology about emotional intelligence or empathy, but without having to name it, read about it, or even reflect upon it, these were the principles that governed my parents' relationships with their guests.

Being introduced to the concept of mortality at a young age also taught me never to dwell on bad news. I often heard my mum and dad discussing the demise of former guests while they played backgammon, sometimes speaking their broken English to keep it private from the guests who were also at the table:

'Remember Foad?'

'Man without nose?'

'Yes. *Mord* (he died).'

'When?'

'Last week. Family call today.'

'*Vasta* (wait). Man with wig like Burt Reynold?'

'No, other one without nose. Face no skin.'

'*Yadam neemiad* (don't remember him).'

'*Bazi kon* (play).'

Cottesmore Court was an austere apartment block bursting with dysfunction and silent turmoil. Built in the 1950s, it was situated in the quiet residential bowels of Kensington. My parents moved in in around 1961. The flats were compact and inhabited mostly by retired members of the civil service, ex-army officers and spoilt children of rich businessmen using it as a central London 'pad'. I don't recall many families in the block except some unfeasibly blond Norwegians in matching jumpers, who rented a flat for six months, and looked like they did modelling for an up-and-coming knitting manual. There was also a family of overweight Americans from Texas, the father of which used to rev his car loudly on winter days to warm up the engine, at 6.50 a.m. After *Dallas* took off in 1979 he sometimes wore his ten-gallon Texan hat, perhaps to appear JR-like and Machiavellian. It worked. No one ever confronted him about his noise pollution at the crack of dawn.

My siblings and I, seeing ourselves as more British than Iranian, often discussed, earnestly, whether you had to be 'middle class' or 'upper middle class' to live in Cottesmore Court. This was a sad reflection of the time: the fascination and obsession with knowing one's place in the class pecking order was annoyingly prevalent. The now famous 1960s sketch featuring John Cleese and the Two Ronnies satirised Britain's obsession with class and was often shown on TV. However, modern-day nuances like 'nouveau riche' or 'colonisation in reverse' had for quite some time been blurring those traditional class and culture boundaries. And we, as Iranian immigrant children from a weird guesthouse, struggled to conclude where we were supposed to sit in this complex, expanding continuum. Class was an especially confusing concept to us as Bahá'í children because in addition to our obvious Iranian identity, we had also internalised a belief in an important principle of our faith – the 'oneness of humanity'. In other words, everyone was equal. Weren't they?

The block's credentials were certainly raised a notch by Lady Elizabeth Bassett, the Queen's foremost lady-in-waiting, who resided on the top floor. Lady Elizabeth was very popular and always smiled benignly when we met in the lift. When the word 'aristocracy' was studied and the subject of social class came up again during my last year of primary school, I remember unashamedly identifying myself as 'upper class'. When asked to quantify this claim I said, 'The Queen's best friend lives above us, and she is my friend. That means I'm not aristocracy but close.' I remember slight rumblings of discontent and amusement from the teacher who instructed me, in my own time, to look up the words 'deluded' and 'misguided'.

I've been inside a number of flats at Cottesmore Court over the years. All seemed tidy, tastefully decorated and modestly populated. Our flat, two knocked into one, defied description. In just about every nook and cranny a distressed-looking person in pyjamas seemed to be lying still, minding their own business, reading, writing lewd poetry, praying, weeping or just staring blankly into space. I often took a book into the bathroom to get some peace, and on coming out, would invariably stumble over a guest prostrate on the ground. Sometimes my home really resembled a psychiatric unit or a community centre.

The kitchen was where the main activity took place. It was the proverbial heart of the home. A large open-plan space where a table curved around the hob easily sat five on square straw stools. Others would stand holding food as they chatted away in bizarre party mode. The radio was tuned to an Iranian satellite station, broadcasting a mix of traditional music and news bulletins, and often caused heated discussions to erupt. It was as close to being in Iran as the guests could have hoped. My parents aimed to please.

Like a lot of Iranians my mother loved bright red carpets. When the flat was refurbished in the mid-seventies, she beamed and asked me, 'What do you think?' I smiled back and nodded enthusiastically. I didn't have the heart or the aesthetic vocabulary to tell her that I thought the carpet clashed with the overly floral and voluminous plastic tablecloth. I couldn't bring myself to say that the unnecessarily ornate gold samovar didn't really sit harmoniously next to the bust of someone we didn't know but had picked up at a jumble sale because 'he looked important' (we later found out it was the German philosopher Immanuel Kant). Everything seemed random and out of place. Pieces were bought and thrown together: a large oil painting of a fox hunt from 1789 (which bothered me as I had decided, aged thirteen, that I was a vehement supporter of the anti-fox-hunting lobby), a stuffed raven on a branch picked up at a car boot sale – even a portrait of the Duke of Edinburgh on his fiftieth birthday was thrown into the mix. In the living area, modern glass and stainless-steel coffee tables, no doubt inspired by the atmosphere of *Moonbase Alpha* on the 1790s TV show *Space 1999*, clashed gloriously with migraine-inducing, geometric-patterned, vision-blurring wallpaper. Throw in a few oddball Iranian gentlemen shuffling around in dressing gowns, and the picture is complete.

My mother and father, Parvaneh and Ahmad Djalili, were supreme multi-taskers. They worked as translator, nurse, counsellor, cook, administrator, mandolin player and entertainer. The 'entertainer' aspect always intrigued me. It was here where I was exposed to the notion of stand-up comedy for the first time. My father literally stood over the stove to cook eggs facing the guests (he cooked, they watched) and often played on the word 'eggs' in Farsi being colloquial for testicles: *'Would you like your eggs scrambled, fried or fondled?'* was a particular favourite. It never failed to get a laugh, although some of it was nervous laughter. I remember once being present when there was a guest who remained unamused. A gentleman suffering temporary deafness, caused by a severe ear infection, wasn't aware that a joke was being told and appeared to be rather confused and upset by my father's antics. My father, generously seeking to make him feel included, soldiered on, raising his voice, and added unnecessarily elaborate mimes that involved, for some reason, going up on his tiptoes. Although the guest was still mystified, the mimes did induce a polite snigger, more a short forcing out of air through his nostrils with a bemused expression in cursory acknowledgement of the effort. My father realised it was best just to keep quiet and make the breakfast, which he did, as he wiped performance-anxiety sweat from his brow.

This was a lesson I never learned – how to give up and shut up. I've wiped buckets, if not bathfuls of anxiety sweat from my brow over the years, mostly because I chose to soldier on knowing deep down what I was doing was funny. The audience just hadn't realised it yet.

CHAPTER TEN

Gainful Employment

'Continuous effort, not strength or intelligence, is the key to unlocking our potential.'

Winston Churchill

Though opportunities for privacy and normal family life (whatever that is) were limited, the guesthouse was a fun place. Relatively quiet during the day when I was at school, in the evening it became like one of those packed restaurants that only the few with inside information knew about. The vibe was part social club, part busy restaurant. It attracted not just the patients who stayed there, but also their friends and family. Add to that my parents' own friends and family, and there was often anything up to thirty people milling around. Impromptu parties suddenly sprang to life. Food was prepared with the aid of one or two guests who were bored and sought domestic activity, and spread out in the kitchen to be consumed like a self-service buffet. There was constant hot tea on a samovar, card games, backgammon, Iranian radio, bandages changed, blood pressures taken, urine samples in marked bottles sitting on the drinks trolley alongside bottles of Canada Dry and Coke, and all in a hazy smoke-filled atmosphere of noise, laughter, music and chat. Romantic intrigue took place between a guest who was partially sighted and another with severe psoriasis. Their bond briefly continued when they returned to Iran but broke up when both realised that they'd felt unnaturally influenced by the atmosphere of that 'happy guesthouse in London'.

I can understand the lure of reality shows like *Big Brother* and *The Only Way Is Essex* because – when truncated into small bite-size pieces – nothing beats watching a heightened version of real life. It's what I did in my own house for years.

My parents often said with the clientele they had built up, my siblings and I could continue the family business. I think they were disappointed that this never appealed to any of us. In terms of making a living, my upbringing gave me an acute survival instinct, probably formed through living with so many ill people. On the one hand this instilled in me a determination never to be dependent on anyone, and an almost pathological rejection of vulnerability within myself. On the other hand, while I continue to hold the view that my parents' generosity and spirit of service to others was an inspirational way to live, I also realised early on that the world can often be cruel and irrational. From childhood I'd decided that, despite an expansive love of humanity, I didn't want to follow in my father's footsteps and earn a living by frying eggs for sick Iranians in pyjamas.

I'd been doing jobs since I was ten, having felt shocked when a random guest bestowed upon me a £5 note, saying, as if he was revealing the secrets of the universe: 'With *this* there is everything. *Without* this there is nothing.'

The very next day I marched purposefully into a newsagent on Marloes Road in Kensington and asked if I could do a paper round. They said yes, but I'd have to start the next day. I was up at 5.30 a.m. and standing to attention by my newspaper cart at 6 a.m. I delivered 500 newspapers on my first shift.

That increased to 700 over the week, when they were satisfied that I was trustworthy (they had you followed for the first two days). It seemed to take about two hours to complete, finishing in time for school. By the end of the week I eagerly waited to collect my hard-earned cash. We hadn't discussed my fee, but I was excited and optimistic. I'd worked very hard and felt I had deserved the £5.25 that was put, albeit brusquely, into my outstretched hand. I was happy enough until I saw the other kids getting their pay. To my dismay it was substantially more generous: £14.50, £15, £18. One boy even got £21. Keeping calm I went back and inquired politely into the disparity. Apparently the other boys had been there longer than me, and were doing bigger shifts and worked larger areas. However, I soon realised that this might not be the whole truth: by now it had dawned on me that they were all blood relatives. They were a large Indian family. I had no chance. I didn't go back the next day. A full week's shift for what turned out to be 75p a day seemed too demoralising. Even as a ten-year-old in 1975 I yearned for my toil and effort to be worth more.

It was around this time that I embarked upon what could have been a burgeoning career as a medical translator. As a ten-year-old, I had a strange gravitas, rare in a child of tender years. I was often put in the position of having to discuss patients' intimate medical conditions with some of the top Harley Street professionals in the country. Pleural effusions, cardiac abnormalities and urinary tract infections were run-of-the-mill topics, and I was obliged to engage with professionalism and compassion. I still remember a top surgeon's expression of awe and pity when he looked at me: 'You're a clever little boy, aren't you?' I never felt it was unusual, it was all in a day's work and worth it for the 50p my dad gave me for every translation job. It certainly enabled me to afford the latest Asterix or Charlie Brown books that I devoured every other month.

Looking back, it seems odd that this was never presented to me as an actual career path. As a bilingual British Iranian child savvy with medical terms (sometimes even in Latin), I had unusual translating dexterity. But it never occurred to me that this was a highly sought skill through which I could have made a decent living. Today it's a specialised job at institutions like the United Nations: top-notch translators are well paid, highly regarded and much-needed. Sadly this career was thwarted before it had a chance to flourish – mainly due to an unfortunate incident involving a man who was recovering from a kidney operation.

I had misunderstood my father's request to go to the Brompton Hospital on Fulham Road – 'and don't just sit there and translate' but 'stay with him and keep him entertained a little'. What he meant was the patient, Mr Rezai, was slightly depressed being away from home and missed his own children. My father thought it would be kind if I, as a child, could sit with him a while, have a little chat and socialise, rather than just translate and scarper. For some reason, though, I got it into my head that this meant I had to actually 'entertain'.

The doctor arrived, and after some pleasantries and the usual surprise regarding my age, we got down to business. I kept my hands behind my back and adjusted my tie to look more official.

'Can you ask him if he slept well?'

'*Khoob khabideen?*'

'*Baleh.*'

'Yes.'

'Ask him if gets thirsty in the middle of the night?'

'*Nesfeh shab teshnatoon shod?*'

'*Yekami.*'

'A little.'

'Does he have trouble passing wind?'

'Sorry?'

'Wind. Ask him if he has trouble passing wind.'

A spanner in the works. I had no idea what he meant. My father had trained me, when I didn't understand, just to ask the doctor to elaborate.

'Sorry. I don't know what you mean.'

'You know, wind.'

'Like the wind outside blowing around?'

'No. You know, when you've eaten a lot and you . . ?'

It was getting tense and I felt I was letting all of us down. How could I know the terms for 'pleural effusions' but have no idea about 'wind'? Finally the doctor made a modest little squat and said 'wind' again to indicate gas being expelled.

'Oh, you mean *farting*?'

'Yes, I suppose, yes. Exactly, yes.'

'Shall I ask did he fart last night?'

'Yes.'

'OK. [Turning to patient.] *Goozeh mohkam tu khaab miza-neen?* (Did you fart hard in your sleep?)'

Here the patient started to smile broadly. I saw he was visibly controlling himself. Having undergone a kidney transplant, patients are told to avoid laughter at all costs. In extreme cases it's known to literally split sides. With anxiety in his smile he said 'yes' to the question about passing wind, but it was the translation that was causing him more discomfort. Over-compensating for my lack of understanding regarding the word 'wind' I had asked him if he farted 'with force' and said it with unwarranted aggression, straightening my arm at a right angle. As I said it I even made a fist, denoting strength, then added the Farsi embellishment '*mesleh toofan*' (like a hurricane), which must have been what set him off.

The doctor smiled, made his excuses and left. I sat by the patient's bedside and stared at him. Remembering my dad said he needed entertaining, I deliberated my next move. He seemed to be amused so far, and stared back at me with wonder and possible fear about what was coming next, tensing up to control his body from possible convulsions.

'So,' I said, 'how are you?'

He looked at me, eyebrows furrowed with trepidation but with a wide smile.

'I'm fine.'

An uneasy silence ensued. I then launched into a joke about a chicken from Qazvin, a region in Iran known for its large homosexual population. The very concept of a ten-year-old starting a joke about a gay chicken from Qazvin was a lot for him to bear and he covered his mouth in anticipation. I finished the joke, and he started laughing uncontrollably. He called for the nurse and with underlying hysteria motioned her with a wave saying, *'Begeen bereh* (get him out of here).' Of course I translated this with the same urgency, not realising he meant me. Before I knew it three nurses had arrived, and a green curtain swiftly went up around him. He was clearly in trouble and I heard the words: 'Stitches – quickly!' I was told in no uncertain terms to get out. I left the hospital feeling traumatised and baffled. I rarely translated again. I was left with a profound sense that a joke is no laughing matter.

What emerged from this episode was an awareness of the importance of keeping my foot firmly in two camps: British order and Iranian chaos. It was also to look out for my parents, who were still not *au fait* with Western ways and clearly needed guidance from their British-born children. This would occur most when it came to their dealings with officialdom. I'm sure this was why I began to use humour as a way of alleviating tension and winning over people in authority. Unfortunately it no longer seems to work with traffic wardens these days.

The authority that unnerved my father the most was the silent disapproval emanating from the 'Cottesmore Court

Association' who ran the affairs of the block. They were exasperated by my parents' misunderstanding of the unwritten laws of the building, and their concerns rumbled on, often gathering momentum. Eviction loomed at every Annual General Meeting where a *'final warning to the Djalilis'* was issued with as much frequency as Lady Bassett's complaints about the dog at no. 66 keeping her up at night. The dog eventually died and the matter was closed. The case of the Djalilis remained unresolved.

A status quo gradually became established, where my parents never stopped taking in the sick guests and the Association never followed through with their threats. What stopped them was probably genuine English fairness and tolerance; 'They *are* sick people, after all, so perhaps we should turn a blind eye?' Possibly there was also a fear that the multitudes who limped in and walked out were miraculously healed through some unknown strand of Eastern sorcery? Or maybe the hordes of people who wandered through our door *were* in fact all family relations – and like the Mafia, we were too big and too dangerous a family to offend?

My guess, though, is that no one *disliked* us enough. They may have been chaotic, eccentric and unconventional but my parents were kind, cheerful and generous. The porters, who had more influence than anyone, were certainly kept happy with their Christmas tips and food hampers, not to mention the many cigars and countless pots of (expensive) Iranian caviar. On one occasion even a random picture of the Shah of Iran was surprisingly well received. The sharing of confusing objects of bribery is still a powerful tactic in Iran today. When I was there as a child, a slightly older boy hit me and made me cry, but came back with the gift of a live snail. I forgave him immediately.

When I think of the service my parents provided these stragglers and unfortunates I look back with awe at their generosity of spirit. As a parent myself now, I'm also troubled by their lack of regard for the boundaries between work and family life. It all seemed to get swept up in a tide of 'fingers crossed' goodwill. Unfortunately, or perhaps fortunately from a child's perspective, it was never without incident.

I remember a day when I was allowed (or possibly required) to stay off school. My parents were out and had asked me to stay behind, aged eight, presumably to make sure I could take care of Mohammad, a man in dark glasses who had lost his sight in a factory explosion. He had a friend, another man with sight issues who also had a leg missing. He was called Elahi, but I secretly renamed him Alan. They were quite low maintenance, as they minded their own business and sat around, exchanging odd bits of chit-chat but generally remaining quiet. Not much else to do really if you're two partially sighted guys in a foreign land. They fed themselves and went to the toilet by themselves so there was no 'taking care' to speak of, but I was nevertheless on duty, to make sure they didn't do themselves any damage. At least I think that's the way it was; it wasn't clear who was in charge. Maybe I was assuming inappropriate responsibility.

I switched on the TV to watch my favourite legal drama *Crown Court*, determined to assert dominance over the living area if I had to be stuck with these two clowns. They sat with me, silent and inert. I remember noting the beginnings of an encroaching heavy sensation, which years later I have identified as depression.

The doorbell rang, which I knew meant tradesmen, as they were the only ones who ever pressed it; the door was usually open as people wandered in and out. Answering the bell, I saw a scrawny man in brown overalls with red hair holding a tatty piece of paper. He said he'd come to fix the television. 'We're watching it now,' I protested. Looking down at his paper, he asked: 'Is this number 56?' – a question that my eight-year-old brain took as a sign of legitimacy, so I let him in. After making a few expert examinations behind the TV he announced he had to take it back to the shop. The guys asked what was going on and I translated that the TV was going back to the shop. They both said they were sure the TV was working fine because they could hear noises coming from it. But the man insisted. He tried to pick up the massive TV set on his own but was clearly unable. Sensing he was having trouble, Mohammad and Alan asked if he needed a hand. 'Yeah, I do actually.'

The sight of an English bloke in overalls helped by two partially sighted Iranian men, one hopping on one leg, edging out the flat and carrying the TV down four flights of stairs is one worthy of early Chaplin films. I watched on, all the while translating as they carefully placed the TV in the back of his white transit van. I even remember waving goodbye and watching the van disappear round the corner. As I guided the two men back upstairs, it occurred to me with a sudden and chilling sensation that we might never see him or the TV again. And we never did. My father was so embarrassed by this incident that he couldn't bring himself to report it to the police. Instead he asked us, incredulously, how we could have let a crook come in and take the TV away in broad daylight.

'*Fekr kardeem bacheyeh khoobieh*' (seemed like a nice guy) was all the guests could say.

My father blew up at them both. 'How would *you* know, you're both blind!'

CHAPTER ELEVEN

Islamic Revolution

'Consort with all religions with amity and concord.'

Bahá'í writings

Iran, 1979. The Islamic revolution (*Enghelabeh Jomhuri*) took place with the overthrow of the Reza Shah Pahlavi dynasty and its eventual replacement with an Islamic republic created under Ayatollah Ruhu'llah Khomeini. It was an event that pretty much took the world by surprise as it occurred when Iran was enjoying relative material progress and prosperity. The revolution happened swiftly and was perceived by many as a conservative backlash in response to the Westernisation and secularisation of Iran by the Shah. Suffice it to say massive changes ensued. It was on *BBC News* daily and affected me personally as it was the first time in my life that Iranians were brought sharply into focus in the Western media.

The Iranian revolution proved to be an intense time – not just for my parents and the guests. It also became the backdrop to everything that happened to me during that period. As a thirteen-year-old adolescent with bum fluff and a drooping nose I sat watching constant images of death and rioting on TV coming from Tehran, and was alarmed by scenes of fanatics beating themselves in so called 'Islamic' fervour. Relationships at school, previously harmonious, became fraught. It was hard explaining what was going on to my friends, who were following events on TV with similar interest, mostly so they would have ammunition to tease me with the next day. In response to their questions I just regurgitated all the random things guests had said at home:

'Khomeini is a puppet put in by the Americans to keep oil prices down.'

'Jimmy Carter is paying people to go in the streets to demonstrate.'

'Iran is going backwards into the dark ages.'

The situation was far more complex than the media were presenting. My father in his job as a photographer had connections with the London-based Iranian newspaper *Kayhan* and had photographed the Shah on many occasions. He was not pro-Shah in a political sense, but had enjoyed his work with the monarch, and was troubled by the various reports of his journalist colleagues that came out of Iran. When seismic world events take place they're often shrouded in confusion, and the Islamic revolution was no exception.

What complicated matters further was the fact that we were Bahá'ís, not Muslims. The Bahá'ís were (and remain) a persecuted minority in Iran. Being Iranians, we were already a minority in Britain. This meant that when dealing with Iranian Muslims in London, my family was actually a minority within a minority. Add that to the fact that some Bahá'ís in the London community thought my family, due to their business, were more than a little strange. So, quite uniquely, I felt like a minority, within a minority, within a minority. Added to this, I felt I was an actual alien within my own family. The levels of cosmic isolation were profound and overwhelming.

News was filtering through of Bahá'ís in Iran being executed.

The Bahá'í faith is seen as an apostate religion in Iran so after the Islamic revolution many people were rounded up and killed. Apart from being emotionally traumatic to my parents, who personally knew a number of those executed, it inevitably affected their work. Their clientele were mostly Muslims, many of whom were severely prejudiced against the Bahá'ís due to government-controlled propaganda. On top of that, it was almost impossible to ascertain which of our Muslim guests were prejudiced against the Bahá'ís and which were more tolerant. So a policy evolved to steer away from any talk of religion. Bahá'ís were being executed because they refused to deny their faith, so out of respect to the guests, as well as to protect ourselves, the question of our religious identity was never discussed. If a situation were to arise where we were required to 'admit' being Bahá'ís (denial was not an option) then there was a distinct possibility that some guests might feel compelled to leave. Moreover, those with deep prejudice would feel they couldn't stay in a house any longer if its inhabitants were in their minds 'najess' (impure), a term bandied about denoting 'those from which one must eschew'. Governed by these beliefs they would have no choice but to leave immediately.

The situation of the Bahá'ís was sometimes discussed amongst the guests and it was always telling. The more liberal guests felt saddened by the regime's treatment of the Bahá'ís and referred to them as 'good people' and their 'fellow countrymen', which always filled me with hope. But others thought the treatment of Bahá'ís in Iran was 'correct and justified'. It was frightening to witness how they had been influenced so negatively. In fact the anti-Bahá'ís propaganda in Iran was so disturbing that I can't stomach repeating it here. As a young boy, what I found most unsettling was the fact that these people were receiving *our* hospitality, happily sitting in *our* house, eating, having fun, talking freely – but not knowing we were Bahá'ís.

I didn't blame them. How would I react if I came into contact with a group of people I'd heard terrible things about? And if they found out we were Bahá'ís, what would they do to me? I had images of guests setting fire to the home and beating me with sticks. As I reached my mid-teens I couldn't take the unpredictability in the house any more. So as a bizarre psychological coping strategy I decided to create a survival alter ego.

I started lying about my nationality. I was going to parties now and meeting a new bunch of boys and girls from a myriad of West London social circles: Mods, Rockers, Bovver Boys, Hooray Henrys, New Romantics, Sloane Rangers. I learned that saying I was Italian was far less off-putting than saying I was from Iran, where men in beards, robes and turbans behaved bizarrely on television screens. The once proud Iranian boy was now a fully fledged Italian called Chico from Palermo, Sicilia (which I learned to pronounce with relish and even threw in the embarrassing add-on 'eh, vaffanculo'). I was now a Catholic who incidentally refused to speak Italian because the Sicilian dialect was so strong that it was difficult, even for Italians, to understand.

At one party, organised by pupils from the International School of London, I stood with a Brazilian, a Portuguese and a Spaniard. The scruffy Brazilian said, 'Hey, if you're Italian . . .' (meaning me) 'then all of us can talk in our own language and we can understand each other! Come on, let's do it!' I froze as the only words I knew in Italian were 'ciao', 'ciao bella' and 'come si chiama?' (what's your name?). As they started to chat, I was the only one who didn't speak. I was exposed. I thought I should just come clean and start a deeper conversation about the soul having no nationality and what lies beneath cultural identity. I also thought I could possibly speak Farsi and just pass it off as that obscure Sicilian dialect. In the end I was asked by the Brazilian, 'Come si chiama?' I stared at him and paused for what seemed like an eternity before saying, 'Abdu'l Mohammad Reza Raysool ya Allah Mamdooha.' It was the first time I'd got a laugh from a new group of people. But it was also the moment I realised this particular Italian job had to come to an end.

To say I yearned for escapism is an understatement. I began to immerse myself in music and films. I went alone to the National Film Theatre on the South Bank on many occasions and I developed passions for less commercial movies like *La Cage Aux Folles* and Mike Nichols' *The Graduate*. The frustrated intellectual in me looked to read everything about the actors and directors of these films. I also developed a deep love for the American folk music of the sixties and seventies, which seemed to be asking important questions about the individual and society. *The Graduate*, especially, had a major impact on me as it featured music by Simon and Garfunkel. I learned all the words to 'Mrs Robinson' and 'The Sound of Silence'. The stereo was in the living room (more like a dying room in our house, given all our sick guests), so a great many hours were spent listening to music on headphones to infuse some beauty into my living conditions. Once I listened to 'Scarborough Fair' while watching a large man in Islamic robes clip his toenails. The music helped immensely.

Although escape and running away were constant preoccupations, a strangely positive by-product of the Islamic revolution was that my home life took on an unexpected element of comfort and sanctuary. In times of difficulty ex-pat Iranians would inevitably sit around a table and lace their political conversations about the revolution with that dark humour that tumultuous events often inspires. I enjoyed the laughter among the guests and felt solace that we were uniting as fellow Iranians in times of adversity, whatever faith. I was also quietly proud that my father led the way with his absurd jokes.

It was one particular joke of his that left an indelible mark on the house. One of the most bizarre events that ever took place happened on a Friday night close to midnight. I lay tucked up on the sofa (my bed at the time) trying to ignore the raucous laughter from the dining table next to me while reading *Asterix in Britain*. There were four men bantering together: a man recovering from open-heart surgery who was about five weeks post-op, my father and two others. I don't recall the joke, but there was a sudden explosion of laughter, the kind of laughter that stops you in your tracks. I looked up and the gentleman with the heart condition was laughing the most, that silent laugh with his mouth open. He then seemed to get light-headed and kept saying, '*Vai vai*' (a generic Iranian sound for 'Oh God, please, no'). He got up and stumbled across the room and, still laughing, went into the bathroom.

As the others were calming down, a moment or two passed and then they all fell silent. On cue, a sound came from the toilet that can only be described as a loud bang. As my mind immediately scrambled to make sense of the noise, I came to the conclusion it may have been the passing of wind. Since my translating catastrophe I had become conversant with the notion of passing wind and it definitely sounded familiar. This was followed by a loud thud as if something had hit the floor, which set them all off again in the dining room. The laughter now peaked, with the men banging on tables, tears streaming down their cheeks. As an observant youth this worried me: didn't they realise something was clearly amiss?

After a while they seemed to forget about their friend in the toilet, so I tried to focus once more on my book. Backgammon and chat resumed and I was up to the point where Asterix and Obelix take on the Brits in rugby for the first time. I was aware that I was probably getting too old for these books, but figured that at least I was learning important historical facts. A full twenty minutes passed after the man had left the table before everyone's concern was reactivated. After calling his name several times and banging violently on the toilet door, my father decided to break it down. There was a distinct pause and even some stifled guffaws as we tried to digest the image that greeted us. A conviction grew that this was all an elaborate joke. Our friend lay slumped over the bath in a position that would have been perfect for him to jump up and shout 'Ta-daaa!' and reduce the gathering to helpless laughter. Unfortunately the silence continued and the body remained motionless. Something was very wrong. My father rushed in and made frantic attempts to revive him. About an hour later paramedics arrived and he was pronounced dead.

A police inquiry ensued. The man had literally broken wind and died. Accidental death caused by heart failure was recorded and to this day the event is rarely spoken of in my family. Yet again I realised laughter was a dangerous thing. Certainly, no one had time to consider whether I might have been traumatised from seeing a dead body at so tender an age. It certainly warranted a few therapy sessions, as it remains – and I have to remember to pretend I'm sorry to say this – one of the funniest things I have ever seen.

Death wasn't the only danger afforded by this chaotic existence. In those days the concept of security was casual to say the least. It wasn't even discussed. Our door was always open, randomers came to stay, friends of randomers hung around all day, and cousins of the friends of randomers showed up and blagged meals and a bed for the night. As a troubled teenager I began to feel protective of my parents and was galled by the thought of people abusing their generosity. It was bad enough I had to give up my bed and privacy, but if money was exchanged I could cope. Freeloaders I couldn't abide. If they were occupying space and taking our time for free, it felt like they were showing the ultimate disrespect to my mum and dad who worked so hard to keep everyone happy. It became exhausting for my parents to keep tabs on who was staying, who wasn't, who was paying and who stayed for free. It all merged into one big mass of people coming and going. This was hugely frustrating, although, looking at it more graciously, it certainly challenged any preconceived or limited notions of what defined 'family'.

In fact so many people came that often when guests would return a few years later and say: 'I'm back! Remember me?' I'd look at them and say, 'No.' My father stepped in and taught me about 'tactfulness'.

'They're back. *Try* to be nice.'

'But I don't remember them.'

'Just *say* you remember them.'

'I don't want to.'

'Why don't you want make them happy?'

I wondered if this counted as lying. According to my parents, it wasn't lying if it was making people feel good. My mother always said a lie was fine if it made sick people feel good because it helped them recover. She was a great believer in the 'placebo effect' and always made wonderful comments to sick patients, bolstering their self-esteem. I could understand the logic but distorting basic facts seemed strange. I honestly couldn't remember the names of half the people with whom I shared a bathroom. They all looked the same to me. When you've seen one guy on crutches with one leg, sunglasses and emphysema you've pretty much seen them all. And quite honestly it was always a relief when they left. To be brutal, it was 'out of sight, out of mind'.

In the summer of 1980 a family who had stayed with us ten years before, when I was five, came back. On arrival they kissed and hugged me like I was a long-lost son and expressed shock at how much I'd grown. They then asked, rather jokily, if I remembered them in any shape or form? I looked at my father and then stuttered:

'Of course I remember you. I was hoping you'd come back again one day. I can't believe you're here. My wish has come true!'

I surrendered myself to their passionate hugs. The mother nearly passed out and declared I was the most beautiful boy that she had ever seen. For the rest of her stay she frequently hovered near me, and for a while I worried that we had become inseparable. Every time I said anything, especially when translating episodes of *Charlie's Angels* and *The Bionic Woman* for her, she put her hands to her mouth and cried with gratitude. My father whispered '*barikalla*' (well done) in my ear and looked at me with pride. To be honest, I did miss her when she left, she was a really nice lady.

By the time I was in secondary school I was coming and going like a guest myself. I played in the street after school and only came up for dinner. Sometimes I hung around outside until I got called in by my mother's shouts from the window. I was leading a very independent life by the time I was fifteen, so it was a shock to come home one day and see the house empty except for a couple of Hell's Angels bikers sat in the living room. Two massive hulking guys, clad in black leather with flowing hair, tattoos and beards, were sipping tea from delicate china. I said hello and saw my father hiding in the kitchen looking nervous. I joined him and asked who they were. He said he had no idea. My sister arrived home and did the same. Ditto my brother. Within minutes we were all huddled together in the kitchen wondering who on earth were these two big burly English men, and what were they doing in our house? Finally my mother arrived, greeted them with warm enthusiasm and asked if they needed anything. Apparently they were fine, so she joined us in the kitchen and started rummaging around for biscuits to offer them with their tea.

'Do *you* know these people?'

'No.'

'But you said hello like you knew them!'

'I don't. Put more tea on for them.'

'Don't make them tea!'

'Why not? Aren't they your friends?'

'No!'

'*Pas qui-an?* (So who are they?)'

'*Nimidoonim!* (We don't know!)'

Even my mother, who always had something to say, was at a loss for words. We sat in silence looking at each other and beginning to worry that these men were going to break into the kitchen and kill us with machetes. My brother, in a lightbulb moment, concluded: 'They might be undercover policemen.'

'What?'

'I heard about this at school: undercover policemen come into the house and wait, usually for the whole family to gather. Then they say what's happened and how serious it is and arrest the whole family.'

Believing it immediately I blurted out: 'I stole something from Woolworths!'

'When?'

'Last year. A Fry's mint chocolate bar. It was a dare.'

Thankfully no one picked up on my terrible admission as at that moment the bikers began to make their way towards the kitchen. This was it. It seemed like a horror film. The silence was appalling; I was sure a sawn-off shotgun was about to be aimed at my head or at the very least I would be led away in handcuffs. Slightly embarrassed, and in the most polite manner imaginable, one of the bikers simply said: 'Well, er . . . thanks for the tea . . . we'd best be off.'

Smock, helmet, water bottle, gun.
The young actor juggling props.

Right: Mum and my sister on an average night out.

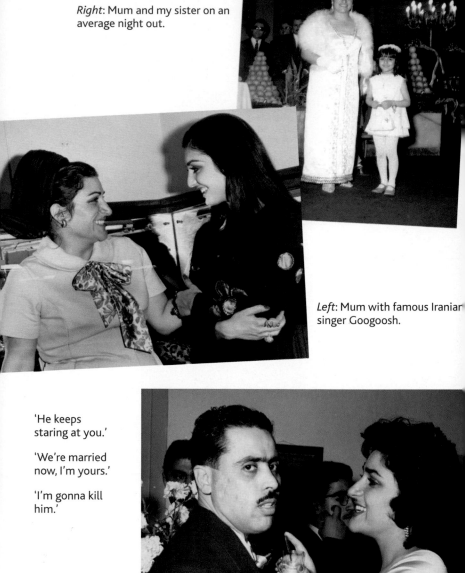

Left: Mum with famous Iranian singer Googoosh.

'He keeps staring at you.'

'We're married now, I'm yours.'

'I'm gonna kill him.'

Mum and Dad

Impossibly cute. What went wrong?

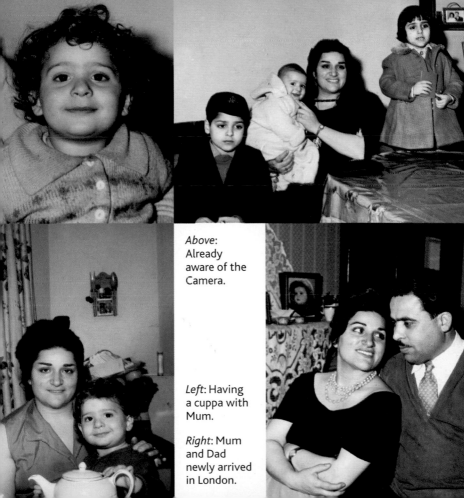

Above: Already aware of the Camera.

Left: Having a cuppa with Mum.

Right: Mum and Dad newly arrived in London.

Left: Dad in sailor suit, 1928. *Right*: Me in sailor suit, 1968.

My Uncle Parviz's wedding where I stole the show.

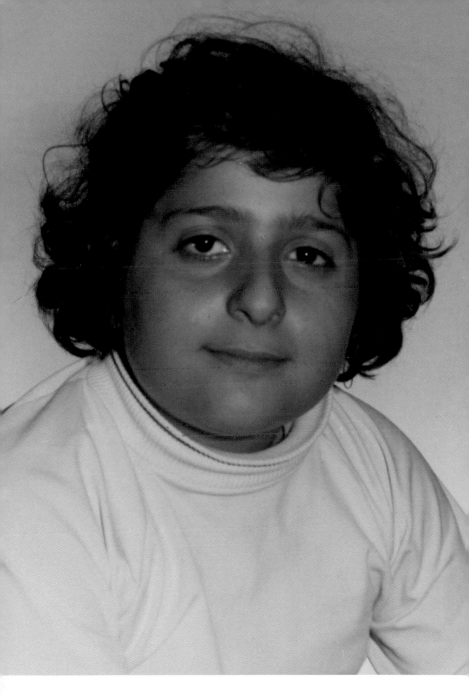

Already worrying about life on other planets
(the day after the traumatic coconuts incident).

Second from the left, front row.
At a Family reunion in 1972 thinking about *The Joker*.

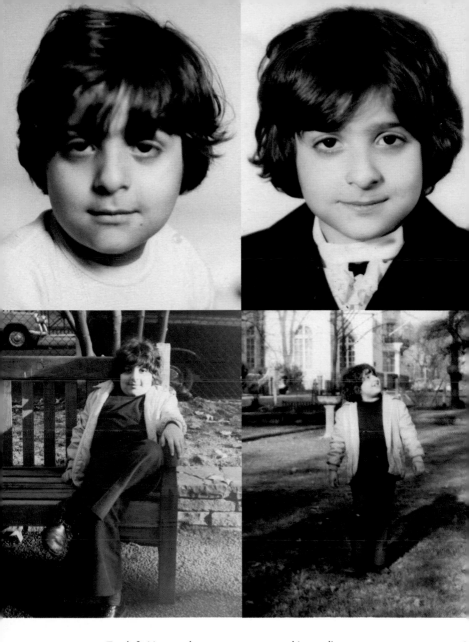

Top left: No wonder everyone assumed I was dim.

Top right: In a cravat just before I fell in the cesspit.

Bottom left, *right*: The young philosopher.

First on the left, back row: A school photo.
Already clear, aged nine, for me, comedy was the only option.

In unison we all got up and said, 'Great seeing you/shame you couldn't stay/pop by again/cheers/all the best/love to the family . . .'

And with that they left. To this day we have no idea who they were or where they came from. Some years later, for a short while, I managed to convince my sister that they were the hairy bikers from the TV show.

It's possible they mistook the house, and with the door being open just came in and made themselves comfortable while waiting for their host. My dad, coming home, assuming they were friends of one of the guests, brought them tea, smiled and parked himself in the kitchen out of harm's way. Realising they must be in the wrong house, the bikers simply decided to leave as politely as they could.

It was the subject of some mirth at dinner that night as we relayed and embellished the tale to a lovely new family of five called the Hashemis from Mashad (the Manchester of Iran). I was intrigued by their accents and their jollity. 'Maybe they were Savak agents [Iranian secret police]!' Mr Hashemi said. 'Could have been worse,' said my father, 'they could have sung rock songs!' He and Mr Hashemi got on very well, as did the two mothers, and by an amazing stroke of fortune each of their three children were the exact same age as myself and my siblings.

We loved the Hashemis. Their youngest, a fair-skinned frail-looking girl with auburn hair called Fariba, was painfully sweet and though not a great conversationalist herself she thought I was very funny. They'd come to England to deal with her mystery illness. There was only one other guest at that time, Mr Kolahi, a flamboyant character who wore loud coloured cravats and was prone to bouts of depression, drinking and gambling. But for a change, that night he sat quietly at the table simply observing the two families. My brother and sister went off with the other two Hashemi kids to play music on the stereo and Fariba and I sat listening to the after-dinner conversation, munching on the caviar and chocolates the Hashemis had brought over for us. 'Not bad, this,' my dad said. 'This is the high life,' which suddenly triggered Mr Hashemi to give an impromptu speech:

'Mr and Mrs Djalili,' he said grandly, 'I need to say something. Your names are very well known in Iran. Well known and well *loved*. When my Fariba got this illness we knew we had to come to England. And from what our friends said there was only one place to come: to the Djalilis. They understand the Iranian mentality, they said. The place is homely and you can relax in the house just like it's your own. If you are sick, staying there will make you feel better. And they were right. We do feel better. We are lucky we found you. God willing Fariba's recovery will be more rapid for staying here. God bless you all.'

Everybody was moved. For the first time I'd heard someone articulate the purpose of this guesthouse. For the first time I didn't rage against it. I now understood why the association hadn't evicted us: good old British decency. To be honest this kind of gentle goodness could never have happened if it wasn't for the understanding of our British neighbours. Sure the business bent the rules, but if it meant people's lives were being helped and enriched like this, then it was for a common good. Cottesmore Court suddenly felt like a cosy bubble of racial harmony. I felt happy that finally there was a family I actually wanted to come back before they'd even left. The Hashemis were friends for life.

That night I slept in a bedroom. The revolution had cut our clientele by half, and at fifteen I was finally able to have my own room. Admittedly it was just a box room by the front door but to me it was an oasis of luxury. I awoke later to noises. No voices, just a lot of bumping and banging. I looked at my digital clock and saw the time was 2.18 a.m. Then the front door closed shut. Silence. I went back to sleep.

It was only when I got up for breakfast and saw the ashen faces of my parents that I knew something had upset them gravely. I learned later that Mr Kolahi had stayed up late drinking and talking to Mr Hashemi till about 2 a.m. In a tipsy haze he had mentioned we were Bahá'ís. There were some remonstrations, some disbelief, and something was said along the lines of: 'But they're too nice to be Bahá'ís.' Without a word of warning or explanation, Hashemi woke his family up, got them to pack immediately and they all left by the front door, bumping and banging their luggage as they went.

This explained the thick atmosphere at breakfast next morning. Mr Kolahi was eating breakfast normally as if nothing had happened, my father standing over him cooking eggs, my mother dealing with the toast. I came in, sat next to him and had my breakfast before going off to school. No one said a word. There was no need. Moments earlier Mr Kolahi had told my father that he had revealed to Hashemi that we were Bahá'ís and that was 'probably' why they left. Keeping his dignity my father simply said, '*Khodeshoon meedoonan*' (that's' up to them), and continued to fry eggs. This upset me later as I considered Mr Kolahi's revelation to be calculated and bewildering. More confusing though was why Mr Kolahi didn't leave himself, and continued to visit us, often getting drunk and needing to be carried to bed, which my father did obediently and without judgement for the next fifteen years.

CHAPTER TWELVE

Fights

'Stop acting so small. You are the universe in ecstatic motion.'
Rumi

I got into a lot of fights during my teens. Perhaps this was due to excess testosterone that eventually led to early baldness. But I've often wondered whether the events in Iran, which dominated my home life, contributed in some way to the pent-up feelings and unexplained aggression I expressed in my teens. Perhaps these tensions in me were connected to the powerlessness my parents felt, far away from their homeland and grieving the brutal losses of people they had known from their childhoods.

Growing up, the concept of fighting held so much ambiguity – was it brave, was it weak, what did it mean? Who was Gandhi? And how did you reconcile his views with an emerging Thatcherism and dog-eat-dog climate when you were an immigrant trying to survive? Where were my principles? What *were* principles? How could it be that members of my faith community were being executed in Iran, while the world seemed to carry on turning and I struggled with algebra? How could I make sense of all this? Why was I always so angry?

There's a saying in Farsi, *'khodesho neshoon dad'* (he showed himself), usually shared in disparaging whispers when someone has humiliated themselves in public, or shown their 'true colours'. Growing up, and being on the receiving end of *khodesho neshoon dad* more times than I can remember, my understanding of this phrase as a youth drove me into the defiant belief that if I didn't 'stand up for myself', no one else would.

Having said that, the need to be seen by others, to show that 'I'm here, I exist and I have rights' is an essential component of survival, and I remember debating this during a break in filming during *Grow Your Own* in 2006, shot entirely in Liverpool. On this occasion a group of us were discussing the qualities of our director, Richard Laxton. Most of us had never heard of him before and were greatly impressed.

'He's an actor's director.'

'I like the way he stays calm.'

'We're definitely in safe hands.'

We were then joined by Roland Manookian, an actor known for his roles in cult films like *Football Factory* and *The Business*. Without hesitation Roland proclaimed, 'Yeah, he can give it all that' – making a talking-hand gesture – 'but he ain't good with his mitts [fists]. One punch and he'd be down like a plank.'

We stressed we were talking about Laxton's *human* qualities, not his fighting skills, but Roland came back with, 'Yeah I know. But he's a talker not a fighter. I'm saying if there's trouble you wouldn't want him about.' It seemed, quite shockingly, to be missing the point, but his words held a certain brutal wisdom. (As an aside, I have no doubt that Mr Laxton is probably a karate expert who can slay a villain with his little finger.)

I first learned self-preservation in the psychological battle-ground outside my apartment block in our cul-de-sac and on the nearby streets. The cul-de-sac was dominated by our posh apartment block, terraced houses and a builder's yard and was usually filled with kids playing outside after school. We got the odd complaint due to the noise, but by and large the residents gave us the freedom to play outdoors and it was relatively safe. Around 6.30 p.m. a mother's elegant-sounding voice would trill 'Toby!' or 'Lenora!' or 'Roger! Time for tea!' and children would scamper inside and remain there for the rest of the evening, presumably drinking frothy milk and reading Enid Blyton while tucked under patchwork quilts. I often stayed out late, sometimes until 10 p.m., occasionally with the odd straggler but usually on my own. I loved that song by the Crusaders, 'Street Life', and often sang it in our West London cul-de-sac. As far as I was concerned, street life was the only life I knew.

It was in this particular street where I bumped into Freddie Mercury, about a week after his iconic 'Bohemian Rhapsody' appearance on *Top of the Pops*. The fact that I was told he had Persian ancestry only added to Freddie's overwhelming mystique. As he crossed the road, he made eye contact with me, as I was riding my bike. His shimmering charisma stopped me in my tracks. All I could think of saying to this dark, vibrant man in purple clothes was, 'You were on TV!' To which he replied: 'Yes I was . . . wasn't I *fabulous*?!' I wanted to chase him on my bike shouting, 'Yes! Yes, you were! Freddie Mercury! Fabulous!' Thankfully I was frozen like a rabbit in headlights. I knew my place.

I also encountered Willie Rushton, a ubiquitous TV personality of the day, at the same spot.

'You're on TV?' (I was getting good at this.)

'Yes I am. But who am I?'

'Willie.'

'That's right. But what do I do?'

'I don't know.'

'Ah, exactly. No one knows what I am or what I do. Actor? Comedian? Politician? Newsreader?'

I hadn't thought about that. He was right. I saw him in lots of shows but didn't know *what he was famous for.*

'Are you an actor?' I enquired.

'No! I'm a wit. To wit too-woo! To wit too-woo!' And he walked off. It was a stock answer he gave to people asking him ignorant questions and it was a good one.

Perhaps I just should have told him he was fabulous?

Celebrities were often spotted around Kensington. I remember seeing Dustin Hoffman stride confidently into Marks and Spencer, and wondered if that's where he bought the flares he wore in *Kramer vs Kramer.* I once gave in a lost wallet to the Kensington Close Hotel swimming pool, and it turned out to belong to the actor Patrick Mower who generously rewarded me with a £5 note. By the same poolside I stood shivering in my trunks while chatting to the affable boxer Joe Bugner who was lunging in the water before his British heavyweight fight.

In those days there didn't seem to be such a distinction between 'normal' people and 'celebrities'. In fact, because of my crazy household, TV personalities became part of a generic group of nice English people 'out there' – members of the 'world at large' who existed beyond the borders of the bizarre enclave of weird Iranian guests but who seemed somehow closer to me than the sick Iranians I lived with. It might also have been that there was more of a sense of community back then, despite Mrs Thatcher telling us that there was no such thing as society. At any rate I wasn't fazed by the juxtaposition of Dustin Hoffman and Marks and Spencer. In fact, I felt comforted by the knowledge that he would have durable slacks for his next movie, especially if it involved running around Central Park in winter.

This was fancy Kensington, sophisticated and well-to-do, where diplomats and celebrities chose to live because it was supposedly safe. But territory disputes in this peculiar patch bristled regardless. While Toxteth and Brixton erupted in riots, and gang warfare raged in Los Angeles, youths in West London ventured out from their leafy mews, and tried to show who was boss by cycling into our cul-de-sac. It wasn't just a guy thing either, it happened with girls, too: *especially* with girls.

Lavinia, the daughter of a banker, lived literally 50 yards away on an adjacent road in a large terraced house. She was pretty for a fourteen-year-old, carried herself with confidence and was very tanned, due to dream holidays in exotic locations, sometimes during term time. Lavinia wandered into our patch, no doubt attracted by the exuberant noise, and seemed to bond intensely with one or two girls, while keeping her distance from others. I felt a little sorry for her, as she seemed nice enough. But I could see that she was an obvious threat, due to her looks and strident elocution-trained voice. Somehow, she incensed the gang of kids in our cul-de-sac and a fight broke out. A girl was wielding a piece of broken brick close to Lavinia's head. To my horror I witnessed Lavinia's skull burst open and rivulets of blood flow into the street.

'She cracked open her head!'

I'd never seen a skull bleed and the image has stayed with me ever since, all the more shocking because Lavinia was so deeply inoffensive. I tried to bring it up with my brother, who was equally traumatised, but he hissed that it was an issue we couldn't possibly understand because there was 'history'. I do remember eavesdropping on the girls discussing it after: 'She had it coming to her./ But she didn't say anything./ She didn't have to, she wore hot pants.' For a few days Kelso Place had become the Gaza Strip of Kensington.

In another road, connected to ours by only a footpath (which meant it was almost a different country), a mean-looking son of a mechanic was a 'face' I came to fear and loathe. I used to cycle past his house on my way to my regular diving competitions.

Incidentally these competitions laid the foundations for my later escapades in ITV's *Splash!* Without wishing to sound immodest, I did pretty well in the West London school diving scene. Competitions generally took place at Chelsea Baths off the King's Road. Unfortunately on occasions when my name was considered too complicated the poolside commentator would announce: 'And the winner is . . . Mr X!' Not that it was a big deal. All we had to do was walk in a straight line, point our toes and enter the water without making too clumsy a splash.

So, to return to the scary boy. I locked eyes with him once every six months or so, and every time he stared back with daggers. We never exchanged words, and I never knew his name (so I'll call him 'Darren' for now). For no apparent or justifiable reason, we had developed an animal dislike for each other. Call it chemistry, call it class or immigration war, call it incompatible astrological star alignment – all I knew was when I saw Darren I felt a reptilian instinct to protect myself.

I would sometimes see Darren on the street below from my window and would observe him with a certain fascination. I was always thankful he couldn't see me, and often ducked down until I was sure he had passed by. After some months, he began to acknowledge me with more focus when I was outside playing with other kids. He'd pick me out with a 'what are you looking at?' glance that sent shivers down my spine. I became acutely aware of the fragility of human sanity, and the thin film of consciousness that separates this life from the next.

One day, a select group of us were playing word games in the courtyard of my flats. Darren sailed into Kelso Place on bicycles with two mates. This vision of three boys in DM boots riding unsupervised into our patch was a terrifying and brazen act of intrusion. The tension was palpable. We immediately fell silent. This wasn't a friendly visit. My animal senses were on red alert and I knew trouble was brewing. Confrontation was inevitable.

'You lot praying?'

Gemma, an awe-inspiringly brave girl of twelve, mirrored back their frosty intensity (I made a mental note to congratulate her later) by asking:

'Playing or praying?'

'You looked like you was praying.'

'No.'

'Wot you doing then?'

'Playing a word game.'

This made them snigger and they mimicked the sentence back at her in an approximation of her high-pitched tone, which admittedly had become rather strangled through nerves. I laughed too, hoping to alleviate the tension. For a second I thought Darren smiled back at me, and I felt a rush of hope that surprised me – maybe we could still be friends?

'What you laughing at?' he snapped. The moment evaporated.

Gemma, emboldened by the raised stakes, came through for the group.

'Why don't you just go away? We don't want you here.'

'Who says you can say anything?'

And the effortless confidence in his voice invoked the presence of a pulsating silence that wafted around us like a sinister fog.

This was war. These boys were only eleven or twelve years old. There were six of us, mostly under-elevens but we had two who were twelve and one very literary thirteen-year-old called Sergio who was the son of an Argentinian dissident. So we felt we had wisdom on our side, and nodded to each other our intention to rid ourselves of these heinous intruders. The problem was, we had no plan.

The 'bovver boys' whizzed off around a corner, presumably

to talk strategy. In a twist of good fortune, some balloons appeared out of Mark and Roger Cazlett's pockets. These two brothers had been to a party the night before and, rather than dismissing the balloons as babyish, had shown incredible foresight to stash several of them away, knowing they might come in handy.

Following Mark Cazlett's instructions, we quietly filled the balloons with water from the hose tap, and made huge waterbombs. In no time at all, we were armed. All of us had a weapon, ready for action.

Mark, a natural leader, got us organised. (I think he later developed a career doing motivational team-building retreats in the Brecon Beacons for large corporations.)

'When they come back, we'll be ready. Gemma, it's your call. You give the go ahead. We'll release the ammunition. Can you handle it?'

It was all set. My heart was beating fast. No one had responded to my idea about code words, but I'd let it go. No one seemed to appreciate my use of the word 'roger' as an ironic word-play between Roger our friend, and the military word for 'OK'. I'd let that one go, too. According to Mark, I was slowing everyone down. He told me that it was about living in the moment, grasping its potential and seeing the bigger picture.

We stepped out on to the road.

'Here they come!'

The boys were by now parading themselves as they swooped around on their bikes, scanning the cul-de-sac as if they owned our patch. They saw us standing in the street and slid arrogantly to a halt. Our gang clocked each other, and with a collective resolve took a step forward. Mark gave the warning: 'If you don't leave now you run the risk of getting very wet indeed.'

The boys laughed.

'Think we're joking?' shouted Gemma, semi-quaking.

The boys said nothing.

Gemma went rogue: 'Well . . . six balloons filled with *petrol* versus NO balloons means we are *very* serious.'

We all looked at each other. Hang on.

Petrol? Why was Gemma bringing petrol into it? It was a ridiculous lie. But somehow it raised the stakes. The boys were visibly shaken. I looked at my nemesis. He stared fixedly at my 'toxic' balloon.

'You wouldn't dare!'

The hateful look of spite on his face, co-mingled with fear, momentarily dissuaded me and I started to recall religious quotes about loving one's enemies. But mob mentality ruled: there was no going back.

Gemma was now drunk with power.

'We're giving you one last chance! Leave or prepare to burn. I've got matches.'

Just as I was thinking: this is such a terrible mistake, Gemma called, 'One . . . two . . . *three!*' All the balloons, except mine, went flying in the air. In a sudden flurry of activity the boys ducked and held their hands up to protect their heads. The five balloons crashed down, bursting on impact around the bicycles. They had all missed. Believing they had dodged life-endangering petrol, the boys became crazed and shouted, 'You've had it now!' They ripped bicycle pumps from their bikes and started flailing them around like baseball bats.

I don't know what came over me: fear, loathing, or possibly just a desperate need for resolution. I started walking towards Darren like a Dalek about to exterminate.

'Go on. Just you try!' he said, egging me on, and I kept walking. He was backing away by now, which was a victory in itself. I walked on in silence. As he finally turned his back to flee, I lobbed the balloon as high as I could, to get rid of it really, in a 'so long, suckers!' kind of way. I just threw, randomly, also preparing to flee. But time stood still. To my horror, and by a complete miracle, it landed and exploded on Darren's head.

An almighty roar went up from our side. Darren was drenched. He took a moment to take in what had happened, frantically smelling for petrol. His long, aggressively curly hair was now lank and dripping. Furious that he'd been duped and enraged by my accuracy, he pointed at me, breathless, and shouted: 'Bastard!'

There was a little beat of shock to settle before the boys gave chase. Everyone scampered away in different directions. Kids disappeared into homes, doors slammed behind them. I was convinced Darren was going to kill me so I ran for my life. I sped around the back of the flats to bamboozle him and shot in through the fire exit. I dived into my room and slammed the door shut. I didn't come out for days.

I avoided the mews where Darren lived for years. If I had to pass by I rode my bike past his house as fast as I could, and kept my head down. I even had dreams about his street being an alternate universe, visualising his family as terrifying rednecks from Alabama. The dream always ended with Darren bursting out of his house with a massive water cannon and drowning me with his rage.

Years later, I saw him from a distance and realised he had grown very tall. I definitely couldn't take him in a fight now. I also noticed that he was wearing a sheepskin coat, which convinced me he was working and/or possibly still into football (he had been a hardened Chelsea fan and I often used to see him and his father on their way to a game).

The last time I remember seeing him, we bumped into each other outside Barkers of Kensington. It was clear he hadn't forgotten who I was, as he grunted loudly, crashed both his hands into my chest, and gave me an almighty shove. It was an undoubted provocation but I didn't react. In fact I prepared to succumb to a beating. It was time for retribution and he deserved to have his revenge. However, although he looked irate, I wasn't sure if he just wasn't in the *mood* for a fight. Or maybe he'd been sent to Barkers by his mum to get something, so he didn't have *time* to fight. Whatever the reason, he left it at that, and I never saw him again. Even to this day, I often think about him and quake. Last I heard he had joined the notorious hooligan group Combat-18 and the Chelsea Headhunters. I just hope he reads this and at least realises I support Chelsea.

Another kid I encountered was Daniel, a Californian whose dad drove a Porsche and whose mum looked like Britt Ekland. Daniel was incredibly competitive and fit and, at ten, already displayed an impressive six-pack.

'A kid with a constant tan can never be trusted,' Gemma said, and I agreed. 'In fact, anyone with a tan can't be trusted,' she said, looking pointedly at my sister. But Daniel was a different kettle of fish. If I saw Daniel across the street we'd instinctively run as fast as we could to see who was faster. He always won. He wasn't friendly and I didn't like him. But unfortunately there was no way I was going to beat him at anything.

One day a fight that had been brewing between us for weeks erupted with surprising rapidity. A disagreement arose about bikes. He said his was better than mine then took my bike (without my permission), declared it to be a piece of junk and threw it on the ground. Before I had a chance to finish – 'hey, be careful!' – he'd taken a swipe at me. Americans didn't mess about.

Kids started egging us on (all on my side) and I gave it a shot. But he was never where I threw my fist. He bobbed up, I went for him and he disappeared. I even punched a wall while he temporarily vanished. Then I remember a flurry of fists, all of them his, raining down on me. My brother finally stepped in: 'You lost. Let's go inside.' The spectators ruefully peeled away. My humiliation was complete. 'We'll call it a draw,' I announced to no one, as my brother gave me a tissue to wipe blood off my lips. Thankfully Daniel and his family moved away and I never saw him again. There was no way round it – he was quite simply better than me in every way.

Having had these two brushes with violence as a child I made a solemn commitment to pacifism. Fighting was fundamentally a useless exercise that had left me feeling diminished and guilty. I wept alone to Elvis's 'In the Ghetto' and vowed never to get trapped in a cycle of violence again.

CHAPTER THIRTEEN

Holland Park School

'Dance in the middle of fighting. Dance in your blood. Dance when you're perfectly free.'

Rumi

Holland Park School was a massive comprehensive that served 2,000 pupils. It was situated in the middle of Campden Hill between Kensington High Street and Notting Hill Gate. I was concerned about some of the 'rough kids' from Ladbroke Grove who attended the school – but on the upside I'd heard they served chips at lunchtime. This was unprecedented and had to be seen to be believed. Despite differences in colour, culture, language and religion, there is nobody, in the entire world, who doesn't like chips.

Things began badly on day one when one such 'rough kid' in the year above me took a dislike to my face (I may have had one of those faces) and purposely bumped into me outside the toilets. I didn't react, and chose to move on with dignity. 'That's Eddie,' I was told. 'They say he was beaten up last year on his first day and wants to do the same to a first year.'

How sad, I thought. But forewarned is forearmed.

The next time I saw him, I was walking to PE, my Adidas

bag bursting with gym clothes and heavy books. Eddie bumped into me deliberately once more. This time I stood my ground and confronted him. His friends shouted, 'Go on, hit him!' as Eddie started dancing around me like a professional boxer, punching me in the face with soft jabs that landed but never hurt. His mates egged him on, shouting, 'Go on! Finish him off!'

Unfortunately my commitment to peace, love and understanding vanished. I suddenly panicked, worrying I'd be late for my next class. In a rush of adrenaline, I took one massive swing and flattened him with the Adidas bag. Sitting squarely on top of him I warned him never to try this again. He got up and ran away shouting, 'You're dead!' But the next day he was remarkably friendly and offered to show me nude pictures from a magazine. He even invited me to join his gang and was always affable thereafter.

Hence I became more confident that I could avert any danger by a modest show of force as deterrent.

My first year was relatively easy. I found my bearings, slotted into a group of friends, joined the school football team and ate copious amounts of chips. I never lost my sense of incredulity that I could eat chips at school. In fact I think this was a major factor in me breezing along so well during those early days at Holland Park. I also did a few sketches in school assemblies that brought me some notoriety amongst the fifth and sixth formers, and was generally good for my kudos. As was (and still is) my tendency, I mostly observed, and didn't get too close to anyone. One half-Jamaican boy called Jerome was someone with whom I shared a rabid musical interest. Jerome remains a friend to this day, and still sends me CD compilations of the latest 'tunes' mixed with some old classics and obscure stuff only he would have heard. I will always love him for that.

My second year at Holland Park turned out to be a whole

new ball game. Consolidating my successful first year, I got off to a flying start with a display of my recently acquired rapping skills.

When rap was first introduced to Britain in around 1979 no one could fathom the sheer volume of words and rhythm that was pumped out. I was desperate to be the first (like thousands of others) to learn how to rap. I knew my own group of friends was too inhibited to memorise the words, let alone perform them to each other, so I hung around different parts of school, waiting for an opportune moment to dazzle the more impressionable first years. I would reel out lyrics from the longer and less well-known twelve-inch versions of the records about eating food at a friend's house, quite different from the 7-inch version – seamlessly giving the impression that I had made up the words myself.

I kept going until the Jamaican and Pakistani kids (whose approval I sought most) were clapping, cheering and shouting, 'Oh my God, man!'

So by my second year at Holland Park I had settled into a jovial gang of about seven boys. Myself, Jason Phipps, Sacha Babic and John Mackintosh had all been at St Mary Abbots primary school and formed the core of the group. Two others from our tutor set were Jerome Stewart (my music friend) and Dominic Curno, whose insistence on wearing a baseball jacket set a fashion precedent. Soon we all wore them, but were mindful not to turn it into a 'gang thing'. Boris Tochiapski from another tutor set also joined us to make up the full complement of seven. We all had similar interests, music, parties and esoteric conversation. We kept ourselves to ourselves. There were also a few girls who joined us most break times and we all went for lunch together, usually in Holland Park (the excitement of chips was by now wearing off). It was great to be outdoors in one of central London's prettiest parks.

Two fifth-year boys called Neil and Ennis came into our orbit because they had noticed the girls in our group. The older boys wolf-whistled at the girls at break times, and after getting zero response, decided to follow us one day, rather threateningly, into Holland Park. The girls, while not particularly warming to these boys, absorbed their macho attentions with friendly laughs and banter, for fear of upsetting them. They certainly looked like they could get violent. One of them was wearing rockabilly jeans and a jean jacket, while the other sported pseudo Marlon Brando-esque leathers and T-shirt à la *The Wild One*. They were almost men to me, so I couldn't understand why they didn't focus their energies on girls their own age. After all, they had Pinky and Sam in their year, the two best-looking girls in school! Pinky and Sam both had traffic-stopping long blonde hair, and modelled all the latest rad-chic styles, including berets, drainpipe jeans and elaborate scarves. Presumably they'd had the sense to put Neil and Ennis in their places, and now these numbskulls were trying their luck with younger women.

One day in the park, Ennis, the taller one of the two, brandished a V-shaped catapult and said to Jason, my gentle, well-spoken mate: 'Oi. If you don't p*** off I'll smack you in the face with this.'

Rashly deciding he'd had enough of this, Jason retaliated: 'Why don't you two just go away? The girls are clearly not interested. It's embarrassing.'

The poshness of his voice probably riled them more than his immense audacity.

'What did you just say?' Neil said, approaching Jason menacingly.

Having assessed the situation in a flash, I made the calculation that a bit of Egyptian dancing would lighten the mood for everybody. I had done this at primary school once and the exotic title of the dance had gone down as well as my moves. I jumped in between Jason and Ennis.

'Please. Don't hit him! I'll dance. Look!'

I started shuffling in a bizarre manner that surprised even myself. A wave of tittering started and within seconds a crowd formed. Even dogs were transfixed as they strained at their leashes to witness a boy dancing to no music for a couple of bullies. The plan was to get some laughs, show them that the girls preferred our zany company to theirs, and then maybe the tension would evaporate and they'd leave on a wave of good humour.

Amazingly it worked. Neil and Ennis looked genuinely entertained. A flicker of life came across their Neanderthal faces along with tiny smiles. Then they started laughing. The more they fired catapults at my feet and ordered me to 'Dance!' the sillier my moves became. I scrambled to build on my repertoire of dances and silly walks – from 'walk like an Egyptian' to John Cleese-style Nazi high kicks in *Fawlty Towers*. At one point I laughed, but things took a sinister twist when they instructed me to 'stop laughing!' So I carried on with a straight face. This somehow made it more entertaining. The girls were laughing, too – I was winning the battle. 'Dance!' they said, with increasingly bad temper and I did, like a crazed but obedient slave. The angrier they pretended to be, the more I pretended to enjoy the dancing. It was a war of attrition. At one point they were shouting at me like an army sergeant major to a subordinate. Spontaneous applause broke out from passers-by. Even a child in a pushchair was clapping. As it all died down, the bullies admitted defeat and sloped off.

Clearly I had averted a potentially catastrophic situation but no one really thanked me. I wondered if it was because they saw me as their own little Dance Superhero always ready to avert danger. Perhaps everyone had so much faith in me that they considered appreciation to be patronising? I fantasised that even if they did thank me I would hold up my hand to stop them mid-flow: *'There's no need, really . . .'*

By the end of the break before the last period, I was walking past the fifth-form rooms to get to my class when Neil and Ennis spotted me again. 'Hey!' they said and grabbed me. I was startled but they seemed friendly.

'Listen, funny boy, before the teacher comes into the class, come in and dance for us.'

'What do you mean?'

'You're gonna dance in front of the class with Neil firing the catapult again. Do what we did at lunchtime.' I wasn't sure. Yes, it was fun earlier, kind of. But no one had realised the degree of performance pressure I'd been under. And to do it again, on school premises, was a whole different ball game.

'Right, this is what's going down . . . you go in, we'll introduce you, like a show and that, then we start firing at you and you do all that stuff that you did in the park at lunch time. Got it?'

I didn't understand why they were so keen, but I reckoned the quicker I got this over with, the quicker I could get to my class. It might even be a laugh. I peered in for a second but to my absolute horror, I saw Pinky and Sam sitting right in the middle of the room. A sudden panic flooded over me.

'I can't do this,' I said.

'Too late.'

Ennis had already gone in and started addressing the class. I felt sick. What had started as a bit of fun was now going to seriously damage my reputation in front of the school's most popular girls. I didn't know Pinky and Sam but I thought I might do one day. In a few years when age didn't matter any more, they might be single and recovering from broken relationships. They might need the attentions of a sensitive younger man to give them some temporary validation and help them bring up their children, who had possibly been abandoned by their previous partners. The three of us might even live together in a modern family type of arrangement, perhaps?

The reality was I was seconds from committing social suicide.

'So please will you welcome, the Egyptian dancer!'

After I heard the half-hearted claps of one, maybe two pupils, I decided to bolt. I was a fast runner and knew they couldn't catch me. I ran out into a forecourt at 60 per cent speed, but suddenly a door opened, and the fastest boy in the school appeared out of nowhere, bolting towards me. He was called Ivan, and had been dispatched after me, with a scream of: 'GET HIM!'

This was serious. Already 20 yards ahead, I flew past kids dodging me, as I headed towards the school gates. I looked behind. Ivan had made up 10 yards and was bearing down on me. I dropped my bag and ran full steam, faster than I'd ever run. I looked behind again and was briefly reassured that I was maintaining the same distance. 'I'll just forget school today, I'll run all the way home,' I thought. But Ivan was creeping up and by the second school gate he was so close that he was literally hot on my heels. As he reached to grab me, his feet got tangled into mine and he wiped out. I stopped in my tracks, noting his moaning, and walked back. 'Are you all right?'

'You broke my arm, man!'

Neil, Ennis and two others had by this time arrived on the scene.

'Ivan, you all right?'

'My arm, man!'

Ennis then turned to me.

'Now look what you've done.'

'I didn't mean it. His feet . . . they got caught in mine'

But Ennis grabbed my arm and started to frogmarch me

back into the school grounds, while his friends goaded: 'Go on, Ennis, teach him some manners!'

He was three years older than me. I realised I only had one option left.

I rummaged in my pocket and took out coins. Knowing this was hopeless, I found my £5 note (given to me as a reward for returning Patrick Mower's wallet).

'I'll give you £5. Don't hurt me. Please.'

But it was too late. A punch swung round and hit me square on the temple. I thought I was going to die. He kept hitting me, punch after punch, each one landing on my face, on my neck, on my forehead, on my other temple. Surely he knew it was dangerous to strike the temples, you could kill someone like that, we'd learned about it in school only a week earlier. He was hitting me with such ferocity that I began to wonder if I had inadvertently committed a heinous crime. Maybe I actually deserved this? I had no idea why no one was stopping this totally unprovoked attack. Then he suddenly stopped, due to his own exhaustion probably, and simply walked away. No final words. No apology.

A thin and mild-mannered teacher came out and weakly asked if I was all right. I wasn't and I didn't trust he could help me so I picked myself up and staggered back into the building for afternoon registration in a semi-daze of shock and a fair degree of concussion.

I hovered outside the class. My form teacher bellowed at me. 'You're late!'

But he became agitated when he realised something was very wrong. My face had already swollen up and my head and temples were throbbing. I explained, stutteringly, what had just happened. The teacher told me I should just come in and we could talk about it later. Against my will I sat down and endured the sight of all my friends gazing at me in blank horror.

'Omid's had a bit of an accident. He needs a moment.'

My face was swollen, my eyes were red and I had leaves all over my clothes. I couldn't say anything. The shock suddenly rippled over me and to my intense shame, I started crying. Like a dam it all opened up – unattractively, I might add – with my eyes and nose streaming. The teacher droned on about something insignificant. I realise now he was trying to divert attention away from my humiliation.

And so what lesson did I learn from this episode?

The psychobabble response: making people laugh was my 'survival strategy' to deal with bullies and the general harshness of existence.

The reality: comedy skills don't always save you from having your head kicked in.

The hope: they were just jealous of me.

CHAPTER FOURTEEN

Healed By RoboKeeper

'True hope is swift and flies with swallow's wings. Kings it makes gods and meaner creatures kings.'

William Shakespeare

Everyone understands the highs and lows of sports. They're a metaphor for life. Harsh lessons are learned through discipline, hard work and application. As a ten-year-old I was invited to a trial in Battersea Park for the primary school district team. My sister had bought me a silver chain with a tiny Coke bottle attached as a lucky charm to wear round my neck. I drank Coke and often became gripped by happy visions of world unity when watching the advert on TV (*'I'd like to buy the world a Coke'*). I kissed the Coke bottle before the game and sure enough, it was the best I'd ever played. I was immediately called up to play for the Kensington and Chelsea under-elevens district team and a career in junior football started.

In secondary school I graduated to the Holland Park school team and by 1980, in my third year, our team was strong. We'd won the West London schools championship and the West London Cup. We had also blitzed our way to the London Cup semi-final, beating teams all across the city over nine gruelling rounds. With 1,000 schools in the greater London region having entered, this was a real achievement. To get to the final would have been a peak moment in our school's history. We were mini stars. The whole school were aware of our triumphs and well-wishers frequently high-fived us in the corridors. This gave us a tremendous boost, especially as our victories were lauded in school assemblies by our jubilant headmaster.

The London Cup semi-final in Stepney Green was looming. This was the home of our opponents and we were full of trepidation. Huddling in groups the week before the game we processed our anxieties.

'It's East London, man, we is tough but they's all criminals tho, innit? S'gonna get nasty.'

'Most of 'em support West Ham and Millwall, they's all hooligans, am serious, guy.'

'All their best players in Borstal tho, innit?'

Mr Armstrong, our coach, told us to eat healthily and avoid trouble leading up to the game. One or two of our boys had already proved they could be 'a bit naughty' and had previous criminal form, but the consensus now was to keep fit and keep your nose clean. Things were now 'serious'. During the days leading up to the game, we had team meetings, training sessions and continuous encouragement of each other over lunch time. I especially appreciated my team members' concern regarding my nervous eating habits. I remember how diligently they removed extra desserts from my tray that week.

The day before the game I was playing in the streets as usual after school. A bunch of kids had discovered 'stink bombs', firecrackers and certain dangerous new flares that became 'smoke bombs'. A boy we called Blind Willy (because he was partially sighted with thick glasses) thought it would be fun to throw a smoke bomb in my direction while it was still flaring. Incredibly it landed on my collar and disappeared straight into my shirt.

I remember the searing pain racing up the side of my neck and the look of shock and horror on everyone's faces as a rather beautiful red mark, like an artist's impression of a contorted flame, suddenly appeared on my skin.

Somehow I staggered indoors and asked my mother to inspect the injury. She calmly reached for Mercurochrome, a bizarre multi-purpose ointment used in Iran, often as an antiseptic to aid wounds to the skin. I yelped with pain – the stinging was unbearable. I read online recently that it was banned years ago in several countries due to associations with mercury poisoning, and had gone from the 'generally recognised as safe' classification to 'untested', which had understandably halted its distribution. Far from being healed then, my injury was made worse as my neck froze up. I was now stiff as a board.

I went into school the next day with a massive bandage all the way round my neck and shoulders. The team was dismayed and nervous that our defence was weakened. I was having none of it, and reassured everyone that I just needed to relax a bit on the ninety-minute journey to East London and all would be well. In those days you only travelled with eleven players, so missing the game through injury was not an option.

We went 0–2 down almost immediately. I was struggling to keep up with the pace but battled on bravely. We eventually steadied the ship and by half time we were 3–2 ahead. We were clearly the better side but against the run of play they equalised to make it 3–3. Stepney Green were fading fast but their vociferous band of about 100 people were cheering them on, especially their star player, a kid called 'Army' who had been quiet all game but now, buoyed by the support, was suddenly their star man. The ref was about to blow for the end of the game and then prepare for extra time when a ball came towards me, but was deflected off one of our players' legs, and spun freakishly around me and behind. Due to my now rock-stiff neck I couldn't turn in time and Army sped around behind me to latch on to the ball. I tried to bring him down but instead collapsed in an ignominious heap.

When Army blasted the ball past our keeper for 3–4 their legion of fans invaded the pitch and celebrated with a wildness I'd never experienced or witnessed. They raised Army aloft and ran around the pitch shouting obscenities. We stood waiting to kick off again for what seemed like an age, but sadly there was no time to restart the game. Stepney Green had reached the final and I was the reason we had lost.

On the bus home Courtney John, one of the more emotional players, broke down in tears. 'If you hadn't burned your neck, man . . !' Everyone looked back at me for a reaction. I had nothing. 'We'd be in the final if it wasn't for that smoke bomb kid!' I just stared into space at the back of the bus. The game was there for the taking and we lost. If it hadn't been for the agonising pain in my neck, I would have hung my head in shame. As it was I carried on staring stonily ahead with what would have appeared to an onlooker as remarkably good posture. We travelled back to West London in strained silence. There was some light relief when Lloyd Moses, who spoke with a slightly more pronounced Jamaican accent, broke the ice: 'See that bwaay who did this? Me gwaan mess up de blind batty man.' It was funny and it made us laugh. Of course the threat was never carried out, and I wouldn't have wished it anyway. Nevertheless it was a comforting recognition that my team was making a magnanimous distinction between the injury Blind Willy had inflicted on me, and my own personal short-comings. And yet, the grim reality remained. An opportunity had been lost. Our teacher's 'it wasn't meant to be' words of comfort didn't wash. There was no consolation to be found. I've played hundreds of competitive games since at university, soccer tournaments and charity matches, and I've won various medals and trophies. But nothing has diluted the nightmare of that moment from 1980.

Until that is, in April 2014. I was booked to appear on *The One Show* to promote a tour and my World Cup song. The producers had asked to show some video footage of me recording the song in the studio. As you'd expect, they introduced the song, I talked about it, they played the video . . . but then they stopped to explain that I had been set a challenge. If I passed, Richard Madeley and Alex Jones promised they would show the rest of my video. It seemed an odd bargain, but I was intrigued when I learned that they were challenging me to take on 'RoboKeeper'. This was a new invention created as a training tool for professional footballers, an automated goalkeeper so perfect that it had stopped multiple attempts by Lionel Messi of Barcelona, the greatest footballer on earth.

I'd seen videos of RoboKeeper. It really is an awesome bit of machinery. The computer can work out the body and eye movements of the kicker and anticipate the trajectory of the ball with unprecedented accuracy. RoboKeeper is basically the best goalkeeper in the world and I didn't have a chance in hell.

A pair of white Fila trainers appeared out of nowhere and I put them on as quickly as I could. I made a calculation that the only way to cushion certain embarrassment was to take the comedy route. I made some jokes about how I was going to give RoboKeeper 'the eyes' (to look one way but go the other). As I moved slowly towards the ball, my only real wish was to get it over with, avoid total humiliation and escape home for dinner.

As I stepped up to take the kick I remained calm and focused. I even put my tongue out which always helps me concentrate when I play guitar.

Seeing the ball miss RoboKeeper's hands by a millimetre and fly into the top left-hand corner of the net is something I still can't believe I achieved. I had done what Messi couldn't. In one go.

I lost my mind. All the pain of past football traumas began to seep away. I allowed my emotions to run wild. I had made history. This one strike happened so unexpectedly and it allowed me to breathe a little easier. It may be childish, but deep down there are thousands who know they'd react the same. Whether it was a great TV moment or not, this one miraculous event, caught live on camera, beamed into 5.5 million homes and now on YouTube forever, is the closing of a chapter about footballing wounds and means I can finally put that awful day in April 1980 to bed.

CHAPTER FIFTEEN

Thank You, Mel Smith

'What matters is how quickly you do what your soul directs.'

Rumi

I was now in my fourth year at school and though it was exciting doing sports I had always fancied trying my hand at being in a play. I had done some absurdist sketches in school assemblies that had made hundreds of pupils laugh. The sound of laughter as a punchline landed, cascading down from the top tiers of the hall's balcony where the sixth formers sat, was utterly thrilling. In my fourth year I auditioned for the school play, an ambitious goal as our drama teacher Mr Fagin was a harsh taskmaster. He gave me one of the main parts but made no secret of his suspicion that I wasn't disciplined enough to take on a major role along with fifth- and sixth-year students. Well, he was wrong. One night I experienced the crowd's delight and surprise when I arranged for my trousers to fall artfully around my ankles on cue at a certain opportune moment in the play. This wasn't scripted and had nothing to do with the plot, but even while Mr Fagin told me off and muttered to himself that he should always trust his instincts when it came to casting, I beamed inwardly and basked rebelliously in the glow of my showmanship and ever evolving comedic instincts.

I'd like to think my arrival into comedy was informed by an appreciation of the Goons, the satire of David Frost, or even an in-depth analysis of the British psyche that spawned *Carry on* films. In other words, I wish I could say that my career in comedy was an altogether more thorough and conscious process. It wasn't.

Stand-up comedy on TV during my teens was rare. *Dave Allen at Large* was the only stand-up show I remember, and even then I didn't connect the word 'comedian' with him. He was somehow above it. He just seemed like a cool Irish guy in a snappy suit with a finger missing who sat and rambled and we listened. I loved the way Dave Allen could stretch a story to the limit, and I can see now that he was a master of his craft. As a teenager, though, I often didn't understand what he was talking about. I also found Dave Allen slightly scary, perhaps because of the snazzy seventies studio lighting that enhanced his stories. All I remember is being completely transfixed by his words and accents, even if the punchlines went not just over my head but over the heads of my parents and multiple Iranian guests who would be watching it with me at home. '*Een chi meegeh?*' (what's he saying?) they would demand. My father would shuffle awkwardly in his seat and say Dave Allen's English was very 'high level', like Hafez or Rumi (Iranian poet-philosophers).

Not the Nine O'Clock News, which ran on BBC2 from 1979 to 1982, was probably the only comedy show I responded to as a teen. I watched all the episodes avidly not just for pleasure but also for kudos because I knew we'd talk about it at school the next day. Having met him in recent years and told him I was a fan, Griff Rhys Jones told me my demographic was exactly who the show had been targeting at the time, namely fourteen- to eighteen-year-olds. My generation, in fact.

Anything Rowan Atkinson touched seemed to turn to gold. Everyone marvelled at his unique, inimitable style. I often observed public-school kids emulating his 'comedy lecture' routine at parties and failing miserably (well, they still got laughs but they were cheap laughs from unsophisticated audiences, I told myself). It was a staple of public-school humour but somehow it translated to us 'comprehensives' too. His timing was impeccable and there seemed to be a deeper intelligence behind what he was doing.

Griff Rhys Jones too had a mad rawness about him that made him seem the most unhinged of the *NtNON* gang, which we loved. I found myself on a boat with him during the Queen's Jubilee flotilla in 2012, an ill-fated BBC transmission, along with Sandi Toksvig and Maureen Lipman. After we were told that the transmitter could not pick us up and the BBC had dropped our feature, Griff, having kept it together admirably for most of the journey, was not too pleased that we were effectively stranded on the boat for the remainder of the six hours with no chance of docking. He dared to voice the question that all of us were feeling: 'Why on earth are we on a flotilla, anyway?' A tired-sounding producer reminded him that HRH Prince Charles was trying to do something special for his mother. Griff reacted with verve:

'Fine. Do something nice for your mum. Have a garden party at Buckingham Palace. Invite some friends over for tea, why don't you? But why are we stuck here with A THOUSAND BOATS ON THE THAMES?!'

I couldn't have agreed more.

Pamela Stephenson, the only female in the *NtNON* group, was beautiful and hugely talented. At school we talked only about how hilarious she was, her considerable physical attractiveness being secondary to her innate funniness. Looking back, this could be considered something of a progressive attitude amongst teenage boys of that time. I'm quite proud of us for that.

But it was Mel Smith who was to have the most impact on me. The fact that he was overweight, balding, but with the audacity to wear his remaining hair long, made him an undisputed people's champion.

Unbelievably, I was to have an encounter with Mel Smith when he came to my school to watch *The Scott Joplin Revue* – my first play, the trouser-dropping one – an original piece written by a Jamie Read, a friend of Mel Smith when at Oxford. There was no real explanation as to why he was there. Maybe Mel had a relative at the school? Maybe Jamie had just called him to say, 'The kids would be thrilled if you came, Mel.' Most likely it was a power play to antagonise the highly strung Mr Fagin, who was always boasting about his various collaborations with notable stars from yesteryear. Tensions and creative differences had been brewing for a while, so Mel was probably Jamie's trump card.

Whatever the political machinations, I was stunned to discover the great Mel Smith backstage. He appeared, unannounced, awkwardly standing alone, and looking like he was patiently awaiting instructions. He was only twenty-seven at the time and seemed to have no idea of his celebrity status. Of course, it may have been that he was simply exhausted from enduring ninety minutes of fifteen-year-olds prancing around in 1920s clothes with bad American accents. Feeling his discomfort I was the first to rush over to him. I didn't know what to do, I just wanted to stand next to him and stare in awe. Thankfully he spoke first.

'Oh you! Hello. You were very good.'

I was overwhelmed. 'Oh *you*.' By pointing at me, Mel Smith knew I existed. Up to that point, it was probably the greatest validation I'd had in my entire life.

'Can I hug you?' I said shamelessly.

'Haha. Of course,' and I remember that ridiculous, classic grin of Mel Smith's as he gathered me to his bosom. It felt so comforting, to be held by a 'daddy bear' type like him. Of course, much later, I would appear (without my permission) on all kinds of websites like hairybears.com so I knew instinctively that I had a fair degree of daddy bear potential myself. Mel would have had no idea, though, that what he was about to say next would stay with me forever.

'I think you're really funny.'

'Me?'

'Yes. You should do it. You really made me laugh. Very entertaining.'

The penny took a while to drop. He said, 'You should do it.' What did that mean? I'd just done it, surely? I'd made my trousers fall down. Wasn't that enough? It took me a while to realise he was talking about a career path. Once I got that, I felt overcome with anxiety and confusion. Nevertheless I carried on hugging him and stayed glued to his side, while he fielded questions from a swarm of feverishly curious teenagers. Eventually he peeled away from me with extreme tact, saying, 'It was nice meeting you,' before exiting rapidly.

Going forward from that encounter, the word 'entertaining' sunk deep into my core. I remember making a mental note that social interaction between people felt pointless unless there was some learning to be had, the exchange of information, or to some degree, the sense of *being entertained*. It's not rocket science to trace the origins of my 'being entertaining' compulsion. But as I got older, I would take it upon myself to alleviate boredom, not just for others, but actually to halt an erosion and a depression that was going on in my own soul. This would invariably involve me doing or saying something outrageous, often getting me into trouble.

It became addictive. I remember a dreary lunchtime at school, when all my friends were lamenting their crushing state of ennui in the late summer term when there was no point even being at school. Before I knew it, I found myself agreeing to a dare to storm into the school staffroom and play the piano with my clothes off. I did it at the drop of a hat, a gleeful homage to Terry Jones' naked piano-playing in the opening credits of *Monty Python's Flying Circus* TV series. Not only did it alleviate the boredom, it also gave me an adrenaline rush for the rest of the week. Even the teachers who issued multiple detentions couldn't disguise their amusement. This was vindication. I was hopeful that my drive to entertain and amuse was at the heart of where my future happiness lay. And not just my own happiness either – somehow I felt that I could make other people happy, too. And that made me happy.

Because suddenly the stakes were being raised and the pressure was on to impress not only my own mates, but also a new potential audience: girls.

Aged sixteen, my social group consisted of geeky boys in possession of poor physical attractiveness, so it was a real surprise to me when two of my gang, Jason and Dominic (admittedly the tallest and best-looking ones), suddenly made it clear that they had developed an active interest in girls. Not only that, they were going to do something about it. They rang one night to inform me that they had arranged with some girls to go on a 'quadruple date'. The boy component consisted of Dominic, Jason, and Jason's cooler older brother Jonathan. Richard Harris, a handsome boy from my primary school who was now at another school, had been involved too, but had dropped out at the last minute. They urgently needed another guy to make up the numbers. I had proved I was 'entertaining' with a Mel Smith endorsement and anarchic piano-playing in the staffroom. Apparently these were sufficient credentials to ensure I fitted the bill.

Overcome with nerves, and never having been on a date before, I told them I had homework to do and it was cold outside. They insisted it was all set but without me they couldn't go ahead. The pressure was high: it was four girls from the posh girl's school down the road, Godolphin. There was going to be dinner, then a movie, then back to Jason's for a nightcap. It all sounded very serious. I embraced the challenge and agreed, telling myself that 'fortune favours the brave'. Rather than thank me, I was instead warned not to mess about and ruin things because they were sure 'something was going to happen'. We'd never really talked about girls this way, and I was curious to see where this foray into unchartered territory would lead.

We met at Jason's house in Notting Hill. When I arrived everybody was already there; the four girls were sporting identical big hair, jean jackets and bangles. They sat close together on the couch, mute and inscrutable. The boys were no better; in their attempts to appear cool, they were veering dangerously into hostility. It seemed to me that there had been zero conversation before my arrival, and certainly no formal introductions were forthcoming. In this tense atmosphere the boys furrowed their brows and took lengthy puffs on cigarettes as if the weight of the world were upon their shoulders. Was this taciturn posturing supposed to impress the girls? If so, it did not seem to be working, as the girls were regarding this display with mild boredom whilst talking amongst themselves.

I couldn't bear it any more. I was spiralling. I had a choice: should I relinquish power and trust others to save the evening? After all, I was a last-minute invitee. I didn't want to impose, and I was unsure of how much responsibility I could assume. The other alternative was to 'step up to the plate' and single-handedly take charge. The girls were obviously not planning to inject energy into the room, and the boys had already proven themselves to be paralysed and misguided. They all needed me.

A quick overview of the dynamics told me that the missing ingredient here was light irony. We were all uncomfortable. Everyone was attractive except me, which I didn't mind because what I lacked in looks I made up for in sociability. It made sense for me to sacrifice myself for the group. I figured when something's not going well, a simple acknowledgement of the status quo is usually a good way to alleviate discomfort. I launched into a snappy routine, joking that the atmosphere was tense, probably because of me (if it wasn't before, it certainly was now), so perhaps I should leave, come back in and start all over again? No one reacted.

It did occur to me at this moment that my original perception of tension in the room might have been a subjective experience based on my inner condition. But I had made a commitment and knew I would lose face if I didn't follow through. Without hesitation I exited the room and waited in the hall for a few moments. I returned, boldly swaggering into the living room, 'in character'. I was now a parody of an over-bearing, wise-cracking 'medallion man'. The choice of a mid-Atlantic American accent was unfortunate. It went horribly wrong. Mostly because I hadn't practised it since *The Scott Joplin Revue*. At one point I sounded Welsh.

After posing in the doorway and delivering an improvised hyperactive monologue (about my life as an ex-cop), I took a running jump and, aiming wisely, I landed neatly on the sofa in a small gap between the girls. I opened with an ironic gambit of, 'Hi. Well, this is awkward!' Looking back this character shared many similarities with Jim Carrey's character in the film *The Mask*. I threw in every line I knew about being the 'perfect man of their dreams' but the irony didn't translate. The girls stared at me in pity and the boys were holding their faces in their hands and looking at me with hatred. The so-called 'cool' vibe they were hoping to create had now evaporated. The whole thing was a disaster. In fact, I don't think I've ever done a stand-up gig, paid or otherwise, that has gone worse.

Worrying the evening was taking a turn for the worse before it had even started, Jason hastily ushered us all outside to the bus stop conveniently at his doorstep and on to the bus to Knightsbridge where he'd booked a table at Pizza on the Park, a popular American diner-style restaurant at Hyde Park Corner. The bus journey was taken in somewhat post-traumatic silence, but once we were seated in the restaurant, my behaviour was called into question. The girls asked why I was 'an attention seeker' and made sarcastic comments such as: 'Have you always been this funny?' It almost turned into *An Audience with . . .* as I struggled to answer all their questions while they ate.

When the dinner was over we all gathered by the bus stop to go to the cinema in Notting Hill Gate. I thought better of it and made my excuses. The ice was broken, everyone seemed happy now, my job was done. I congratulated myself that I'd been pretty funny towards the end. Best quit while I'm ahead. I had 'turned it around', which is always the toughest situation in life – when a bad impression is initially made but you manage to leave the audience wanting more. As they climbed up to the top deck of the bus, I smiled and waved, feeling the satisfaction of a good night's work. A job well done.

The beauty of language is such that a single word can conjure up so many meanings. The word '*zerrang*' in Farsi for example can mean 'gumption, having initiative and tenacity' all in one. The same can be said for 'non-verbal communication'. A wave can mean 'see you soon', 'I'll be back in a minute' or simply 'nice meeting you'. As I waved goodbye, to my horror, I witnessed the girls were flicking V-signs at me from the top deck. And not any old V-signs: multi-layered, multi-dimensional V-signs accompanied by a multitude of V-sign-inspired faces. There was the 'thank God that's over' V-sign, the 'finally got rid of him!' V-sign, the 'oh my God, can you believe we just spent an evening with this twat?' V-sign, the 'let's get outta here!' V-sign, the 'I thought it was never going to end' V-sign, the classic 'now HE'S out the picture you guys actually seem quite attractive now' V-sign, the 'let the party begin!' V-sign.

And the particularly crushing V-sign that signified: 'If he ever comes near me again, I want a lawyer and a restraining order.'

It took me a while to get over the shock of that evening. I realised I needed a break. I was exhausted from multiple humiliations. On top of my social and academic struggles I had also just been fired from a temporary job doing deliveries for a wine merchant on Church Street. This ended in disaster when I left a crate full of Domecq Double Century sherry (as advertised on TV by Orson Welles) on Kensington High Street when I nipped into the toilet in McDonald's. Strangely the crate got stolen. I had to prove to the owner that I was a non-drinker who definitely had no intention of stealing it myself. Needless to say I was fired for my 'poor attitude to alcohol'.

I was down on my luck; I needed a whole new challenge, a new perspective. I sensed, as a rather jaded fifteen-year-old, that it was time to broaden my horizons.

CHAPTER SIXTEEN

Escape To America

'Where there is ruin, there is hope for a treasure.'

Rumi

Fuelled by the influence of US TV shows like *Starsky and Hutch, Taxi, Hill Street Blues* and *Cheers,* I believed America to be a magical land where anything and everything was possible. My older brother constantly fantasised about living in America; after all, my extended family, having emigrated there after the 1979 Iranian revolution, were already dotted across California. After my last O-level exam I made a decision: I was going to live in the USA. I thought I could start out living with my grandparents in Los Angeles for a while, and then cut loose in pursuit of the American Dream.

So this was the plan. I would enroll immediately at UCLA, the University of California in Los Angeles. (In 1982 you could go from the UK to the US with O levels only, as long as you did a short three-month foundation/conversion course. At least, that was what I had been told.) There I would study astrophysics, graduate with top grades, get a job in a science lab at Cape Canaveral and be the first to work out how to ride space tubes and gravitational corridors around the solar system. When the world was on the verge of self-destruction I'd exit the planet with a group of visionary scientists in a privately funded space vessel and start humanity up again on the first manned colony on Mars. All I had to do was physically get myself out of England and into America.

Looking back, I'm impressed by my parents' detachment from this crazy scheme. Having said that, I may not have actually told them that I was planning to leave London for good. In their minds I was just going to visit my extended family who lived in LA.

The day finally came. Pan Am flight 001 to Los Angeles, 14 July 1982. I settled into my seat, pulled out my diary and wrote: 'The day my life starts.' An air of hysteria filled the cabin. A raucous group of American students on their way back home were making their presence felt. I'd never been in close proximity to such a vibrant bunch of young people, mostly blonde, healthy-looking and dressed in summer shorts and T-shirts. Their teeth were brilliant white and in excellent condition. 'What do they brush their teeth with? Americans are better than me in every way,' I jotted down in my diary.

Soon after take-off, some of the students chatted to me by the toilets. Talking to girls often made my mouth go dry, so I talked to the guys instead who seemed unusually open. One, a bloke with blond dreadlocks who – a bit out of step from the rest of the group – looked like he hadn't washed in a month, hung on my every word as if I were the Dalai Lama. Everything I said was undercut with a low hum of 'far out' and 'amazing'. When I went into the toilet, I spontaneously started exchanging drumbeats with him from inside the walls of the cubicle – him drumming back at me on the outside. It was a spontaneous and intricate 'question and answer' routine: confident, skilful and lasting for about ten minutes. 'Unprecedented levels of creativity among their youth,' I wrote down later.

Every American I came across, every thing that happened around them, seemed drenched in star quality. One particularly radiant air steward – Brad – proved a fascination for me the whole flight. Every time I asked for something he would reassuringly say, 'Why, *of course*,' and immediately came back with the desired item. He was tall and chunky with that thick Hollywood dark hair that I associated with wonder showman Liberace. He was theatrical and vivacious and had an ease about him that was disarming. He was so attentive I scribbled in my diary: 'Wish Brad was my dad.' I considered elongating this into a poem but I couldn't think of any more rhymes. Later Brad seemed to want to pass me a piece of paper with a number on it and a stewardess stopped him saying, 'Brad! Enough already. Stop it!'

When the jumbo touched down the students burst into spontaneous applause. I joined in the whooping and cheering and shouted, 'Yeah!' I even raised a fist in the air. This single eleven-hour flight convinced me that I was one of them now. As the plane taxied along the runway the dreadlocked dude silently mouthed to me from across the aisle, 'We're home buddy.' I mouthed back, 'I know, man.' In solidarity he nodded back. It made perfect sense to him. I told him I lived in Malibu. I scribbled a final note: 'Dreadlock dude – far out,' and closed my diary.

When you step off a plane on to the tarmac of a new foreign land in searing heat there's a distinctive smell. It's unfamiliar and indescribably thrilling. With the plane's engines winding down, we all surged on to a bus, the hubbub of excited students ringing in my ears. I'd had an amazing flight but I was feeling nervous. 'America is awesome,' I thought. I'd heard the word 'awesome' on the plane and I was already using it in my head. To me that was awesome.

My handsome uncle Parviz (now a Californian with wild hair) picked me up from LAX (to this day I have no idea what the X stands for) and took me to Cypress, Orange County where most of my extended family on my mother's side had settled. They had moved two years previously, but already seemed like bona fide Californians. Sporting a Tom Selleck moustache, dressed in shorts, a Hawaiian shirt and huge sunglasses, Uncle Parviz looked like a superstar driving 'an American car'. That's what we called them back then: long cars that glided and made a deep humming noise. For a boy used to small English cars buzzing and zipping around, just being in such a car this was mind-blowing. Parviz mocked my accent, reminding me Brits said things that were outrageously different from Americans: 'You say MOTTTOR VAY,' he'd say with his bad English accent, 'but we say FREEVAY!' I don't think he meant it to be funny but I took it as hilarious observational comedy and laughed uproariously.

A summer with my cousins! I couldn't think of anything more exciting. Getting to know them by visiting Disneyland, Universal Studios and the legendary Magic Mountain (a theme park with the terrifying 'Freefall' ride in which people are taken up in a container 100 feet high and just dropped) was about as much fun as I could take. We did things I'd seen on TV but never imagined I'd ever do in my lifetime: ten-pin bowling, late night drive-in cinemas, eating in restaurants (my family *never* ate in restaurants). An unlikely highlight was walking along Venice Beach watching body builders, dodging the skateboarders and gawping at dangerously cool Bohemians as they strutted their stuff and hawked their wares. Camden Market is still about the closest thing we have in London to Venice Beach . . . in comparison Venice Beach makes Camden Market seem like a village fête.

The old days were gone: struggling to do homework on the dinner table, cleaning rice off my exercise books on grim rainy nights. No longer would I be surrounded by guests and forced to breathe in the conflicting odours of food and medication. I used to think, 'There *must* be a better life, somewhere, somehow, sometime?' Well, it was here and it was now. Looking back, I realise this was probably the first time in my life I'd been on a holiday, not counting my trips back to Iran.

My head was so pro-America I would chant 'USA! USA!' ironically in the car as we drove around with all my little cousins. We chanted it for real at a cinema in Orange County at the climax of *Rocky III* when he knocks out Clubber Lang. The whole cinema audience was up on its feet cheering. I was hugging strangers and punching the air like I was ringside at Madison Square Garden. Even though Clubber Lang was also American the crowd bonded by chanting 'USA! USA!', regardless of there being no foreign opponent to rail against.

Even a slightly worrying incident when visiting Disneyland I interpreted as a sign that explained why America ruled the world. Taking a break from the roller-coasters with my Austrian cousin Ramin, we observed a bloke in a Snoopy outfit padding through the crowds. 'Hi there! Wanna picture?' he'd say, seemingly undaunted by the possibility of a negative reaction. Some stopped for a photo, many moved on when realising a payment was expected. I looked at Ramin and said, as an expert on *Peanuts* comics, and rather audibly, 'What a *douche* . . .' (another word I'd picked up on the plane). 'He shouldn't be talking. He can't say "Wanna picture?" Snoopy is a SILENT dog. Charles M. Schulz wrote him as being *too cool* to talk. He can't expect to make money by talking. That's embarrassing.'

Snoopy snapped his head in my direction. I smiled but immediately felt nervous, as he seemed to be making a beeline for me. I froze as he arrived, uncomfortably close. 'Hey there, buddy!' he said in his super-friendly Snoopy voice. From the grille of the snout of the costume I could see the darkened shape of an angry man inside the dog suit, unshaved and sweating profusely.

'Picture?'

'No, thanks.'

'Wanna picture?'

'Really, it's fine.'

'Come on. Take a picture with Snoopy!'

'I . . . er . . . I don't have any money.'

Suddenly his tone changed.

'You making fun of me?'

'No.'

'Wanna try working in this suit in 100-degree heat?'

'No.'

'Make fun of me again and I'll snap you in two. Got that?'

'Yes.'

'Wanna picture?

'Yes, please.'

'Five bucks, kiddo.'

Shamefully I unrolled a bunch of notes from my pocket, dropping three $20 notes and picking them up awkwardly in front of him. Ramin chimed in rather weakly with, 'I will take the picture.' I gave Snoopy one of the $20s and he gave me back $10. I didn't ask for the other $5. He said, 'Thanks, buddy!' in his Snoopy voice.

I respected his right to verbalise a silent character in popular fiction. I respected his right to work without being mocked. I respected his right to be whoever he wanted to be in the free market economy. I shouted, 'Bye bye, Snoopy,' and he muttered 'Kiss my ass' as he padded away. Later that evening I lay on my back on top of my kennel and silently stared up at the sky.

The summer passed very pleasingly. Every day an activity was arranged by Uncle Parviz (who didn't seem to work) to keep us all amused. Before I knew it, five weeks had passed.

Fun on Brighton beach with guests.

Above: Relaxing at home with guests ('Alan' who helped with the TV removal, is far right).

Right: Beginning to crack under the pressure of being a six-year-old tour guide.

Friends, family and guests on an average mid week dinner at the Djalilis'.

Me, pigeon, guest.

My brother before a James Bond premiere. What you can't see is a golden toy gun in his hand.

Uncle Iraj's acting headshot that bagged him a role on *Starsky & Hutch*.

Having a blast with American cousins.
Austrian cousin Ramin on the left, mute and isolated.

My brother and I on a motivational walk before January re-takes.
Facial expressions convey sky-high confidence.

Me and my parents enjoying midnight backgammon.

Graduation. Me in unexplained tails. Dad trying not to keel over in the Coleraine wind.

Will somebody take me seriously?

'Come on smile, you've graduated! Come on let's have a smile. No smile?
Oh come on. That's better. Bit more. Bit more. Ah there it is!'
Click.

My signature Berkoff vomiting audition.

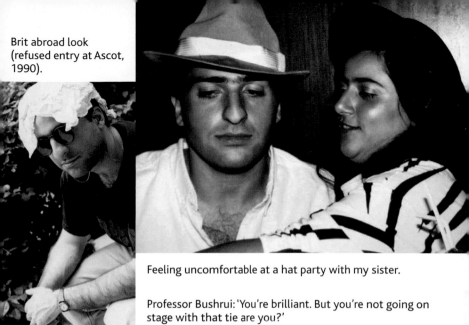

Brit abroad look (refused entry at Ascot, 1990).

Feeling uncomfortable at a hat party with my sister.

Professor Bushrui: 'You're brilliant. But you're not going on stage with that tie are you?'

Unfortunate publicity shot.

My cousins had all settled back into their routines. I was patiently waiting for my exam results so I could get my new life in LA kick-started. The date arrived: 23 August. I stayed up until 1 a.m. LA time waiting for them to arrive by post at 9 a.m. London time. The phone rang and my mother read out the information on the slips of paper. She was struggling to understand them, and it took an agonisingly long time to get the results, as I jotted them down in my diary.

The initial shock was hard to digest. I remember the feeling of my heart physically sinking. A coldness trickled over my body as if from an invisible leaking tap. I had failed Maths O level. My vision slowly started to evaporate. I sat silently in my room for an hour. You can't do astrophysics without maths. Depression, that familiar feeling that had beckoned with increasing intensity throughout my childhood and youth, started to creep in again. But I knew I couldn't allow it to swamp me now, so I started packing my bags immediately. I couldn't stay. My summer was over. UCLA was over. All I knew was that I needed that Maths O level. I just had to go back and retake it, didn't I? All else melted into insignificance. I had an open ticket and booked myself on the first plane back to London the next day. My grandfather, who had been overtly taciturn during my stay, sprang to life and seemed delighted I was leaving. He gave me $50, almost as if to make sure. Not speaking much English, he never really understood why I'd come to stay in the first place. I never got past explaining what astrophysics was. In fairness we never really got past the meaning of 'UCLA'.

CHAPTER SEVENTEEN

A Levels – A Debacle

'Success is stumbling from failure to failure with no loss of enthusiasm.'

Winston Churchill

I arrived back in London on a cold, rainy August afternoon and immediately moved back into the guesthouse.

Optimistically I rolled out plan B: re-enroll into Holland Park School.

There was one snag: they didn't want me back. The head-master pointed out that 'chasing first years on your scooter in the playground' last term was a contributing factor. He also pointed out that 'bursting into the staff room and playing the piano with your clothes off' was not appreciated. I had the cheek to say, 'Yes, but it was funny though,' which elicited zero response. Did that mean I had been expelled? Apparently it did.

I was devastated. I'd been so convinced of my bright golden future that I had become arrogant and had thrown caution to the winds somewhat during the previous school term. Having been well behaved for most of my life I had reasoned there was no harm in a bit of wildness. After all, I was moving to America. Sadly this had come back to bite me.

It was at this time that I entertained the idea of scrapping education altogether. I could be an entrepreneur! I could make big money, quick. I'd heard of 'traders' and the 'stock market' but never really knew what it was all about. This was the eighties and there were a lot of yuppies in shiny suits. Everybody was forming companies and trying to get involved with import–export. Even my brother Javid got in on the action and had created a company, Gentle Enterprises, with a business card offering 'Bespoke Travel Agency & Import & Export & Miscellaneous'. To be honest the company wasn't really going anywhere and in many ways didn't actually exist. But to prove that it did, my brother rented an office in Ealing and had me man the phone for a while. I sat at a desk for two weeks waiting for the phone to ring. It never did.

There was a moment of excitement towards the end of that second week when it appeared that I had hit a massive deal: an obscure acquaintance of my father's cousin in Iran put me in contact with someone who needed 10,000 low-grade Romanian truck tyres. I found a company based outside Bucharest who could supply these and send them to the buyer in Turkey. It couldn't have been more random. Fevered phone calls with dodgy connections, grappling to understand broken English, incoherent faxes going backwards and forwards . . . It was exhausting. But I persisted because I was convinced this was going to be the deal of a lifetime. My brother and I could be pocketing an unbelievable £10,000. It all came down to one long day of cliffhangers. I waited hours for an answer. Was the deal going through? The lines went dead and I had to face facts. It had come to nothing. Gentle Enterprises folded shortly afterwards and, with relief, I decided that pursuing A levels wasn't such a bad idea after all.

In a vulnerable moment it did occur to me that 'maybe this whole science thing was misguided'. My brother, perhaps sobered by his recent business collapse, offered some words of wise pragmatism: 'You're crap at science, you *have* to do the arts. There's no choice.' I had passed English and French, subjects for which I had no affinity. Could I take them for A level? Economics seemed a great third option and I imagined myself on *Panorama* talking smoothly about philosophy and politics with a beret and an isosceles-triangle chin beard, holding my own with politicians and journalists. I was hooked.

I scrambled to register myself into sixth-form colleges that were already full, so I had to divide my studies between two separate colleges: Westminster College (where I could retake Maths O level to keep the astrophysics dream alive) in the daytime and night classes at Hammersmith and West London College. French A level twice a week after 6 p.m. with mostly 'mature' students, who included:

1. A man from the Ivory Coast who spoke French fluently but always chickened out of the exam every year due to unexplained fears.
2. An ex-con who thought learning French might make him more attractive to women.
3. A Sikh Labour Party member replete with red turban, who talked a lot, always in English, with the only French he spoke being: 'Je m'appelle Opinder mais ma famille m'appelle Pinder.'

The challenge was the decision to take all three A levels in one year. It was an impulsive decision, mainly to prove to the world that my maths failure was a blip. It was a high-risk strategy. Relying mainly on a hugely inflated sense of my ability, I went for it. I put in the hard work, did no extra-curricular activities for a whole year, and launched into exam season brimming with confidence.

As I awaited my results that summer I found some work as

a driver with a chauffeuring company run by a friend of my dad. The company had contracts with the various stars associated with rock bands and movie premieres like *Rocky IV*. I wasn't lucky enough to drive one of the stars myself but I remember, with some of the other guys, surrounding the driver who had been ferrying Sylvester Stallone around. He proudly showed us the $100 bill he had received from Sly as a tip. My time for excitement finally came when I got to drive the rock band Metallica to their now-iconic gig at Knebworth. I drove lead guitarist James Hetfield and a close female companion on the two-hour journey from the Athena Hotel in Picadilly, and in those few hours I was on an adrenaline high. I wasn't even a heavy metal fan but I knew the significance of Metallica. I managed to maintain eye contact with James Hetfield for a few seconds and even made him laugh once. The boost I received on hearing James Hetfield say to his lady friend, 'This driver is crazy. I love this cat,' is unimaginable. 'Rock bands is where I should be,' I thought to myself and made a mental note to pursue this once I'd secured my A levels.

YEAR 1 EXAMS: JUNE 1983

My prediction: Two As and a B.

RESULTS

ENGLISH: E
FRENCH: F
ECONOMICS: F

ANALYSIS

I remember laughing when I opened the envelopes and then furtively looking around to see if there were hidden cameras about recording my reactions. Mistake, surely? I'd really failed everything? OK, so it was another blip. I always had the January retakes. And by the time I'd get the results in March I'd still be way ahead of the game.

YEAR 1 RETAKES: JANUARY 1984

My prediction: Two Bs and a C.

RESULTS

ENGLISH: E
FRENCH: F
ECONOMICS: F

ANALYSIS

The *exact* same grades? What were the chances? On the bright side: no regression.

Remaining hopeful there had been some sort of a mistake, I ordered an inquiry into all three exams. For a fee of £20 per A level, results can be reassessed. £60 was sent and I waited two weeks. Letters arrived informing me the original results for English and French stood. My 'F' in Economics, however, was downgraded to a grade of U (unclassified). There was also an apology that they got it wrong. I got £20 back as recompense. From a purely economics point of view there was a certain irony to the refund that I had failed to see until this very moment.

On to the June exams and I was in bullish mood. 'Bring it on, my friends, bring it on,' I kept muttering to myself. I was now armed with a great deal of exam technique so I was still, gloriously and triumphantly, way ahead of the game.

YEAR 2 EXAMS: JUNE 1984

My prediction: B and two Cs.

RESULTS

ENGLISH: E
FRENCH: E
ECONOMICS: O LEVEL PASS

ANALYSIS

Economics had moved up a grade to 'O level pass' – a special grade, not quite a fail but as good as a basic pass at O level. The bright side: two previous Fs in French now graduated to E – a significant progression. A third E grade for English meant at least there was no regression. These two years had proved I was a tortoise not a hare. 'Slow and steady wins the race,' I kept telling myself. What I chose not to dwell on was that after two years I was at exactly the same point at which I'd begun.

RESOLVE

I had the January retakes to look forward to. Focus. Knuckle down. 'Never, never, never give up,' was a Winston Churchill quote I'd heard at school and had decided to live by.

YEAR 2 RETAKES: JANUARY 1985

My prediction: Three Cs. (I'd learned now to be more realistic.)

Before the last French paper I'd stayed in all morning listening to 'Eye of The Tiger' and a progressive rock band called Camel hammering out esoteric rock instrumentals to help pump myself up. I could feel a spiritual energy flowing from somewhere above, cascading into the crown of my head and coursing through my veins. French was going brilliantly. Four papers had been completed and I was tremendously focused for this last exam. In fact, I was euphoric.

Screaming my battle cries through the cold winds on my scooter I reached the exam venue of the American church on Tottenham Court Road. But something was odd. The hall was completely empty. It was 1.45 p.m. and I was fifteen minutes early and no one was about. By 1.55, overwhelmed with panic, I asked the cleaner if I had got the venue mixed up. She told me the French exam had taken place in the morning. I said this couldn't be because the exam started at 2 p.m.

'No, love, it was this morning at 9 a.m.'

I produced the exam slip to show her the evidence. But with a heart now sunk to below my bowels I saw my exam schedule: everything had been in the afternoon *except* this one paper. I had screwed up. I had missed my exam.

RESULTS

ENGLISH: E
ECONOMICS: O LEVEL PASS
FRENCH: U (A)

ANALYSIS

There is some distinction in having a 'U (A)' grade in French. Essentially a grade in two parts: the 'A' being the grade for the oral exam (it had gone miraculously well) and the 'U' being the overall grade of 'Unclassified' due to the no-show for that paper, thus nullifying the whole A level. The oral grade is indicated out of the kindness of the London Board.

'O level pass' for Economics meant I had not progressed. Remotely. On the bright side, despite having four consecutive E grades in English I was – after two changes of syllabus – the most well-read of all my peers. By now I was studying with people a year younger than me. No shame in that, I thought. I could help others who were struggling. I had that one quality money couldn't buy: experience.

In a spirit of wise pragmatism, I started playing bongos and conga drums with a jazz funk band called The New Quartet. Clearly a back-up career plan was needed. If I'd learned anything, it was that exam success was more elusive than I'd anticipated.

So I embraced a vision of myself as a surly, charismatic muso, despite being clearly out of my depth in an impossibly cool new crowd. I'd met them through my friend Niko Frangoss whose brother was a brilliant bass player. I literally auditioned in the kitchen, banging on tables and chairs and using cutlery on Formica. The band leader was keyboardist Robert Tei, a wonderfully talented half-Spanish half-Chinese musician who seemed to symbolise a new modern multicultural zeitgeist. And, unbelievably, Courtney Pine, the now world-famous super-talented saxophonist, was in the band too. Sadly he only played two concerts with us before he got a record contract and informed us that he couldn't play in our next gig as he now had 'other commitments'. I was outraged and impressed upon him, with brutal showbiz honesty, that if his dream fell apart, under no circumstances could he re-join. He left the band. Part of me hopes he might be regretting this even now . . .

The band suffered a terrible blow when our brilliant drummer Jason died of a drugs overdose. We never really recovered from this loss, and we never played together again. My short-lived rock-and-roll dreams crashed and burned. My fallback career had fallen through. With grim determination, I pressed on with my plan to get into university.

YEAR 3 EXAMS: JUNE 1985

At this point I really should have been finishing my first year at university, not doing retakes for the fourth time. Three years after I'd started, realism arrived. Long gone were the days in which I dreamed of space travel. I needed a back-up plan. No more A levels. No more retakes. This was it. If I failed I decided I would join the French Foreign Legion. I was an exam soldier and if I was to fail then perhaps joining the Legion was where I was meant to be. I followed through with a letter written (in French) to the French Foreign Legion assuring them of my commitment, and in the unlikely event of my final attempt at passing my exams proving unsuccessful I would join them immediately. They wrote back congratulating me on my academic success and assuring me that I could join them with immediate effect. It was good to get this letter before the final exam, they had obviously misunderstood me totally. A sobering reminder that I still needed extra revision on French tenses.

My prediction (defiant): Three As.

RESULTS

ENGLISH: E
ECONOMICS: E
FRENCH: C (A)

THE MOMENT OF TRUTH

I'll never forget opening those envelopes in my bedroom that day. My final grades were on pale blue certificates. C in French (A in the oral exam) was some sort of an achievement. I never really understood economics from day one so an E was an achievement in itself. And for the fifth time in a row, an E in English – maintaining my personal best.

That was it. Thirteen A levels. Forty-nine papers. Three years.

I sat at the desk where I'd slaved over the last three years and put my head in my hands. It was official: this set of results would get me nowhere. I lowered my head even further.

All I had achieved in three years was a terrible Scrabble hand.

How could I face the world? How could I tell everyone I couldn't pass a few poxy A levels? Was I that stupid? It seemed so easy for others. Friends had just finished their first year at Oxford, Kent, Durham and Cambridge. I alone had an uncertain future.

I couldn't tell my parents. I couldn't tell anyone. In fact, I wasn't going to. A voice in my head spoke to me:

'No one *has* to know.'

Interesting. I listened to the voice.

Go on.

'No one should know.'

What do you mean?

'Tell *no one*.'

I have to tell someone.

'*Then lie.*'

About what?

'*You know what to do.*'

Do I?

'*Yes. Do it. Do it now. There's no time.*'

What I did next I have no explanation for other than it was an instinct of desperate self-preservation. I grabbed a pen, hovered it over the certificate directly over the E grade of English and paused. It was a big moment. My future could change in the next few seconds. With tender care and due diligence I changed the English grade from an E into a B.

It surprised me how easily it worked, with two curves. Those doodlings of mini bums I used to draw as a child were clearly not in vain. What surprised me was how I'd never thought of doing it before; I'd received so many E grades. It was perfect. Had I given it to a professional forger he couldn't have done it better. It was one of those magical – and in my case utterly rare moments – when I'd actually got something so accurately and so marvellously right. In an exhilarated state, I ran to my parents and showed them the certificate. 'I did it! I got a B in English!' Disbelieving, they took the paper in their hands to check for themselves (that's how little faith they had in me). Then they cried with relief. 'Thank God! You were alone in your room so long we thought you'd failed! Bravo!' They both held me in a clinch. 'See? You're NOT an idiot!'

I fooled them. I fooled everyone. I even fooled myself. 'The B in English was deserved,' I told myself. 'So it's B, C and an E. Not great but it was all about finding a university place now somewhere.' No time to dwell. I got in the car and drove north.

Up the M6 in four hours I found myself at Salford University. My mate Dana who lived in Manchester at the time came with me to the registrar's office. A stern-looking man appeared from behind the window.

'Yes?'

'Hi, I've come up from London. I know it's a long shot but I haven't got into my choice of university with my grades, so I was wondering if there are any places left here at Salford?'

To my surprise came the answer: 'That depends. What subject are you looking to study?'

'English.'

'What are your grades?'

'B, C and an E. The B was in English.'

'Do you have the certificates on you?'

'Of course.'

I passed them over. After a long pause he said, 'Yes, that might just be enough.'

I clenched a fist.

'All seems fine. I just have to check the results on the computer. I'll be back in a minute.'

Check what? What computer? I'd shown him the certificates; that was enough, surely? I hadn't banked on the results being on a database! He left my sight for what seemed like an eternity. Dana reassured me all would be fine and he'd later take me for a pie and pilgrimage around Old Trafford. However, after several minutes had elapsed, the man behind the window came back with an ominously solemn face.

'There seems to be a problem.'

Dana, sensing my imminent humiliation, started backing out the door.

'Problem? What problem?'

'The English grade does not correspond.'

'Correspond to what? I just showed you the certificate.'

'I'm afraid Salford cannot offer you a place this year. Thank you for your interest.'

'I don't know what your computer is saying, but I have a B in English. You see that, don't you?'

He stared at me with a look that combined pity, empathy and disgust.

'The computer says otherwise.'

'Please. There must be some sort of mistake . . .'

I fixed him with a stare. The kind of stare that says: *'Listen . . . the power is with you. You can get me in. I'm a good guy, I've just had a few problems. Deep down you can FEEL I belong here. Please. Help a brother out.'*

A moment passed between us.

I fixed him with one last look of desperation – rather like the people you see these days on *The X Factor*, pleading with Simon Cowell for redemption.

With all the professional sensitivity he could muster he apologised: 'There's nothing I can do. If your certificate states a B and the database says otherwise I suggest you take it up with the London Board.'

Shaken but not stirred, I got straight back in the car.

I drove to Cardiff University and Exeter St David's. No luck. Perhaps it was a mistake to tell the registrar in Cardiff, 'You should let me in on the basis of my Welsh roots alone,' and to the registrar in Exeter that: 'My family connections with Devon go back centuries . . . my forefathers laid the cornerstone to this university before you were even born!'

I contemplated suicide. I walked up to the roof of the Tara Hotel in Kensington and thought about throwing myself off. Thankfully, I got distracted by a view of the floodlights at Stamford Bridge, home of Chelsea football club. I spotted Fulham FC's ground too and then tried to spot all the London clubs. I could see Crystal Palace but that could have been the athletics track not Selhurst Park. I could also see the Millwall ground. Well, I couldn't see the ground itself, I could just make out the cloud of hopeless anger that hung over it, like the one hovering over my own head. I wondered if I could hear the crowds on match days and made a mental note to come back at 3 p.m. on a Saturday to see if that was the case.

A week later a letter came through, telling me that I could apply for a place through what was known back then as the UCCA clearing system (now UCAS). I had to fill out a card with my A-level grades which would go into a computer database, in order to identify what university places were still available. I filled it out: English B, French C, Economics E. A final defiant lie that was sure to be found out. I didn't care. I had nothing to lose.

Out of the blue, a letter came through a week later: 'You have been offered a place at the University of Ulster in Coleraine.'

I was stunned. Was this a mistake? I didn't even know where that was. All I knew was that it ranked fifty-fourth out of fifty-four universities at the time. I'd heard the word 'Ulster' on the news but it conjured up images of the IRA and terrorism. I could at least visit the place and see what it was like, so I flew to Belfast the very next day.

Coleraine is in the north of Northern Ireland, a strange place but a friendly one. The campus wasn't particularly inspiring and looked more like an oil refinery than a university. I noticed the main supermarket was called 'Crazy Prices'. I couldn't help feeling that perhaps more exciting things were going on elsewhere. The place reminded me of sunny Sunday afternoons at home, when the world was revelling outside and I was stuck indoors with guests in their pyjamas semi-conscious in front of some fishing programme they didn't even understand on BBC2. I would be desperate to watch *The Big Match* on ITV, but was told I couldn't change the channel as it would disturb them, so I just had to live with it.

I sat in a room with a socially awkward but very genial professor who made me feel welcome and explained what was to happen.

'Thank you for making the trip. Before we show you around, erm, quick formality, did you bring your A-level certificates? Sorry, it's just something we need to check.'

I hadn't bothered to bring them, as I was sure I'd be found out.

'Er, no matter, let's take a look at the computer printout. All the results from the university database are on a desk in the main hall.'

Database. I'd had it. He led me out of the office, where we saw pages and pages of computer printouts. They showed all the incoming freshers' grades, their names alongside the sequence of A-level results. 'Murray, Susan: B, C, C / Davis, Kieran: A, B, C / Campbell, Elaine: B, C, B.'

He perused the printouts. 'You'll be here somewhere . . .'

Scrolling up alphabetically with my heart beating. There it was, my name, blurry at first and then coming into focus, almost as though it was emerging from a dense fog: 'Djalili, Omid . . .'

I pretended I hadn't seen it but the professor pointed it out. 'Ah, there you are, Djalili, Omid: B, C, E. Clearing system, was it?'

'Yes.'

Stunned and confused, I followed him on a tour around the campus. All I could think of was 'English: B'. How on earth was that possible? Was it a computer error? Was it divine intervention? Did the UCCA card develop a mind of its own, and defy the system to land me a place? I had no time to find out. I was already there. I even felt special that I'd done the campus tour alone. The professor told me that students usually did this in groups of twenty. Everything seemed to be shifting and taking a new shape.

So it was that I started university life on my birthday, 30 September 1985, at the ripe old age of twenty. And though two years older than everyone else, I was convinced that a miracle had just taken place.

CHAPTER EIGHTEEN

Iranian In Coleraine

'There is a secret medicine given only to those who hurt so hard they can't hope.'

Rumi

'I'll take it.'

When I like something I cut to the chase and get impatient. I was keen to clinch the deal and move in straight away.

'Cottage in Castlerock £30 a week.'

I'd arrived at the university blind. Expecting to be found out, I hadn't brought much with me other than my car, my bongos, my precious Panini football sticker albums I used to carry with me in a briefcase at all times (a weird compulsion that gave me great comfort), and a bin bag of mismatched clothes. I hadn't arranged anywhere to stay, and found myself by the accommodations noticeboard with a gaggle of people, presumably in the same boat, staring at dozens of cards advertising one-room bedsits, single rooms and digs with families.

Almost everything was around the £15 mark, which was the maximum students were prepared to pay. A post-graduate bloke sporting the classic 1970s Open University ponytail and beard, pointed to the £30 Castlerock cottage card in derision: 'Jesus, way too steep, man.' But for me, a central London boy raised on a couch surrounded by noisy, eccentric strangers, the idea of living alone in a cottage was thrilling. All my life, the dream of a rural idyll was as ridiculous as it was unattainable. But this small white card told me that my dream could become a reality.

The cottage did not disappoint. Beautiful and cabin-like, low ceilings, two-up two-down, tastefully furnished, all mod cons. It was behind a house on Sea Road, owned by a lecturer and his wife who were renting it out for extra cash. After my initial zeal, even I had to admit that £30 a week was rather a lot, but my hesitation dissolved when I saw the fireplace. The wife of the lecturer, Orla O'Leary, said she would teach me how to make a fire. She was small, sweet-faced and pregnant, with a geometric Plantagenet-type hairstyle that reminded me of the front cover of my anthology of Shakespeare's history plays. I'd never made a fire before and I had images of late-night chats with students by the fireplace as we wrestled with Plato and Aristotle. If Immanuel Kant ever came up in conversation, I'd brought a picture of me with the bust from the guesthouse to cement my 'deep thinker' credentials with my comrades.

'Do you need cash or a cheque either way I'm fine I've got cash if you want cash I can even pay cash a month in advance I can move in now my car's outside should I bring it into the drive or leave it on the road I don't mind you say I'm easy you say.' I realised I was talking very fast and sweating profusely.

Despite my eagerness, she hesitated, and instead gestured apologetically towards another student loitering outside. My sense of disappointment overwhelmed me, only to erupt into outrage when Mrs O'Leary suggested, 'Well, he's come a long way and who knows, maybe he'll like it too and you can share?'

Was she out of her mind? I couldn't *share*. With *anyone*. I felt hot and nauseous. Couldn't do it. I'd seen a BBC documentary about student life, which convinced me I would have to spend my evenings lending a lone polite ear to poetry recitals from social outcasts, while eating stale Quavers. Or absolute worst-case scenario, I would have to endure earnest monologues about alternative fuels and compost from the needy Dutch environmentalist I'd just encountered by the accommodation noticeboard. He'd said he was looking for somewhere to rent in the countryside too and had looked covetously at my bongos. The anxiety that it was him waiting outside induced such a panic within me I could feel my heartbeat pounding in my ears.

I experienced a momentary relief when I saw that the other student was a second-year Indian boy who had dyed his hair red. Mrs O'Leary welcomed him in for a viewing. It took him much longer than me, and they seemed to be talking in hushed tones. They finally came out and approached me with trepidation. The Indian boy declared, 'I like it. Obviously. I'd like to take it. But . . .'

Yes, big 'but' there, mate, I thought. I was here first. Not knowing what to do, Mrs O'Leary just stood there.

'Well, you like it, and you like it . . . haha. What to do?'

Was this *Annie Hall* all of a sudden? All I needed now was for her to say 'ladi da' and I was ready to punch someone, probably the Indian bloke for dyeing his hair red; punk was over five years ago, for God's sake. We stood in painful silence looking at the ground. This was not a time for vagueness. I took charge.

'Well, I want it.'

'So you're OK with the rental?' Mrs O'Leary said.

'Yes.'

'I like it, too,' said the Indian guy. 'I mean, maybe we could share the cost?'

I looked at him, fighting not to be influenced by his *'we're*

Asian brothers, man . . . let's do it' pleading gaze. Struggling to calm my nerves, I decided the least I could do was get to know something about him.

'What's your name?'

'Zebedee.'

I needed a moment to take this in. The theme tune to *The Magic Roundabout* went off in my head.

Mrs O'Leary nervously chipped in: 'It might be *fun* to share.' She was trying to ease the situation she had created.

Zebedee said, 'Yes, is that your car? We could share the petrol costs.'

No.

Mrs O'Leary chimed in again. 'It's always safer to live with someone. It can get lonely out here too . . . gets very cold in the winter.'

Was she suggesting Zebedee and I cuddle up together to stay warm on cold nights? This wasn't going to work.

'Mrs O'Leary, I'll take it and I need to be alone. Sorry.'

And that was that. I'd never been more blunt in all my life, and was almost shocked by my own directness. But I needed this cottage. It was a need of the soul. Perhaps that was why forthrightness flowed out of me that day. After all those years of sharing my house with a procession of ailing, random strangers, being alone was essential to my sanity. Who knows, I might think great thoughts once I had a place to myself.

Besides, I was never going to share a house with someone called 'Zebedee'.

Accommodation satisfactorily sorted, I went along to Fresher's Week thinking it was going to be an exciting introduction to my fellow students. I walked into the grand hall called the Diamond and merged into the sprawl of people. I didn't speak to anyone, just observed for a few minutes. I wondered when the initiation would start but everyone seemed already busy and engaged talking to various university societies who were pitched up at makeshift stalls dotted around the room. I looked to see if there was some wacky society who would dress me up in a banana costume and start a chase through the campus. Sadly, no such society existed.

For some reason I stumbled upon the canoeing society and stood with two depressed-looking freshers, listening to a bloke shout about their activities, clearly trying to make himself heard above the crowd. The canoeing society members themselves not only looked dull but were also surprisingly rigid, with their endless lists of rules and regulations. I showed an interest and asked questions because the other two freshers were shockingly mute and seemed to lack the social skills to speak. The society members were older, mature students but so set in their ways that it felt like the canoeing society was an obscure religious sect. To my surprise, after rattling through the information in a monotone, they suddenly singled me out to test me on what I'd absorbed. I had only feigned interest because I felt sorry for them and hadn't really been listening. They said they had to check my commitment. I hazarded guesses and got them all wrong. I was denied membership on the spot. Supposedly to make me feel better, they said, 'If it's any consolation you might be the wrong *shape* for canoeing.'

Over the next three years whenever I saw them approach me on campus they always dropped their eyes as they walked past. Fortunately they had found that Dutch environmentalist who seemed to fit in perfectly. He would occasionally invite me to join in, and I would pretend to be gutted that they'd told me I was the 'wrong shape'. He offered to take this up with the other members, I always said 'no need to rock the boat', and he would laugh hysterically.

Prioritising privacy and solitude, I promptly did nothing, academically speaking, for the next eight weeks. I went to one lecture but fell asleep. I attended a seminar on Shakespeare's clowns, but left early and instead drove to the Giant's Causeway. I did manage to sit through one lecture on the Norwegian dramatist Henrik Ibsen (who I thought was called Henry Gibson) but didn't take a single note. All I remember is feeling baffled by how it was possible for the lecturer to be standing in front of a large crowd talking and yet be so far removed from them. I'd fought tooth and nail to get to university and almost immediately I lost all motivation. I was bored rigid by academia.

So I rented a TV instead, retreated to my cottage, and stayed there for two weeks, gripped and fascinated by the 1985 party political conferences, first Labour, then Conservative.

Cameras were allowed into the conferences for the first time. Labour leader Neil Kinnock gave a great speech about 'the Loony Left'. I was very impressed with how he took on the scary Derek Hatton and Liverpool city council, always in the news then, a thorn in Kinnock's side. As someone who had been raised in an Iranian bubble, I realised I needed to firm up my awareness of the British political scene, I remember standing and clapping alone in my front room, in my underwear. I felt I was marking history.

It wasn't just political programmes: I watched everything. I really was a child of the TV generation: *Blind Date, Call My Bluff,* the first year of *EastEnders, Grange Hill, Brookside, Blankety Blank, Question Time, That's Life, Emmerdale Farm, World in Action, Mr and Mrs, The Old Grey Whistle Test, Tenko, The Paul Daniels Magic Show, Game for a Laugh, Juliet Bravo* and *Pebble Mill at One.* I still get a flutter in my heart when I hear the theme tune to *Sportsnight.* It's with a mild shame that I admit I even watched the 'ill-fated' *Albion Market* and at the time couldn't for the life of me understand why it just disappeared from our screens.

However, *Just Good Friends* with Paul Nicholas and Jan Francis was the BBC romantic sitcom of the 1980s. I built my whole week around it. Tuesday nights was boil-in-the-bag Vesta chicken curry time, as I sat wondering what on earth would happen next in this roller-coaster of a show. One minute you were laughing aloud. Next minute, you had brimming eyes and a lump in your throat. I became so engaged that at one point I almost believed it was actually real, and unfolding live. She (Penny Warrender) was a middle-class girl who was a secretary at an advertising firm and he (Vincent Pinner) was a former ice-cream salesman and son of a scrap-metal merchant. It was Shakespearean, with classic *Romeo and Juliet* undertones but with the added premise of wondering what would have happened if Romeo had done a runner on their wedding day. What if he had left her at the altar? We pick up the story five years later when they bump into each other in a pub and decide to become friends. We at home knew they still loved each other but empathised with the fact that Penny just couldn't trust Vincent wouldn't hurt her again. It often finished with me weeping and standing on my porch, trying to calm myself down with deep inhalations of sea air, before taking myself off to bed thinking about their back stories: 'Why *did* he leave her at the altar if he loved her so much?' and 'Why can't Penny's family be more supportive? They obviously still love each other! Why can't they be together?'

University life really was stimulating. I felt I was getting far more out of these programmes than if I had watched them back in London.

Not being drawn by anything else I sought out the University of Ulster Association Football Club, notoriously the most difficult club to join. Eighty guys showed up at the trials. They asked for my name and not wanting to lose points for having a complicated foreign name I told them it was 'O.J.' – sort of my initials.

Tom Stark, a Scottish coach in his fifties, had been running the club since 1968 and his assistants Micky Willis and Dez Wallace kept a close eye on all of us playing over three pitches. It was clear there were a few boys who were professional standard. They would go into the first team who played in the professional Irish B division league, nothing to do with the university league. The others would join the Colts. I liked the sound of a team that was named after a young, vibrant, masculine animal.

I gave a good account of myself in the trial but I worried it wasn't enough. We were told to look at the Soccer Club noticeboard on Monday to see who had been selected for the 'invitation-only' training on Tuesday night. Only ten places were up for grabs so we were warned not to be too disappointed if we were not selected. Monday came and I ran over to the noticeboard, desperate to see my name up there, having worried about it all weekend. I looked. I hadn't been selected. My morale dropped.

Thankfully, like a default setting, the indomitable spirit that governed me to blag my way into university reared its head again. Refusing to admit defeat, I went along to the 'invitation-only' training session anyway. A trait I'd no doubt picked up from my mother who often showed up at weddings when not invited. When my father would plead with her not to go she'd brush him off saying, 'They'd never *not* invite me. It's a mistake.' She did this often. She was never challenged and she was never turned away.

I arrived at the sports pavilion and Tom Stark asked me what I was doing there. I said my name was on the list. He said it wasn't. I said it was. He said it wasn't. I said there must be some mistake. He asked what name I gave. I said maybe there was some confusion because I gave the name 'O.J.' when in fact my real name was Omid and anyway he should let me play again and judge for himself. He said he *had* seen me play and had already judged for himself. I said I thought he was wrong and should be given another chance. He looked at me and – no doubt beaten down – looked at his watch and said, 'Get changed.'

There was so much running in the training I nearly puked before we'd even kicked a ball. When the training match kicked off I got stuck in and played as if my life depended on it. When it finished I looked at Tom Stark, and in a rush of euphoria, said, 'Thank you, Starky.' On the Wednesday I went to the noticeboard to see if my name was included for the match on Saturday. Yes! My blagging was vindicated. My name was selected to start. 'No.10 Djalili.' Not just any number. No. 10 was Pele, Zico, Maradona. I started shaking. In my head I'd become a footballer. A deep thrill welled up inside me.

I enjoyed a great relationship with 'Starky' after that. The next training session on the Thursday we prepared for the game with me as the playmaker, the focus of the team. 'Get the ball up to O.J. as quickly as you can' someone was instructed. The boost was immense. My ego ballooned. As it was I got injured in the first game and didn't play again in my first year.

For the two years I played I had a wonderful time winning trophies. Starky's only drawback was he never quite got to grips with my nationality. From the start he had it firmly in his head that I was from Egypt. He understood I was from Iran but just couldn't differentiate between the two countries. I tried to reassure him by suggesting that it was a bit like getting the old-time actors James Coburn and Lee Marvin mixed up. I don't think that helped.

'O.J., where are you from?'

'Iran.'

'Is that the pyramids?'

'No.'

'Is that the Pharaohs?'

'No.'

'The Sphinx?'

'No.'

'River Nile?'

'No.'

'Sharm el-Sheikh?'

'No.'

'Alexandria?'

'No.'

'Is that where they set *Raiders of the Lost Ark* with Harrison Ford?'

'No.'

'Luxor?'

'No.'

(Pause.)

'So . . . why do you say you're from Iran then?'

CHAPTER NINETEEN

The Aimless Arab Of Antrim

'Personally I'm always ready to learn, although I do not always like being taught.'

Winston Churchill

It feels obvious to me now, three decades later, that after the struggles of the previous few years, I was burnt-out. Lying to get into university, I believe, had left a profound psychological scar. I had lost self-esteem, affected by the old Groucho Marx maxim about not wanting to be part of an establishment that had me as a member. I couldn't take university seriously and I was unable to absorb anything given to me by 'authority'. To reinvigorate my persistent fantasy of the scintillating academic life, I decided to take a week off. Clearly, it had not occurred to me that becoming a hermit and a telly addict had anything to do with my dysfunction and dissatisfaction. The reason for my malaise was simply that I was in the wrong educational establishment.

I concluded that I had to go on a research mission. I somehow convinced myself that all I needed to do was show up at Princeton University in America and persuade some official person in a tweed jacket to let me transfer. When I consider that Princeton is the equivalent of Oxford or Cambridge, I wince at my naivety. And yet, I'm also quite impressed by my ability to grab firm hold of seemingly ridiculous ideas and follow them through with blind conviction to the bitter end. This was a case in point. With supreme confidence, I booked a flight to Newark, New Jersey and lurched inelegantly into a bold and audacious challenge.

This particular adventurous impulse had come to me during 'reading week' so I told myself that the timing was auspicious – I wasn't missing much. Besides, I was going to Princeton, so what did it matter if I didn't stay in my cottage studying during reading week? I would read on a transatlantic flight instead. I arranged an overdraft with the bank, and flew with a calm sense of personal destiny from Belfast to London. Two hours later I climbed aboard a flight to Newark, whereupon an elderly American Jewish lady sat next to me started quizzing me.

'So do you have business in Newark?'

'I'm going to Princeton University.'

'That's great.'

'Yes, it really is.'

'Are you joining mid-semester?'

'No.'

'Are you getting ready for next year?'

'No.'

'Are you on a scouting mission?'

'No.'

'Well, Princeton is known for helping their overseas students.'

'Actually they don't know I'm coming.'

'Where are you staying?'

'I haven't got anywhere to stay.'

'What are you studying?'

'I don't know.'

'You sound a little confused.'

My bubble had burst a little, and harsh reality beckoned. Admittedly I was a little confused. We didn't exchange another word for the rest of the flight. I shoved my doubts aside and assured myself with even greater conviction that a bright future lay ahead, all I had to do was believe.

Having said that, when asked at passport control regarding the purpose of my visit, I said I was coming for a wedding. The elderly lady overheard this and frowned in my direction. I could feel her eyes scrutinising me as we waited together in baggage reclaim. It seemed that she was genuinely torn as to whether she should insist I sorted out my confusion, or report me to airport security. Perhaps as a compromise she offered me a bag of Mint Imperials and wished me luck.

On the train to Princeton I got friendly with a black guy called Troy who was on his way to Trenton. I happily chatted with him the whole way, feeling the same affinity with Americans as I had on that first trip to LA in 1982. Troy was very 'street' but gentle, educated and a firm believer in fate. His kindly presence calmed me down and renewed my sense of purpose. We became so friendly that I took him into my confidence, and shared my ambitious plan to get into Princeton. Troy seemed fascinated and excited.

'You crazy. But I love it. Gonna happen for you, man.'

I thanked him profusely for his enthusiasm, and he was gracious in his reply: 'I'm just blessed to be a part of your journcy. May God and the Lord above protect you.'

This actually moved me to tears. I suddenly felt that I couldn't go through the rest of my trip without him.

'Troy,' I said, grabbing his hand, 'come with me!'

'Sure man!' he replied, holding my hand in both his own, 'Sure!'

I breathed easier, knowing I had made a firm friend.

A couple of stops before Princeton Troy excused himself to go to the restroom. I loved the way Americans called it that. So much 'cooler' and more refined than the ugly English word 'toilet'.

'Have a good rest,' I quipped and he chuckled as he walked down the carriage. He found me hilarious.

In his absence my attention was drawn to a map on the wall. Just before Albany and to the right, there was a small town called Troy. This was serendipitous! I couldn't wait for him to come back so I could show him what I'd found and bathe once more in his warm laughter.

As the train began to move again I was aware that Troy seemed to be taking a long time. I looked down the carriage, eager to show him his namesake town and felt sure this was going to be amusing enough to have us laughing all the way to Princeton. As the train started to pick up speed I glanced out of the window and saw him, standing on the receding platform, with his bags.

He'd left me.

I stared out at him, my face and hands pressed against the cold glass, like the daughter from *Sophie's Choice*. To give him his due, he did wave.

Alone now I mulled over what had transpired.

Apparently people will be nice to you just so they can get away.

Luckily Troy had given me information on where to stay in Princeton. I checked into a small guesthouse very close to the main Princeton campus. Once settled, I went for a midnight wander round the town and was awestruck by the atmosphere of 'Old America' that Ivy League university towns always evoke. I half expected to see the ghosts of F. Scott and Zelda Fitzgerald cheering me on and telling me to write my own 'undergraduate' novel (I had just learned about this genre and had been trying unsuccessfully to finish *This Side of Paradise*).

The next morning I sat at a free-access university bar and got chatting to some students, who told me that I couldn't get into any of the main buildings on campus without a photo ID student pass. Security was tight but I refused to be daunted. I trawled around the bar, driven by a gut instinct that if this *was* 'meant to be' an opportunity would present itself. My father once lectured me on this subject:

'Sometimes an opportunity is placed in your hand and you drop it; sometimes an opportunity is placed in your mouth like a sugared pill and you spit it out. Be aware of opportunities. Sometimes they're right in front of you but slightly hidden. Always be ready to pounce.'

An hour passed and sure enough, there it was, an unoccupied and messy table. Like a Scorsese zoom my gaze suddenly focused on a student card lying next to some books and empty coffee cups. I surreptitiously grabbed a cloth from the bar, pretended I was a waiter, cleared away the cups, wiped the table down and swiftly popped the card into my pocket before exiting the bar. Unfortunately, once I was outside I saw, to my horror, that the card belonged to a girl called Kathleen Madigan, who was the proud possessor of a flowing mane of blonde curls. This was a problem.

Not ready to accept defeat I went straight to the toilets and practised walking in with the card in my mouth, then nonchalantly taking it out to present it with my thumb strategically placed over the picture. Speed was key. I needed to perfect an attitude of moving with a brisk and slightly neurotic purpose, as though I was preoccupied with an essay, and had been to-ing and fro-ing within the university for months. It worked like a dream first time. Swiftly moving past a security guard, books in hand, while saying, 'Morning, my dear fellow,' in an enunciated English accent, I breezed past with ease and familiarity.

The main library was a massive building, each of its five

levels the size of a football pitch. I wandered around for a couple of hours and came across all manner of fascinating tomes. Marvelling at how comfortable I felt, I settled down with a photographic history of New York. I came across a photo of some early designs of the Chrysler Building by its architect William Van Alen. I remember being enchanted by the beauty of this magical skyscraper. Unfortunately, with my head on the book, I drifted off into a contented slumber. Perhaps it was jet lag, perhaps it was the shock of actually finding myself in Princeton. I was awakened in due course by the aggressive prodding of an outraged librarian who told me that snoring was unacceptable in a place of study and maybe I should see a doctor as it really was unusually loud. I left hastily, only to meander around the campus for another hour.

Luckily I still had Kathleen Madigan's card and so, like a tadpole, I began following a group of students who seemed to be swimming their way towards a lecture hall. They all seemed so excitable and earnest. Being with them but not of them, I still needed to rely on the card, and so flashed it up casually, congratulating myself on my enterprising spirit. Sadly I saw Kathleen Madigan herself looking very stressed, as she rummaged through her bag and tried to explain her lost card to an unsympathetic security guard.

As the lecture began, Troy's words about fate resonated afresh in my brain. In a flash, I experienced a certainty that all the angst, the travelling and the overdraft was all worth it. The lecture was on exactly the same subject as the one I'd attended recently in Ulster – Nora's slamming of the door in *A Doll's House*, and the assertion that the sound of that slamming reverberated throughout late nineteenth-century Europe and gave voice to the feminist movement. I felt an immense rush of belonging and scribbled furiously on the back of my travel insurance documents and the envelope containing my return ticket. (Note to self: remember a notepad next time.) I experienced a rush of joy to the roots of my curly-haired mullet – and even had the presence of mind to wonder if my hairstyle was an appropriate homage to Art Garfunkel. 'Sound of Silence' echoed in my head and I was transported to my own imaginary movie – a tender biopic featuring my early academic forays – reminiscent of the Berkeley campus scenes in *The Graduate*.

I was amazed at the commitment of the professor. He was magnetic. That Ibsen lecture to this day remains one of the most stimulating, dazzling, high-octane performances I have ever witnessed. I was left in no doubt by the end that Ibsen *must* be taught in primary schools everywhere, let alone universities.

I lamented the fact that the lecture at my own university had been so poor in comparison. Then I realised, of course, Princeton is an Ivy League university in the United States, in the same bracket as Harvard, Yale and Stanford, recruiting the best, highest-paid professors and enrolling the best students. It was reserved for the cream of society. People don't just go there, they *belong* there. I didn't belong there and never would. Of course what I needed was someone to sit me down and say, '*This is crazy. You can't just show up and enrol at Princeton! You can't keep living in a fantasy world,*' but as the visit was secretive (my parents had no idea I had flown to New Jersey) no one could sit me down and deliver me some home truths. There was also the worrying issue of the overdraft that seemed to be mounting irrevocably due to stress-eating of Wendy's burgers and expensive Chinese food.

Needless to say, after a rather frosty and humiliating encounter with the vice chancellor, Princeton did not feel I would be an asset to their 1986 cohort. To put it mildly, my sojourn there had given me a great empathy with those on the receiving end of Nora's door slamming. After some soul searching on the plane journey home, I knew I had to stick it out at Ulster. University was what you make of it, after all, so I made a commitment to pull my socks up, knuckle down, and take myself in hand.

Upon my return, the first decision I made was to skip all lessons for a bit longer. I was jet lagged, so it made sense to take it easy. I knew I had to turn the telly off and get out so I decided to explore the Antrim Coast. I discovered mountains, found isolated clearings in the middle of dense forests, and sat alone praying and meditating and imagining I was Tarzan. I even climbed a tree and got stuck for an hour. I tried to climb down gingerly but failed. I then tumbled down fast and hit a twig on the way, ripping the seat of my pants. The dull ache in my buttocks lasted for days. But I felt a sense of primal oneness, a calm centredness that everything would be OK. A kind of cosmic unity with my surroundings. Sadly a photo of my solitary excursions ended up in the university magazine. I'd been caught in the foreground of a picture in a holiday brochure and this snap was put on page two of the rag with the caption: 'Anyone seen the Aimless Arab of Antrim?' This may have raised an alarm because a week before we broke up for Christmas, I was called into an office by the same man who had welcomed me on my first day.

Surprisingly Mr Jones introduced himself as my 'tutor'. I said I didn't know I had a tutor. He said he was my tutor and that he had been trying to contact me for the last eight weeks. His manner was extremely kind and he spoke with great gentleness.

He informed me that he was aware that I had been absent from all lectures and seminars for my subjects and asked if I was aware that I had to give in some essays? I said no. He informed me there were sixteen essays outstanding across three subjects. I said it was the first I'd heard of it. He said that was understandable if I hadn't attended university events and outings. I asked him to elaborate on the words 'events' and 'outings'. He said the drama department had already put on a major production, the English department had made several trips to the theatre in Belfast and Dublin and the French class had been to Lyon and back. I said it was sad I'd missed out. He said he was glad to hear I was sad because my behaviour suggested that I wasn't. I asked what he meant. He explained that he was required to ask me formally if I wanted to stay at university. I was stunned and said of course, why ever would I not? He said, well, because this kind of behaviour was usually associated with people who didn't want to be there. Or people who had undergone or were undergoing some sort of severe mental stress or nervous collapse. I remember not having the words to explain my state at that time and said all I knew to be true – that I had needed time to be alone. He said he understood perfectly and reassured me that 'these things happen'. I agreed and ventured that you never know how you're going to react when you relocate. Nodding compassionately he assured me that starting something new and being out of one's comfort zone was tough. I thanked him and got up to leave, feeling rather shaken and embarrassed. Unfortunately my tutor, straightening his back, coughing and looking rather awkward, said he wanted me to understand that given the gravity of my situation, I really had to hand in all sixteen essays on or before 6 January next term by 10 a.m., or I would be kicked out of university.

I was shocked but kept my gaze steady, and my smile casual. I told him I would do it. No problemo. He looked relieved and wished me 'a productive Christmas'. He then shook my hand as if I were his best friend and for a moment I imagined what we would do together as pals. I was happy to be his friend. I then realised I had no friends, so this served as extra motivation to get the essays done. Perhaps we could go for coffee in January.

Back at home I noticed just how warm London was, even at Christmas time. It was at least five degrees warmer than in Northern Ireland. An insulated city with millions of heated houses and apartments in close proximity was very different from the seaside expanses of Antrim and Londonderry. When I didn't make a fire my cottage was so freezing I began to wonder if maybe cuddling Zebedee on cold nights was a trick I had missed. I remember nothing else that Christmas other than writing out by hand all sixteen essays. It's bizarre to think now how hard I worked with the sole motivation of preserving the right to be alone in a tiny, cold cottage, miles away from civilisation.

As it was I enjoyed writing the essays and they were given reasonably good grades, especially the one about Nora slamming the door on nineteenth-century Norwegian patriarchy, in favour of pursuing an autonomous life as a modern woman. I quoted everything the professor at Princeton said. It produced the highest mark on the course for the Ibsen module. My tutor was ecstatic, convinced there had been some sort of pedagogical breakthrough. The marker's notes read: 'Inspired. Great to see a young man so conscious of the feminist struggle!'

Thus my time at university finally kicked off 'for real' in January of 1986. I roused myself from my solitude and started going tentatively to lectures like a 'normal' student. Even if they did not share the panache of Princeton, there was still much to enjoy. For example, I often sat next to Charles the narcoleptic who dropped off during English literature lectures. He'd write down long involved questions intending to challenge the lecturer, while shaking his leg to keep awake. Invariably, Charles would fall asleep in the middle of the lecturer's response, leaving the lecturer tapering off with an embarrassed 'Oh, dear, er . . . he's gone again.' A supportive round of applause would start up, along with cries of, 'Come on Charles! Wakey wakey!' Charles would generally 'come to', take the applause and carry on listening politely. I sat next to him during an exam once and, at his request, kept prodding him with my ruler every ten minutes to wake him up. It eventually became too onerous and debilitating a task, so he was obliged to take exams on his own with a supervisor on hand, briefed to keep him awake with loud clapping, constant prods and forceful barks of encouragement. Had I not been focused on my own exams, I would have happily shouldered this important duty.

I was doing English, French and Theatre Studies but somehow, I couldn't really engage with the other students. It may be that they never quite got over their initial mistrust of me given I'd previously been so absent; they were all clearly thinking, 'Who is this bloke on our course who's been missing all these months?' When asked where I had been, I would defensively reply, 'Around.' People seemed indignant that they had all been working hard while the 'Aimless Arab of Antrim' had been generally cavorting around the countryside and disappearing abroad. Remarks like 'how nice of you to drop in' were probably meant in the spirit of banter, and had I been a little more alert and conscious, I might have bantered back. Instead I reverted to my default setting of disengagement and sank deeper into my rich fantasy life.

Feeling uncomfortable around students my own age, I gravitated more towards the 'mature' students, many of whom were angry activist types in their thirties who sold copies of the *Morning Star* outside the main canteen on Mondays. Although I seldom read it, I often bought copies of this socialist newspaper in the vain hope that if they thought I was 'one of them' they would leave me alone. I had witnessed them carry out aggressive challenges to others' beliefs where many buckled. I once saw a Christian Conservative renounce God, and promise to pledge allegiance to the Chichester Communist Collective on his return to England at half-term.

Luckily the 'mature' crowd also included aspiring writer types who were more easy going: Malachy Martin and his partner Maria were a popular couple who had come into a mysterious inheritance and seemed to be constantly travelling. They often held court like a comedy duo in the bar, delivering lengthy anecdotes of multiple misunderstandings in Japan, bareback horse riding in Texas and bathing in goats' milk in Outer Mongolia. And then there was Ron Blakely from White Abbey in Belfast. Whilst looking like a beery 'Ulsterman' in the most stereotypical sense of the word, Ron had the most poetic soul of them all. Over the course of my time in Ulster, I began to spend most of my time with Ron. He was one of the funniest and most stimulating of my friends whilst possessing an insatiable capacity for esoteric conversations and laughing deep into the night. Our evenings usually ending with Ron saying, slightly drunk, 'What's it all about, Omid?'

After a while, probably thanks to Ron who was also studying drama, I found my place amidst the Theatre Studies crowd. Admittedly I perceived drama students initially as fellow misfits rather than kindred spirits. But the theatre lot were definitely 'my people'.

My first collegiate theatre performance was in the curiously titled *Dosaberd* (stupid bird), an amalgamated version of six Chester Mystery Cycle plays, written and directed by our head of theatre studies, Paul Hadfield. I got the impression that there might have been some 'pastoral care' cajoling from my tutor Mr Jones, but there was certainly some surprise when the course director Lynda Henderson (partner of Paul Hadfield) handed me one of the lead roles as Herod. The production was to take place at the Riverside Theatre and we were to be joined by two professionals: the late Wolfe Morris, the perfect casting to play God with his heavyset figure and white hair, and Paddy Scully, a wiry and waspishly camp actor from the Lyric Theatre company in Belfast, who was to play the Devil. The rest of the cast were the first-year students, most of whom didn't know me, so there was a lot to prove. Unfortunately my only interaction with them up to that point had been a disastrous seminar a couple of weeks earlier.

There was no question that I was judged harshly by the group, and not just by the 'activist' element. Frankly, I could understand their point of view. I had missed the first term and yet had not been kicked out. I wore white cricket jumpers slung casually over my shoulders. I think I had also taken to wearing cheesecloth shirts in the middle of winter. I drove a Renault 5. I think I basically gave the impression of an archetypal 'London twat'.

Somehow Lynda Henderson saw my potential and felt something had to shift. She asked me to research and conduct a seminar on playwright John McGrath's controversial '7:84' theatre company. The numbers denoted a popular fact that 7 per cent of the population owned 84 per cent of the country's wealth. The company specialised in 'agit-prop' (agitational propaganda) theatre to highlight social injustices, in particular the unequal distribution of wealth. Their shows often included anti-right-wing rants with a heavy pro-communist leaning, but usually ended with singing and dancing to soften the didacticism. Based in Scotland and steeped in tradition they referred to this regular shindig at the end of their shows as a 'ceilidh' – the Celtic word for a traditional Gaelic social gathering, pronounced 'kaylee'. My hermit-like behaviour during my first term had deprived me of the benefit of learning the important fact that Celtic words had very different pronunciations – for example, it took me an embarrassingly long time to realise that the girl's name I heard phonetically as 'Shavaun' was in fact spelled 'Siobhan'.

Considering I was giving my presentation to students of mostly Scottish or Irish Celtic origin, my pronunciation of the word 'ceilidh' resulted in an excruciating baptism of fire. Arms folded in confusion they confronted me, gently at first, led by curly red-haired Lenny Mullan, Communist mature student ringleader if you will, who interrupted me through tight Scottish lips:

'Hold on. What's that?'

'What's what?'

'That thing you just said.'

'A saylid-huh?'

'Aye. What's that?'

'You don't know a saylid-huh?'

'I don't mate, sorry.'

'Well, you must know.'

'"Must know" what?'

'It's in your culture . . .'

'Never heard of it. What is it again?'

'A saylid-huh.'

'Never heard the word.'

'You know, a kind of, you know, a get-together. Like a shindig? When people gather and sing and dance together. Sounds like a lot of fun if you ask me.'

'You mean a ceilidh?'

'A what?'

'You're describing a ceilidh.'

'I don't know what that means. Well anyway, it's called a saylid-huh . . .'

'A what?'

'A saylid-huh . . .'

'It's called a celidh.'

'Well, have a look for yourself. It says it here in this book, see? Saylid-huh!'

'Aye, that's ceilidh.'

'No, saylid-huh.'

Not an auspicious start by any standards. But there is always 'a moment' in the life of a student artiste, a moment that kick-starts artistic life: a moment when you think 'I can do this'. Here was the moment:

Once cast as Herod I began to tackle my scene depicting the killing of the first-born. This proved to be a stumbling block. I was given a large chopping knife taped with Sellotape (an old theatrical trick which blunts the blade but maintains the appearance of a violent weapon) and was directed to use it on little white cotton sacks filled with baking flour and sawdust, which represented babies. In the dress rehearsal I just couldn't accept that plunging the knife into the little white sacks to depict the slaughter of the innocents would work. I just thought the idea was silly. I actually believed that the horror of that moment would be best served by using baby dolls and ripping their heads off. Much to my shame, I even pitched for this several times. Thankfully, no one responded to my ideas. I was going to have to go for it on the night.

Keen to please, I put aside my misgivings and did just that. To signal the start of the mass murder – Herod's vain attempt to kill the baby Jesus – I plunged the knife into the sack to 'kill' the first child, producing what Lynda described as an 'unearthly shriek of pure focused evil'. The sight of me desecrating the sacks with all my might seemed to overwhelm the audience. For those moments I transformed into a raving lunatic. Flour and sawdust swirled frantically around me as I ransacked the set. The combination of sweat, panting and white powder all over the theatre seemed to shock the audience into a disbelieving silence. Lynda approached me afterwards telling me earnestly that, for a moment, everyone believed that the white powder was actually the blood of the children. 'Omid, you really understand evil. That was chilling.' I actually had no idea what she was talking about. I had simply been relishing this chance to emulate Al Pacino in *Scarface* when he is engulfed in white powder, in his case cocaine, albeit with a different accent. I'd even considered shouting 'say hello to ma little friend' before bringing the knife down for the final plunge. I was as shocked by the audience's reaction as they were to my performance of Herod. In a lightbulb moment it dawned on me: 'Can I make a living from this?'

CHAPTER TWENTY

The Portstewart Near-Death Experience

'Better three hours too soon than a minute too late.'
William Shakespeare

Nationality was always a problem in Northern Ireland because there were so few minorities there in 1985. The entire list of 'foreigners' on campus comprised about four Indians (including Zebedee), two black guys, some exchange students from Hong Kong, a German guy with a moustache and mullet called Klaus and of course Johannes, my Dutch environmentalist canoeing friend. There were five other Iranians, all science students, whose five-a-side football team (aptly named 'The Persian Empire') I joined. We did very well, powering through six rounds of the university five-a-side tournament and making it to the final. Sadly, after they found out I was a Bahá'í, I was quietly dropped before the last match of the tournament.

Incidentally, years later, one of the team came to one of my comedy shows and apologised about me getting dropped. He was adamant that it had nothing to do with prejudice. He explained kindly that they just didn't particularly like me. He hoped that I would be reassured by knowing that it was nothing to do with religion. I was doing drama and they were all engineers so it made sense.

On my way back home to Castlerock during the spring of 1986, I'd become aware of an elderly gentleman who often seemed to be trying to hitchhike but didn't quite know how. He would put his thumb out nervously and shake it from side to side. But as cars came near he would draw his thumb anxiously back in again. Feeling sorry for him and curious to find out if indeed he was attempting to hitchhike, I stopped and asked him if he needed a lift. 'Aye, Portstewart,' he said with a heavy accent and a lisp. Quite against university protocol I told him to get in.

'Very kind of you. Very kind. Aye. Cheers, all the best.'

He sounded like he'd already said goodbye as he got in. After some initial chat he noticed my swarthy appearance and asked where I was from. I said Iran and all hell broke loose. He started yelling at the top of his voice: 'Akh Jaysus, lemme out! Lemme out!'

Despite us travelling at 60 mph he tried to open the passenger door to fling himself out. An almighty struggle took place as I leaned over him to slam the door shut. In a terrified voice he asked, 'You've no got any bombs in here, have ye?!'

A minute of frantic explanation ensued. I reassured him that I was raised in Britain and I didn't carry bombs in my car. He finally calmed down. When he realised I wasn't going to blow us both up in an act of terrorism, he immediately relaxed and went off on bizarre tangents and streams of consciousness:

'I had ma tooth out, my sister had her tooth out too but she's got Parkinson's, so it's not easy, you know? So I says to Gerry Adams what about that wee baldy specky bastard on ITN? Don't look Tibetan to me.'

I listened impassively, realising that once people have overcome their prejudices, more often than not they won't shut up.

The irony seemed to be lost on him that someone in Northern Ireland at the height of the Troubles was worried about a young student from Kensington being a terrorist.

March 1988 saw a horrific incident in the Andersontown district of Belfast when two British corporals inadvertently drove into a Catholic funeral.

A few days earlier three people had been killed at another funeral, so tensions were already high. Corporals Howell and Wood then found themselves driving into the wrong place at the wrong time, surrounded by the funeral crowd who were convinced they had come to kill Catholics. The corporals fired warning shots to clear the car of people who were surging around them. Sadly and tragically they were later executed by IRA gunmen.

This tragedy, like many others in Northern Ireland, and indeed around the world, showed me how deep fear, hatred and religious prejudice could go. For a few days Northern Ireland was on red alert and the university upped its security with armed guards in the form of soldiers in berets and fatigues walking the perimeter. The toilet graffiti near the library, never complimentary towards the British, now involved human excrement being smeared over Union Jacks. I remember looking at this and feeling despair that someone could have felt driven to commit such an extreme act.

Preparing for a mock exam the next day I revised into the early hours one Friday night. Portstewart was always busy on weekends with students, locals and out-of-towners coming up from Belfast and gathering in the bars along the promenade. By 1 a.m. I was throwing stones on the beach to clear my head. I heard some shouting but had no idea it was directed at me.

'You! Throwing stones!'

I looked back, pointed a finger at my chest and the voice shouted, 'Aye! You!' proceeded with some random obscenities.

Picking up some large stones as security, I made the long walk back to the middle of the promenade to face my abusers. Two men, possibly students, were looking out of a first-floor window above a row of shops, with what sounded like a party going on in the background.

'What de ye want?' they said, spotting my fists clenched round the stones. Presumably they were regretting their aggression and were now worried as they could see I had weapons. Believing they were first-year students I felt morally bound to teach them a lesson, so I kept walking steadily towards them. 'I'll give them a little fright, they'll be thankful afterwards,' I thought. After all, I was reasonable, I wouldn't do them any damage and I'd see them at campus on Monday and they'd look up to me and maybe even see me as a role model. I could possibly even mentor them at some point, socially, religiously or mentally.

As I got close they got excited. 'Aye, that's right, come here Shaymee.'

I knew this was a nickname for Seamus. Said in a derogatory way it meant they were Protestants. Calling me Seamus meant they thought I was Catholic. Or at least from Southern Ireland, some Irish people having inherited dark genes from the Moroccan Moors. Now I could see they weren't students at all. They were the very roughest of that breed we called 'locals'. And drunk. Still, I was the one with the stones.

'Did you call me something back there?' I said, caressing the stones as if to say: 'I'm the one with the weapons here, you better be careful.' They obviously had no regard for the threat but I held my ground. I wasn't going to be scared of them, not with my two handfuls of stones.

'You want your kneecaps blown off?'

A chill went down my spine. This activity was associated with paramilitaries. Victims have kneecaps blown off with guns pressed to the legs. I weakly said, 'Well, not really.' One of the men disappeared inside; the other changed his tone and said with urgency: 'Jeez boy, you better run. He's serious.'

I didn't move. I didn't have time to think at all before the man reappeared with a double-barrelled shotgun. He took aim and fired. A loud bang rang out and I heard female screams, obviously from the party inside. Dropping the stones, no use to me now, I ran for my life. A second shot was fired (I heard the bullet whistle past my ear) and then I heard: 'Get him!'

I had never been chased like this before, not since one time on the West London party circuit when I was chased by a group of skinheads called the 'Nutty Farmers' who were only intent on a skirmish and a slap. Here a gun had been produced along with a threat that my kneecaps would be used by Protestant children to clop together to make a noise like a horse trotting (instead of the more traditional coconut shells I used back in primary school). My football training came in handy. I was fast. After a lightning sprint I jumped behind a wall and hid behind a bin as the locals ran past screaming, intent on murder. I had escaped almost certain death.

The next day I went in to see the head of the English Department, a man called professor Robert Welch, my favourite lecturer and an Irishman I trusted at this difficult time, to report the incident and consult him as to what I should do. He told me I had a lucky escape and to speak no further about the matter. I said that I'd nearly been killed. He said I should report it to no one, not to the RUC, nor the Special Branch nor the police in England. If I did then I would run the risk of getting killed. That was the reality of the situation. Shocked, I asked if there was anything else we could do. He said that was the best help he could offer. He then reminded me I had six more essays to hand in by the end of the week. I asked if I could have an extension. He said no.

CHAPTER TWENTY-ONE

The Mentor

'O, had I but followed the arts!'

William Shakespeare

University is a time to process what your life has been, what your life could be and, most importantly, to decide what your life is going to be. For some, the university years are a chance to go crazy and reinvent themselves away from parental preconceptions and expectations. For others, the way isn't so clear. I'm baffled to look back and see how very little comedy did for me when I was at university. It's not that I didn't enjoy humorous pleasure. Perhaps I was simply too preoccupied with myself to be able to laugh at anything. I remember watching comedy performances where comments were made on stage that transported me into a tunnel of insecurity, I just got lost and zoned out.

The first live comedy I was exposed to was a duo called Skint Video, big on the comedy scene at the time. I even know one of them now, Steve Gribbin, a lovely and very funny man. But I didn't laugh once that first night. I actually couldn't understand what they were on about. People were laughing hysterically but I didn't get it. I know now that comedy has a language to it and you need to be attuned to that language to get the jokes. That's why I never judge people who come to a gig and don't laugh. They could be highly humorous people, but if they are not used to watching comedy, not used to the rhythm of it and how it works, it can leave them cold. After my first taste, I must say I didn't care for it at all.

'Cabaret is not real art,' I used to say. 'Anyone can get up and try to be entertaining. Doesn't mean you're an *artiste*.' If I had been studying self-importance I'm sure I would have got a First. After three years of theatre studies I was well on my way to becoming a drama ponce.

But I did it. I finished university with a 2:1. Looking at the results table I was amazed, after all my blagging and A-level disasters, as my eyes went up the list of names to see that I had actually come eighth out of 160 students studying combined humanities. I must say it was an emotional moment.

I'd also blagged my way into the university football team and played fifty-five games over the three years, winning a total of four trophies, even one for Personality of the Year. These achievements set me up. There was much to be hopeful about, but I still didn't really know what I was going to do with my life.

Although I'd enjoyed performing, acting was not something that had ever truly appealed to me as a career, and it certainly was not the reason why I had been so desperate for a university education. I'd wanted to escape, I'd wanted to better myself, I'd wanted to expand my horizons, but I'd also wanted to emulate a family friend of mine who had made an enormous impact on me during my disastrous exam years. His name was Professor Suheil B. Bushrui. He was the reason why I wanted to come to university in the first place. Although born and raised in Lebanon and then Palestine, he always considered himself a citizen of the world. Looking back I believe that he was the first person I ever considered as a role model. He was portly, short and bald (no surprise there – I must have seen my future self in him) with a light moustache. He had style and wore fine suits (there the comparisons end). He was passionate and articulate and, though a professor of Anglo-Irish literature at the University of Maryland, he spoke with a highly engaging Arabic accent. It was Professor Bushrui in all his zany refinement and excitability that I used to channel as a character in my early stand-up act. I never truly mastered the nuances of his slightly posh Oxford tones, which laced in superbly with his Arab accent. I was never doing an impression, just channeling his spirit.

I first came into contact with him when I was seventeen and he was staying in our family home. Unbeknown to me, Bushrui was a respected member of the international Bahá'í community, and my parents were delighted to offer him a room whenever he was in London. I could see from the way they treated him that they considered him to be beloved and special. He breezed into the flat one Sunday afternoon and took over the house with his fresh, enlivening presence. Bizarrely he smoked a cigar, which seemed to me to be sophisticated and defiantly eccentric. His very energy made me shake. Professor Bushrui was a completely new entity in my life: highly intellectual but with a great sense of humour, and importantly, enormous amounts of soul. In my (limited) world, intellectuals were never funny, and funny people were never considered 'intellectual'. On top of that 'soulful' people were mostly flakey and boring.

I was still at the very beginning of my tormented A-level saga. He seemed thrilled and delighted that I was studying English. 'But this is fantastic! Young Iranians usually do the sciences. Well done for choosing *the soul.*' I loved his enthusiasm but confessed that I was struggling. He asked me to give him some of my work to read one night. Feeling slightly nervous I handed over two recent rather weak and disappointing essays. I'd just received a D+ for a question on Shakespeare's *Measure for Measure* about 'whether Isabella was justified in not saving her brother', and a C– for a question about 'the use of song' in Ben Jonson's *Volpone*. Professor Bushrui looked at the marks with impassive distaste. I noticed this and, feeling embarrassed, apologised and admitted that these were not great essays. He fixed me with a steady gaze and told me that he would be the judge of that, not the teachers. I was amazed at his confidence. True to his word, he approached me the next morning.

'Omid, I have read your essays. You are clearly a misunderstood genius. Your hypothesis that Shakespeare's Isabella is schizophrenic – this is extraordinary – as is your costume design of a fox's tail for Volpone. Both essays were incorrectly marked and deserved A grades. Your teachers are obviously either racist or corrupt or both.'

Never having received an ounce of academic encouragement, I fell in love with this man immediately. I didn't care if it was disproportionate praise based on pity and compassion. It was encouragement nonetheless.

From that day forth, I followed Bushrui closely, watching him speak at a number of gatherings, private parties and conferences. I drank in his words, his wisdom, his interpretations and his funny stories. His commitment to 'the life of the spirit' was intoxicating. He gave me an appreciation of writers like Kahlil Gibran and James Joyce, and awakened a curiosity in me to understand the similarities or even the underlying fusion between eastern and western literature. His favourite saying was: 'Walk the spiritual path with practical feet!' I saw him attempt to do this many times, in ways that were often bonkers, but never did I cringe. He also loved football, playing for teams in Egypt, and he was known for his headers that always seemed to find the goal. He was nicknamed 'bullet head', which for one so short was highly amusing to me.

During my very last summer at university, in a miraculous

and fortuitous twist of fate, Professor Bushrui arrived in Coleraine. My campus was host to the annual Anglo-Irish Literature Society conference. Unbelievably, Bushrui was chairman and convener that year. He encouraged me to attend, and to assist him for the week. Naturally I jumped at the chance. I listened to his talks, observed his interactions, fetched him water and drove him around, all the time absorbing his pearls of wisdom. I even wrote them down.

1) 'Nothing is wasted. Ever.' This was in response to my worry that I had wasted my first term at university lounging around my cottage in my underpants, watching television and staring blankly out the window, mammalian and non-cognisant. He may have been wrong on that point.

2) 'It's noble to be hurt and to forgive. But how much better to have the power to comprehend and not be hurt at all?' I protested that this was hard to put into practice. Whereupon he offered his favourite Oscar Wilde quotation: 'Forgive your enemies, nothing annoys them more.'

3) 'You only live once. Why not enjoy?' This advice related to food. When I commented that we were both slightly portly he retorted: 'I always judge a man by his weight. Never trust a thin man,' and promptly quoted Julius Caesar referring to Cassius who he said had 'a lean and hungry look . . . Such men are dangerous.'

Having already familiarised me with W. B. Yeats and James Joyce (he was an authority on both) he told me with glee about his interview with Samuel Beckett only a month earlier. Bushrui claimed that he was privy to a 'breathtaking revelation' made by Beckett in conversation about his play *Waiting for Godot*.

Bushrui, visibly controlling his excitement, told me the story: '. . . And then I said to him: "Mr Beckett, I believe *Waiting for Godot* is your most misunderstood work." He said, "How so?" I said, "Two tramps wait for a Mr Godot who never arrives. Thus critics deduce the message that God does not exist. To me the message is far deeper than that." Beckett looked at me with that intense glare and said, "Go on . . ." So I said, "Perhaps your play is saying that it's not about *waiting* for God but telling us that we have to go and *find* Him, or have the courage to *seek* him. As it says in the Bible, 'Seek, and ye shall find.'" Beckett leaned forwards and looked me in the eyes, grabbed my arm and said, "My dear Suheil, you may just be right."'

Bushrui told this story to me, but bizarrely he didn't mention it to any gathering during the conference. I pulled him up on this.

'It debunks all their theories about Beckett,' he said. 'They'd never believe it anyway. But you should know it.'

As I was pondering this privileged information, Bushrui suddenly became aware of the time: 'We have to hurry! J. P. Clarke's lecture is about to start. We cannot miss it – he's going to say something sensational.'

Bushrui had already told me about this obscure academic, describing him as a highly controversial figure. I imagined one of those scruffy personalities who regularly appeared on BBC2 for the Open University, deciphering complicated diagrams in front of a blackboard. Whoever he was, there was no doubt J. P. Clarke was going to ignite the conference with his incendiary remarks. 'We're very lucky to have him. He's flown in especially from Lagos. God knows what the reaction is going to be.'

When we arrived at the sparsely populated hall, I saw J. P. Clarke was a serious-looking Nigerian gentleman with thick glasses. He was sitting quietly, awaiting his introduction. An elderly English academic who must have been about eighty-five years old with long, flowing white hair, wearing inexplicable lederhosen and sandals, struggled to his feet, and began a lengthy speech. This introduction was filled with accounts of shocked reactions and splinter group formations from previous conferences. 'What happened at Yale was remarkable.' Suffice to say this made the atmosphere even more pregnant with expectation. We braced ourselves for tumult.

Unfortunately there were some technical difficulties, and as J. P. Clarke started his speech, the microphone stopped working. Undaunted, he carried on despite the resounding echo in the hall. This, coupled with his extremely strong Nigerian accent, rendered his words unintelligible. Furthermore, after a calm and measured beginning, J. P. Clarke burst into unexpected ranting and gesticulating. I'm pretty sure no one had any idea what he was talking about, although the eighty-five-year-old in lederhosen seemed to be mouthing along with J. P. Clarke's speech like a fan before eventually falling asleep with his mouth open. Academic life was certainly not as earth-shattering as I'd hoped it to be. I asked Bushrui afterwards what he made of the speech and all he could offer was: 'The acoustics leave a lot to be desired in this place.'

In the evenings I observed Bushrui in full swing, hosting the evening programmes with wit and charisma, making audiences roar with hysteria at his off-beat stories, whilst still finding time to engage in emotional conversations about poetry. He even initiated the late-night dancing that took place in the university canteen, with a makeshift beatbox doubling as a sound system. Taking his jacket off and dancing with all the ladies of a certain age, he did the foxtrot, the quickstep and the jive, having been taught to dance as a young man. All the while he delivered breathless tips, as he paused to wipe sweat from his brow with his flamboyant blue polka-dot handkerchief. It was as if he were training me to be his protégé: 'Try and dance with everyone. Leave out no one. The ladies get very jealous. Margaret! Where have you been? I've been waiting!'

Bushrui was an orator, a comedian, a scholar – and a dancer.

But it was what he said to me on the very last day of the conference that was to cement the direction my life was to take. I asked: 'What's the secret of your talks? They're by far and away the most entertaining of anyone I've ever seen.'

He said, almost ruefully, the passion he put into his talks was fuelled by his love of theatre. True, he was theatrical by nature, but I had not realised his yearnings for the acting profession.

'You know, Omid, all I ever wanted to do was act. I loved the theatre! Shakespeare, David Mamet . . . the world of passion, ideas and emotion! Nothing is more exciting! I always wanted to be an actor. Sadly my father would never let me. I was good, too. It makes me sad to even think about it. So I made the classroom my theatre.' I told him I thought it was wonderful to be such an influence on so many people. He said: 'In the classroom I can only affect hundreds. You can reach more. And I know that you will. I'm jealous of you because you will do it, not me.'

I laughed, knowing that my twenty-two-year-old self really wasn't up to much.

'But it's about what you're going to *become*. Never lose sight of that. Never lose hope.'

At last, I had a mission. I was determined to fulfil what my hero could not fulfil in his own life. Had I not been with Bushrui that summer, I might have attempted a misguided career as a university lecturer somewhere. I would have probably been appalling and certainly unsuccessful in any attempts to emulate Suheil B. Bushrui.

Luckily what Bushrui wanted was for me to be my future self: an actor, equally short, portly and bald, but an actor nevertheless.

CHAPTER TWENTY-TWO

Chauffeuring – My Soul In A Car Crash

'These pains you feel are messengers. Listen to them.'

Rumi

So fresh from my summer with Bushrui I knew what I wanted to 'be'. The problem was, I found myself back in London, in the guesthouse, with a cashflow problem. I needed a job while I figured out my next move. My employment history had been rather chequered to say the least. But I'd usually managed to find driving work to tide me over in times of transition.

My first driving job came in the summer of 1984, the second of my A-level years. Back in the seventies my father had been particularly helpful to a Persian gentleman called Jam (short for Jamshid) who was trying to find a job. My dad had used him as a driver and tipped him well. So well in fact, that Jam talks about the night he and his wife danced around in their bedsit together, so grateful for the extra cash. Jam loved my dad and the feeling was mutual. Jam went on to start a chauffeuring company (bizarrely called Denis Carter despite the fact that most of the drivers and clientele were Middle Eastern), and often cites my father as having been his chief supporter during his tough early days. I've since wondered whether my dad was rather disappointed in Javid and me that we didn't get further ahead in the chauffeuring business. Jam was always held up as an example of what we could have been if we'd had more business acumen/work ethic/vision . . .

Anyway, in just a few years, Denis Carter became established as one of the top limousine companies in London and Jam managed to acquire a number of lucrative contracts with Arab royal families. He was kind enough, as a favour to my dad, to use my brother and me as auxiliary drivers during the holidays when they were especially busy. Being assigned to one of the royal families was seen as an excellent job, as long as you could avoid having to drive the royal children.

And so, upon leaving university I approached Jam for some temporary work and was pleased to be given a short contract for the remainder of the summer.

I was assigned to a prince – we'll call him Prince Kamil – one of the dozens of royal family members who summered in London. Prince Kamil had two sons, let's call them Princes Tariq and Saud, and they were aged five and eight respectively. And sure enough, driver to the children was to be my task. At twenty-two I was one of the youngest drivers on the books and probably not really accomplished enough to be manoeuvring limos bearing royal cargo. Luckily, I looked more like a thirty-year-old, as I had been shaving from the age of eleven. We all hoped this would lend me an air of authority – a crucial tool when dealing with recalcitrant royal children.

Walter, a thin English butler, oversaw all the family operations but I had little dealings with him. He wore a prominent moustache, spoke in a slightly louche manner, and had a nervous tic. Oddly, he seemed to dress as if he were on permanent safari in Kenya. He had forged links with the royal family through his involvement with the military. Walter was the go-to man the Arabs could trust. He dealt mainly with the dishevelled, bespectacled Prince Kamil, who was forty-eight but looked seventy, as he was hardly able to walk due to the various after-effects of a misspent youth. He spent most of his time indoors wearing dark glasses at casinos and the Playboy club.

I dealt mostly with the Filipino nannies and servants who looked after the boys. I had to be outside the block of flats at 9 a.m., waiting in a road adjacent to the Park Lane Hilton. They often didn't emerge until midday. The car was a massive Oldsmobile, a left-hand-drive American station wagon that was larger and wider than most cars on the road but easily fit my five passengers. It also had a huge trunk to house the crazy amounts of shopping they did every day. I was nervous about driving this massive car through the narrow streets of London, but within a day I was finding motivation by singing along to the likes of 'So Emotional' by Whitney Houston, which seemed to dominate most radio stations at the time.

My shift was long but straightforward – mostly Mayfair to Regent's Park where the boys would be let loose like dogs to burn off their pent-up frustrations. After that, possibly a trip to Hamleys toy store on Regent Street to buy sacks full of toys which often got destroyed but were replaced on subsequent visits. Sometimes the children's mothers wanted to go shopping, and would jump in the car too, demanding 'Wigmore, Wigmore!' which I understood to mean Wigmore Street and then 'take me Bimboo' which I came to know as a children's shop called Bimbo on the same street. Once they said 'Hala Street' repeatedly and I had no idea what they meant. Through a bizarre and increasingly frustrated game of charades they made me understand they had a medical appointment. It took me a full five minutes to understand they meant Harley Street.

The children themselves were spoiled materially and sadly deprived of any perceivable personality. For a quiet life the defeated Filipino nannies simply let them do as they pleased, and if we got through an outing without meltdowns, breakdowns, visceral tantrums, primal writhing, injuries, and objects flying around, then it was classed as a good day. Much as I may have felt indignant and rather too accustomed to hardship in my childhood, having slept on the sofa for many years to make room for the guests, I did not envy these children their upbringing. If anything it made me want to renounce materialism forever and go and grow vegetables somewhere and make sculptures out of driftwood.

Prince Tariq often liked slapping the back of my head for fun. Nothing malicious. I think he liked me actually. They decided I was fun when early on I pulled a few faces at them and showed I wasn't like the other drivers, usually overweight middle-aged Egyptian men who only spoke Arabic. I was young, lean (well, leaner than I am now) and more accessible. Plus with me they were forced to speak English, something the nannies encouraged out of a sense of educational duty. I even joined them in the park sometimes, chasing them about to give the nannies a rest. But the constant hitting actually hurt, so one day, as tactfully and playfully as I could, I grabbed Prince Tariq by the arm to warn him that if he did it again I would growl like a monster. He screamed as though I had physically and mentally assaulted him. Fearful of lawsuits, I eventually decided it was easier to just endure the assaults. Even when he wasn't concentrating and looking out the window in the car he would still hit me distractedly. I just came to accept it, and I felt an unspoken solidarity with and respect for the nannies.

One day the nannies were given massive mobile phones (this was 1988 and like shoulder pads everything then was big and larger than life) and asked to keep in close contact with the mothers. I dropped them off at Whiteleys in Queensway and parked in the car park. Half an hour later I was reading quietly when the two boys and the three nannies suddenly bundled into the car laden with shopping bags, shouting urgently that they had received a message and we all had to return immediately.

I drove fast out of the car park to the bottom of Queensway. Unfortunately, a massive traffic jam prevented me turning right towards Park Lane. I turned left along Westbourne Grove, the opposite direction, but most of the roads back on to Bayswater Road were blocked. The nannies were getting hysterical – 'Why you go this way?!' – and I struggled to explain the traffic situation. We then found ourselves near Moscow Road and the only option now was to go up Ossington Street. This was a dangerous slip road to drive an Oldsmobile: it bottlenecks towards the end and becomes extremely narrow, even for normal-sized cars.

By now, I could see two cars following as I hit Ossington Street. Approaching the bottleneck I stopped. To my horror, I realised that the car was definitely too wide. I'd learned through practice to navigate this massive car around London and congratulated myself that I could drive confidently through tight spots in town. Now I knew we couldn't make it. If I were to drive ahead I would take off the wing mirrors of every car parked on both sides of the road, not to mention scratch them all, severely.

I froze.

'Why you stop?! Go!'

'I can't go. The car won't fit.'

'MUST go. We late!'

'I can't. I have to go back.'

I turned my head to reverse, but there were now five cars stuck behind me, honking furiously. By this time all I could see in the car were snarled faces and terror-stricken eyes screaming at me to go forward; in the mirror I saw the tense red faces of English businessmen and outraged white-van drivers yelling expletives, not understanding why I was holding everyone up.

I contemplated getting out of the car and calmly explaining the situation. Surely it was self-explanatory? Perhaps if I shrugged my shoulders and said, 'Arabs, eh?' then everyone would understand. But the screaming was hitting new decibel levels and Prince Tariq saw this as his cue to sit up behind me and start whacking the back of my head with all his burly five-year-old might. I pleaded with the nannies to call him off but they just kept screaming at me to move as if their lives depended on it. I emphasised that if they didn't call him off I might do something drastic, something I might regret, but they just started slapping my shoulders while the kid was smacking the back of my head. The clamouring felt like it was both inside and outside my skull. Clearly, the emergency to get back was more serious than I had imagined.

At this point the cars behind me were blasting their horns in short angry stabs of noise, and eight-year-old Prince Saud, who really should have known better, decided it was legitimate to completely lose control and started wailing like a banshee. I'd reached my own cracking point. I opened my mouth and roared. Then I put my foot down on the accelerator and crashed into the first pair of cars, tearing off the wing mirrors immediately and scratching the side of their doors. It was the perfect squeeze, the Oldsmobile gliding snugly along both sides of the parked cars, lurching forward, bouncing up and down, its wooden panelled sides smashing everything in its wake. All the way up the road, thirty cars one side, thirty the other. We had obliterated everything in sight.

The noise of smashed metal, revved-up engine and screaming eight-year-old all subsided at once. I drove the car out the other side and everyone fell calm and quiet. I looked back and saw the carnage I had caused – wing mirrors of BMWs, Mercedes,

Fords, Renaults, all their debris lying in the middle of the road. No one said a word. I drove the mile back to Mayfair in silence. All was calm in the back apart from Prince Tariq, who was still standing behind me, but now hitting me gently, just little brushes, no doubt a reward for doing thousands of pounds of damage to other people's property. When we got back we discovered that the 'emergency' was that the medication for Prince Tariq's 'slight temperature' had arrived and his mother had wanted him to take it immediately. I hadn't even realised he was ill. Neither, in fact, had he.

Within a week it was all forgotten. I told Walter what had happened and over the coming weeks I saw him calmly issuing cheques and fielding indignant phone calls from the understandably irate car owners and residents of Ossington Street. There was no CCTV then, so Walter had simply reported the incident to the council and invited claims. Only twenty of the cars did so. He even praised me for my honesty and said the family was grateful I had risked all to get their sick son back in time. Actually I felt it was me who was the most sickened by this debacle. It left a bad taste in my mouth for months.

I knew I had to do something to get out of this dead-end job. I was trying in vain to 'better myself' by reading as much as I could, often taking four books along with me in the car. Usually I was lucky if I managed a few paragraphs a day. Constantly distracted by a yearning for a more meaningful life and suffering from a deep loneliness, I also felt permanently exhausted and found that I needed to catnap in order to catch up from sleepless nights spent worrying about my future. Boredom sometimes begets more boredom. In fact boredom became comforting as a device to numb myself and remain sane. Driving around London, I was fascinated by glimpses of people who seemed to be having the time of their lives; groups of people, young, old, tall, small, attractive, well-dressed, laughing, joking and obviously free, while I was hopelessly stuck behind the wheel of a car peeling rowdy children off my back. One low point involved a stint of a few days driving an elderly royal relative to casinos where he would blow more money in one night than I would earn in a year. The fact that our journeys were punctuated by his violent coughing and unpleasant hawking up of phlegm plunged me into such deep despair that at times I doubted the very point of my existence.

It was all so far away from where I instinctively knew I could belong. I wanted to be around 'evolved' people – without really knowing what 'evolved' meant. The family's other drivers irked and dismayed me with their low-vibration conversations. Sometimes we were invited into the kitchen to sit in an enclosure reserved for minions. We had snacks, tea and coffee on tap and a television to keep up to date with things going on in the world, providing images to the news stories we'd only hear on the radio. Inevitably group discussions would break out and heated debates would ensue over the most inconsequential of topics. For example: 'So, Omid, when you read a book, don't you get bored?'

I remember internally debating whether this companionship was better or worse than languishing suicidally alone in the car. After a while, I cultivated a special capacity to zone them out. I was happier alone, I decided; even if I wanted to die, at least my thoughts were my own. And anyway, I wanted to keep out of Manouch's way.

Manouch was one of the older drivers, and whenever he was on duty everyone was on edge. I began to wonder if being around Manouch was the tiniest taste of what it might have been like to be in the presence of Saddam Hussein's fearsome sons Uday and Qusay. At six foot two he was as sinister as he was volcanic. When driving, the slightest roadside misdemeanour could cause him to jump out of his car with a baseball bat and issue screaming death threats at drivers. In gentler moments, he often approached me, sage-like, one bejewelled hairy hand resting on my shoulder and the other gesticulating as he offered me dietary advice. He would scrunch up a piece of pitta bread, plunge it in Greek yoghurt and place it delicately in his mouth, declaring this combination to be 'the most balanced food in the world'. No one argued with him. This one sentence, shared prescriptively as if it were a medical secret between the two of us, somehow captures and symbolises the world in which I felt stuck. I began to feel like the pitta bread, drowning in a sea of thick yoghurt, unable to hear my own thoughts, or feel, or escape . . .

A more resilient part of me insisted that this was all good. Take the nonsense; it's going to be character-building in the long run, I told myself. I concocted a coping analogy: the further you pull a catapult back, the further the missile will go when released. In other words, the more you suffer for something the better it was for you and the more it propelled you to go on and achieve your heart's desire.

Unfortunately, by the end of the job with the royal family, I had forgotten what my 'heart's desire' was. I wondered if I even had a heart at all. I had become blank.

Until . . . out of nowhere a girl came into my life.

CHAPTER TWENTY-THREE

Girl Of My Dreams

'You don't love someone for their looks or their clothes, or for their fancy car, but because they sing a song only you can hear.'

Oscar Wilde

I've never been very good at relationships. The quadruple date in my teens had squashed my confidence and sadly throughout my youth most of my passion and romantic energy was channelled into Chelsea FC in the old second division.

Annabel was a friend of a friend who lived in Kent. One day I had a random dream about her, which was strange, as I had only met her on three brief occasions. I'd been struck by her loveliness but assumed she was one of the 'unattainables'.

I awoke from the dream with a compulsion to track her down and tell her we were soul mates. Fortunately, even though I believed this to be the case on an intuitive level, I had the sense to realise that she may be alarmed by this kind of information from a relative stranger. I resolved to err on the side of caution. My first task was to ring Shirin, our mutual friend. Still half asleep, I stumbled to the telephone, and was a little stunned by the voice on the other end.

'I'm sorry, Shirin's not here, can I help?'

The voice sounded strangely familiar. I forced myself to go on.

'Well, actually I'm trying to contact a friend of hers. A friend called Annabel . . .'

'I'm Annabel.'

Oh my God.

Garbling my words, I told her that I needed to see her. Could I come and visit her? It was very important. I needed to tell her something. After a slightly tense pause, she said she was very busy with her work, but was going to a party the next evening and was sure it would be fine for me to come. I deduced from this that she didn't want to find herself in the company of a nutter without back-up. Sensible girl. I liked that.

Within twenty-four hours I found myself at an awkwardly small party amongst a bunch of strangers, waiting for Annabel. They seemed like arty student types and wondered who I was. I said I was a friend of Annabel's and remained mute. When she finally arrived, she greeted me warmly and invited me into the kitchen for a chat. After my incoherent recounting of the dream, she smiled and said kindly that she was sure we were meant to be friends. I agreed heartily – adding that perhaps it meant we might play a significant role in each other's lives. She smiled again but seemed a little unsure, suggesting that perhaps we should rejoin the party. I was delighted she hadn't dismissed me outright as a nutbag or a stalker and was thrilled I'd established a connection with a girl who didn't seem to think I was weird, or 'too much'.

Later, she dropped me off back at the train station in a rather battered yellow Ford transit van. I was suddenly struck by a twinkly quality that emanated from her. She was a petite blonde with big eighties hair, hippy-chic clothes and, rather incongruously, DM boots – a staple fashion statement among artsy intellectual girls of that era. It seemed like such a cliché but her blue eyes really did sparkle. On the train back I was suddenly filled with so much energy I jumped around all the seats on the empty carriage with nerves and elation, only to be caught by a ticket inspector who reprimanded me severely.

At that time Annabel was working with an educational theatre company in Kent. Shortly after our conversation at the party I learned that they were going to be performing at an outdoor festival in Canterbury (something to do with Chaucer). I pretended I was interested in the festival and showed up with a bag over my shoulder in the hope of giving an impression I was there mainly for research purposes. The bag actually had nothing in it, but I felt it gave me purposeful gravitas. The performance itself was an alarming piece where Annabel seemed to spend a lot of time doing acrobatics and sitting on people's shoulders reciting poetry to audiences of schoolchildren. When it was over I had a ten-minute chat with her under a tree, but there were so many annoying kids milling around that it was difficult to have any meaningful conversation. I felt grateful for the bag because without it I was convinced I would have felt naked and exposed. Those ten minutes with Annabel were the highlight of my life that month. It's all I thought about when back in my driving job. I simply had to get her alone again.

Annabel's theatre company actually specialised in working with people who had learning difficulties. She seemed to spend most of her time conducting drama workshops and perfor-mances. This was tough work, sometimes doing three shows in three different centres a day and driving all over Kent in the company's yellow Ford Transit van. The job also included putting on some performances for psycho-geriatric patients in homes and hospitals. Annabel described this as 'reminiscence work' – the theatre company would research songs and poems from yesteryear and perform them for frail elderly people who seemed barely cognisant and would more often than not heckle her quite rudely. One of her colleagues told me that an old man recently exposed himself to Annabel when she was mid-song. Thankfully he was bundled away tactfully by exhausted male nurses. Like a true pro, she didn't bat an eyelid. I had never met anyone like her. She even had a dog, a grey whippet called Joe who used to sit next to her in the van and had his own seatbelt.

In a moment of inspiration, I remembered I'd done a module on 'Theatre in Education' at university. I could pretend I was researching this line of work and ask to accompany her on a 'scouting mission' as an excuse to follow her about. Although seemingly surprised by my request, she agreed that I could come with her the following week to a community centre on a farm in the Kent countryside.

I noticed she was a fast driver. Like the DM boots this seemed to clash with her gentle and empathetic nature. I liked that. 'Dynamic,' I thought. When we arrived I saw that she was very well received; the group she had been working with, about twelve people with varying degrees of learning disabilities, all had a great affection for her. Some were hugging her and some just stood next to her holding her hand and smiling benignly. I blended into the background and watched her work. Annabel invited me to join in but I felt rather daunted and pretended I was making notes.

The workshop started with simple ball games and clapping exercises. Then a bubble machine was introduced which filled the participants with joy as they expressed themselves with free-flowing movements – popping the bubbles mid-air and swaying to the music of Clannad. I watched from the sidelines, dazzled by their amazing moves. Others were wafting multi-coloured scarves in the air with incredibly intense expressions on their faces, I'd never seen anything like it. After that, they all settled down and the atmosphere got very serious. Role-plays unfolded, mostly scenes designed to familiarise the group with emergency-service procedures. The participants practised dialling 999 on a specially provided phone, and enacted dramatic scenarios involving mugging, injury and theft.

However, the *pièce de résistance* for the afternoon came from the two stars of the group, a couple who seemed to be romantically involved. They performed verbatim a scene from *Coronation Street* they'd apparently been working on for several weeks, a marital altercation between Ken and Deirdre Barlow. Annabel quietly explained that she'd tried to engage them in broader and more artistic themes, but they'd preferred to take their inspiration from TV. I said 'spot on' and that I knew 'exactly where they were coming from', which momentarily confused her. I loved the way she worked with total acceptance of their reality, no judgement and a generous sense of humour.

There was one girl called Claire who was tall and seemed very attached to Annabel. She kept looking over at me suspiciously. Annabel told me she was the most sensitive of the bunch. I immediately made it my mission to win Claire over. It was a subtle window of opportunity. I began smiling at her. She didn't smile back.

Just before the end of the workshop, the group told the story of a stolen wallet and got very excited. There was a dramatic chase scene that resulted in the stolen wallet landing by my feet. This was my chance! Claire, who was playing a policewoman in the sketch, came over to pick it up but I got there first. I decided to join in by pretending to be a concerned member of the public. 'Here you are, madam. I believe this is yours?' Claire took the wallet coldly from me and stared deep into my eyes. I fixed a stare back.

'It's working,' I thought. I knew I had magic in my eyes.

'Who is he, Annabel?' said Claire, rather loud.

'Oh, he's just a friend.'

'I don't like him.'

Panicking, I smiled and upped the radiance.

'I don't like him, Annabel! Who is he? Why is he here?'

I needed to shut this down. This girl was beginning to get hysterical and I could feel my chances with Annabel were slipping away.

'I'm a nice man. Don't be scared.'

'TELL HIM TO GO AWAY, ANNABEL!'

Claire was beginning to hyperventilate, which alerted two other members of staff who had been involved in the workshop but were now relaxing in the corner doing crosswords and enjoying a well-earned cup of tea.

'I DON'T LIKE HIS EYES! TELL HIM TO GO AWAY!'

My eyes? They were my best feature! This was getting out of hand. All I remember was a lot of shouting. Annabel said to me quietly, 'Maybe you should just wait in the van,' while the carers were calming Claire down by stroking her back and saying, 'It's OK, Claire, the man is leaving now.'

The train journey back to London was miserable.

Once again I was thwarted and drove around the streets of London in despair. My clients were killing me too. I was being given more and more passengers who didn't speak English but who shouted at me nevertheless. Some asked to be dropped off at casinos at 9.30 p.m., telling me they had no more use for me. I would make my way home and collapse wearily into bed, only to receive a call from the casino at 2.30 a.m. saying my client needed a lift. He'd lost all his money and didn't have enough cash for a cab. Clearly there would be no tip. Once or twice I got a depressed grunt which I interpreted as some kind of thanks or acknowledgement.

I was beginning to lose hope of making any progress with Annabel. I was feeling imprisoned and stultified. My life wasn't just going nowhere, it seemed to have stopped. At one point I told myself that perhaps this was my lot and I had to accept it.

It was at this lowest ebb when, out of the blue, an opportunity arose to drive a lady who was referred to as a 'Patron of the Arts'. She was wheelchair-bound and had requested a strong driver who could carry her and transfer her from the car to her chair. It was a coveted job because it was well paid, and by all accounts she was a very nice lady. My boss Jam went with his gut instinct in proposing I took this job. Perhaps he felt I'd served my apprenticeship with the royals and I deserved to enjoy more refined company. I went along to the interview in a maisonette opposite Kensington Gardens.

A maid ushered me in, and motioned me to an ornate ground-floor office. The wheelchair spun around and I saw that Pamela was still a relatively young woman, late thirties or early forties, with thick, flowing blonde hair and a business vibe that gave her an air of authority. She was quite beautiful, and I was suddenly overcome with emotional curiosity as to how she could have ended up in a wheelchair: was it a horse-riding accident? A car crash where she had lost a husband? She seemed to me to be someone who had once led a very active life, and been suddenly hit by this terrible misfortune.

'Polio,' she said, swiftly noting my distress. 'I had it as a child.' Her matter-of-fact approach relieved me. Her study was almost completely surrounded by old, thick, leather-bound books on wooden shelves. I loved the smell of the books and felt privileged to be soaking up the atmosphere. We chatted about life, art, music and culture. We even talked about Kensington, where we were both raised, the pros and cons (more pros). We laughed as she said that in all her years living so close to Kensington Palace, she'd only ever seen Prince Charles in the flesh once and even then it was from the back when sat in a car. She'd only guessed it was him from his ears. I laughed and told her I'd seen HRH in a convertible surrounded by security and stuck in traffic outside Barkers on the high street. A group of blokes had started a chant of 'There's only one Charlie Windsor! One Charlie Windsor . . . there's only one Charlie Windsor' and he'd waved enthusiastically at enthralled motorists.

She had deeply intelligent eyes and a keen interest in everything I said. Empowered by her engagement with me, I began crowbarring every literary reference I could think of into the conversation. It worked; she seemed impressed.

'Gosh, you know your literature, don't you?' and 'You came from Iran? Oh, but your English is exquisite!' I didn't have the heart to tell her I was born in London.

Talking to her helped me access parts of my ancestry that I rarely contemplated. I told her that my background in literature was not just from my 2:1 humanities degree (which I was wont to mention to all and sundry at the time) but also from my father's family, five generations back. They had been roaming poets, part of a band of troubadours who pitched up in towns across Iran to perform poetry 'gigs' at the turn of the nineteenth century. She seemed genuinely fascinated and asked me to tell her more. I said they were unofficial poet laureates, if you will (I always said 'if you will' when I tried to sound intelligent), but when they became Bahá'ís they were violently persecuted, made to walk barefoot in the snow, paraded around a town wearing dunces' hats on their heads, connected to each other's necks with chains and pelted with stones by unruly mobs. When I told her that the poets disarmed their captors by laughing at each other, no doubt overwhelmed by the absurdity of their situation, we had a long discussion on the power of humour and its place in society. I was on a roll.

She was clearly moved by these stories. A fantasy gripped me; I would become her confidant and would assist her in the work of writing about whatever it was that she was writing about. I wasn't quite clear what this was, but it must be stimulating and important. I felt I could talk to her for ages. I even felt comfortable with her startling assertion that she knew I came from a noble background because of my gait, and the way I carried myself when I walked into the room. By this time I was so puffed up with my own importance that I had come to the conclusion, under her generous gaze, that I was actually a pretty fascinating person. Just as I was expanding on her point about my noble gait by suggesting that my good balance came from playing football she suddenly interrupted me by wheeling herself past me and out of the door.

'Come on then, let's get on with it.'

This was a job interview after all . . .

'Where's your car?' she said, as she wheeled herself outside. Approaching the Mercedes 230 CE class I was driving, she asked me to pick her up and put her in the back seat. She warned me that as a paralysed person she was much heavier than she looked. And she was right. I wasn't able to even lift her out of her chair. After her repeating, 'It's all right, put me down. Put me down!' and me saying, 'No, I can do this, please, I can do this!' I gave in. The dream of working for a worthwhile employer had vanished. I was devastated. This experience was pivotal nevertheless because, despite my intense mortification, the incident had somehow restored my hope and given me an inkling of the kind of person with whom I wanted to spend my time, as well as the kind of life I wanted to have and the kind of person I wanted to be.

Professor Bushrui had opened my eyes to the path ahead of me. Annabel had hit me with Cupid's arrow. And now Pamela had reinforced the sense that there was more to life than driving spoilt miniature royals around the West End.

I wanted to be an artist. I wanted to be an actor. I decided that there was only one thing for it – I had to get into drama school.

CHAPTER TWENTY-FOUR

Drama School Auditions – A Catastrophe

'Speak the speech I pray you as I pronounced it to you, trippingly on the tongue.'

William Shakespeare

Had I known then what I know now about the acting business I would *never* have become an actor, let alone thought about drama school, but back then all I knew was that I felt most alive when I was on stage. I loved the freeing sense of 'nothing else matters' that occurs when you are in the elusive 'moment'. Unfortunately, along the way, I had also acquired a remarkably grandiose vision of myself as one of those actors who would write books like *My Life In Art* by Constantin Stanislavski. I remember reading about Stanislavski's famous conversation with a like-minded gentleman called Danchenko. Apparently they spent eighteen hours thrashing out their ideas and concerns regarding the lamentable state of late-nineteenth-century Russian theatre. Whilst acknowledging that I may not be up for such lengthy chats, I nevertheless felt inspired by their conviction that theatre *deserved* such macho levels of commitment. I began drinking espresso so that I could stay up late pondering my own ideas about art in between driving jobs. Sadly I had to abandon that plan because I didn't like the bitter taste, and realised I was developing a sugar addiction.

Perhaps I could become a theatre radical like Augusto Boal from Argentina who created 'Theatre of the Oppressed' or 'forum theatre'. I loved Boal's vision of 'simultaneous dramaturgy' where scenes of oppression from individual's lives could be re-enacted in front of an audience who would suggest ideas for more positive or healing conclusions to painful social and personal narratives. The dialogue that it inspired would contribute to healing. I imagined myself creating dramatic scenes in my workplace in which fellow drivers and Filipino nannies would give impassioned speeches to their royal employers and we would clear up years of wounded feelings and misunderstandings. Sadly it was not to be . . .

At university I was most drawn to Polish theatrical pioneers like Jerzy Grotowski who created the concepts of the 'theatre laboratory' and 'Poor Theatre'. Truthfully I did not really understand Grotowski's philosophy, but was intrigued by the photos in his textbooks that featured sinewy, bald actors in loincloths who appeared to be screaming, holding on to cushions and crying and generally writhing around.

The point was, after three fruitful years at Ulster University I'd developed a body of knowledge regarding the various strands of theatrical influences available to me, and in my head I imagined I could bring all these eclectic approaches together and effect monumental social change as well as personal and career fulfilment. I could become an impresario, an actor-manager, who, together with a band of faithful and dedicated actors, would push every artistic and social boundary and invent a new style of theatre altogether. Admittedly, this was not as easy as it sounded. It was complicated by the reality that acting is also a desperately insecure profession. I had frequently encountered artsy types with overblown egos and actually found the theatre

I usually play left-back but my belly clearly fancies itself playing further forward.

Above: Mother's funeral.

Left: Me aged 16 with Mum in Montreal.

How I like to remember Mum. Always having fun.

Right: Dad is in his nineties and still going strong.

Below: My Grandfather. The perturbed expression he often had in my presence. I always thought he looked a bit like Spain manager Vincente Del Bosque.

Above: Annabel at work. The intensity of Theatre in Education.

Right: Me in my *Miami Vice* look. What was stopping her?

Below: Secretly filming her behind a chair.

Annabel still not sure.

Portrait of a smug fat husband.

Bongo night with my Moroccan friends.
Brendan Fraser and Arnold Vosloo bored out their brains.

Training in the desert, thinking that's what Hollywood stars did.

Day 1 filming on *The Mummy* with Rachel Weisz.

Right: Free as a bird on *Splash!*

Below: Preparing for Arab Action Hero.

My kids. Already signs they've inherited my insanity.

world alien and intimidating. The stark truth was, I greatly doubted whether I could belong, let alone make any kind of meaningful contribution.

Naturally, as was my pattern, this drove me to forge ahead. Regardless, in spite of, because of and anyway . . .

In those days drama schools were the main portal into the world of professional acting. But the world of the stage seemed to have numerous mental obstacles for me to overcome. For example, I was clearly the wrong shape, size and colour and emitted the wrong vibe. Scrutinising *Spotlight* (an actors' directory, featuring headshots and details of everyone registered as an actor in the UK), it seemed to me that there were specific young actor 'types' in the late eighties – the most prominent being the moody model English public schoolboy with floppy hair and wistful good looks. These boys were labelled 'sensitive' and 'interesting' by adoring drama school luvvies. Then there were rather more sallow young guys with pockmarked faces and fiery eyes. They were considered edgy and dangerous, especially as they tended to be proficient in acrobatics, circus skills and ancient musical instruments.

So, not belonging to any perceivable category (apart from panto villain) I girded my loins and put myself through a gruelling audition process, believing the hype that a post-graduate course at drama school was the necessary platform to launch myself, torpedo-like, into show business. Looking back, my A levels debacle was a doddle compared to this hard-nosed, head-banging-against-a-brick-wall, deluded dull ache that I put myself through sixteen times. Repetitive strain injuries I've sustained over the years have been less painful.

My first audition was September 1988. After my work with Jam finished I had gone on to do a sandwich delivery job, which was a little soul-destroying, perhaps because I was fired shortly after being discovered comfort eating the sandwiches in my car. So, 'in between' jobs, I rocked up at Mountview Theatre School in Wood Green, North London. Forty of us had gathered. We were all given number tags for identification purposes and I was given number six. This felt fortuitous, as it was the same number worn by Patrick McGoohan in the popular 1960s TV series *The Prisoner*. Hoping to break the ice in the rather tense waiting room, I mimicked McGoohan's intense voice, shouting rather too energetically for the time of day: 'I am not a number, I'm a free man!' This seemed only to increase the tension in the group, as they were now worried they had a basket case in their midst. It also didn't help that I was chewing bubble gum and blew a huge bubble, which I then proceeded to try and run away from before it promptly burst all over my face. Their opinion of me sank ever further. Maybe the chasing bubble reference went over their heads? It had terrified me when I watched *The Prisoner* on late-night ITV.

The audition process required us to sing a song and perform a 'modern' piece. However, this was not just for the benefit of a faceless examining panel – we had to perform our pieces in front of the other auditionees. I was not comfortable with this at all. What if I was terrible? Everyone would see! Witnessing the other candidates would presumably put everyone's talent into context – clearly there was a humiliating logic in this, or rather, a method to their madness.

Singing was the first ordeal, and first up was a candidate from Glasgow in his late thirties who really could sing. He was obviously some sort of folk singer who was trying his luck at acting. He nailed the loudest, most powerful rendition of Gershwin's 'Summertime' I'd ever heard. This resulted in thunderous, albeit jealous, applause. Watching him had reminded me of another category of actor – 'rough diamond' – and this gave me hope. As the next number was called a young girl got up hastily and rushed to the door, crying. A painfully audible brief chat with an administrator-type woman ensued. The girl, receiving and scrunching up a plentiful supply of tissues, apologised and said she would be sticking to her office job. After a split second's pause I applauded and mouthed 'that was brilliant' to the candidate next to me. Her tears had seemed so real. It wasn't until she actually left without singing that I realised she was serious. The tenseness of this scene, whilst touching some of us with compassion for the poor girl, also bonded the group; we had all shared the cynical realisation that there was one less person to compete with.

My turn was up. I had the sheet music and gave it to the elderly lady at the piano. She started the intro, but to my horror, it went on for quite a while before I realised I'd missed my moment to come in three times. I'd chosen 'Careless Whisper' by George Michael and had imagined combining some of George Michael's opening 'woh-woah-oo woahs' with some opening 'la-las' to replace the classic saxophone opening to the song. To be fair, I sang badly and immoderately. The pianist found it hard to keep up with me, as due to nerves, I was racing ahead and ignoring the piano accompaniment. By the time we got to the chorus I was getting carried away as I struggled to convey the confusion in the song with jerky head movements, doubled-over stomach convulsions (I was a forerunner of JLS or One Direction's performance style) and closed eyes. At this point, the pianist understandably gave up and lit a cigarette. Unfortunately I had also compensated for my lack of singing prowess by introducing a tortured anti-rhythmic dance routine during the lines about guilty feet not having any rhythm. Receiving a lukewarm and somewhat stunned round of applause I collapsed back into my seat feeling nauseous and giddy.

Then we moved on to the 'modern' pieces. The only prop we were allowed to use was a chair. One of the meeker-looking boys decided to throw it against a wall in an unexpected piece about football hooliganism. The rest of us were immediately warned not to be reckless with the furniture, as this was the only chair at our disposal. One tattooed man defiantly stood on the chair for the entirety of his bizarre pirate speech. I remember he even placed a hand over one eye to conjure up the image of an eye patch, and lifted one leg up to indicate a peg leg. Sadly the Geordie accent he adopted didn't seem to fit, and it was a surprise when he announced, quite aggressively, to the impassive panel that this was a Robert Louis Stevenson piece. The suspicion that he was lying felt awkward, and I hung my head in shame for him. One girl performed an interesting piece called *Abuse* that she had written herself. She circled the chair as if it were a boyfriend who had wounded her and even hit and kicked it a few times until a cold, tactless voice from the panel interrupted her to reiterate the earlier advice that we should be careful with the chair. Undeterred, she skilfully carried on and threw herself on the ground, as if pinned down by the chair, and pretended to be smacked by it repeatedly before symbolically walking away with dignity. Powerful stuff, I thought. Everyone clapped enthusiastically as she sat back down, flushed and triumphant.

Next up was a very serious-looking girl with a posh, breathy voice, who had chosen a speech from Chekhov's *The Seagull*. For the first time, the panel seemed to be humming with approval. I watched them nod to each other and scribble furiously on their notepads. She was obviously the right kind of student and fitted the bill.

Still traumatised by my singing audition I was determined to stay in the game. I announced confidently that I was doing a piece by Steven Berkoff from the play *Decadence*. There was an immediate murmur of concern as the piece was 'very modern' and not considered suitable for auditions. In fact it was a huge risk, as drama schools were generally rather conservative in those days and Berkoff was seen as anti-establishment. 'Truth by exaggeration' was a bold, over-the-top style and my audition piece involved ordering and eating a meal at a high-class restaurant. This was an excellent opportunity to showcase my well-honed mimes as I tasted and digested an array of fine foods before throwing it all up again, replete with violent actions and textured sound effects. The other candidates looked on in amazement, astonished by the bad language and the ferocity of the performance. I sat down to hearty yet confused applause as if the others were querying whether this kind of thing was even permissible. A member of the panel quipped wryly: 'Well, that's ruined my appetite for lunch,' and everyone laughed sycophantically. I knew then I was in with a chance.

The moment of truth came. We were thanked for all our 'hard work' and told that if our number was not called out to participate in the next round, then we should not be deterred, rather we should feel free to come back and try again. (I wondered later whether the £50 audition fee had anything to do with their warm and welcoming invitation to reapply.) Only four numbers were called out – 'number six' being the last. My heart leapt. This was a huge deal.

The four of us were ushered into a room as the others packed up and left. Some were in a huff that their talent had not been acknowledged, others were more angry and declared that Mountview would 'definitely come to regret it'. A few bold ones even stayed behind to remonstrate and demand another chance. It was a very dramatic scene, with the tragic backdrop that some chances had gone forever. Shame hung thickly in the room where the unlucky candidates were hastily reconsidering the future and taking stock of their options.

We only had moments to prepare for our second audition, a Shakespeare monologue of our choice. It was to be in front of an extended panel of people. 'How many?' said the rough diamond Glaswegian, amazed he'd got through and now terribly nervous at the prospect of performing the next piece. He seemed totally out of his comfort zone. 'Who are they? How many? I've no' done this before.' He was quickly taken to a corner where someone in a beret and John Lennon glasses appeared to be helping him with some breathing exercises. This calmed him down considerably but I could still hear him periodically muttering, 'Ahm gonna shite myself.'

These nervous predictions were not helping my mounting nerves so I moved away to focus on my own preparations. I'd only performed Shakespeare to myself in the mirror a few times. I'd chosen a light piece from *Hamlet* where Hamlet gives his Players (actors) advice on how he would like the actors to act: 'Speak the speech, I pray you, as I pronounced it to you, trippingly on the tongue.' Frankly, I thought it was a clever choice.

No introductions. The panel now consisted of eight people sitting behind a long table sipping glasses of water and whispering to each other. An administrative minion announced my presence as 'number six'. This surprised me, as by now surely they'd want to get to know me a bit? Maybe my name was just too complicated. I was a bag of jitters and considered doing my *Prisoner* gags again if only to make the experience more enjoyable for myself, but felt I should stick with my hard-won gravitas and status as a candidate who had made it through the first round. After all, the piece I was about to perform was relatively serious. I did get a hello and a perfunctory 'What piece are you doing?' to which I replied, 'Hamlet, to the Players.' The minion said, 'In your own time,' then a heavy silence fell and they all looked at me expectantly. This was all a bit clinical, I thought. But no matter, if that's how they're going to be, I'll roll with it.

I felt the panel calm down as I opened, strong and confident. By the second sentence they relaxed back in their chairs and looked like they were relieved at last: here was someone who could act. They could sit back and enjoy a performance. They began to smile. This was going well. At one point the whole panel were beaming like an audience at Stratford-upon-Avon. Potential headlines ran screaming through my imagination: 'IRANIAN HAMLET TOUR DE FORCE!', 'BREAKTHROUGH HAMLET!' and 'RSC UNEARTH NEW LAURENCE AL-OLIVIER ETTIHAD EBRAHIM MAMDOOHAH!'

Distracted by this vision of my meteoric theatrical future, my Shakespearean self came crashing to a halt, mid-flow. I'd forgotten my lines. The already silent room plummeted to new levels of deadened hush. I found myself just staring, helpless and aghast, at the panel. Thinking this was an intentional dramatic pause no one shifted. Breaking the spell, I apologised: 'I'm sorry, can I start again?' A bald man with moustache and glasses said, 'Just pick it up where you left off.' I frowned back, incredulous.

'Well, that's why I asked to start again, I have no idea where I was.' My mouth went dry due to tension and the potential for conflict.

The smiles began to evaporate. I just couldn't find my bearings. Beads of sweat formed above my lip. I repeated my point – 'It's easier if I just start again' – but the bald, bespectacled gentleman insisted that I should pick up where I left off. Nothing came. The silence was interminable and horrific. A woman on the panel looked at her watch. I racked my brains and settled on a line. Relieved, I picked up from there, but unluckily this remembered line was from the end of the speech. After a sentence or two, the speech came to a grinding and incoherent stop. After an awkward pause someone said 'thank you' and I left.

Still believing I had a shot, I waited two weeks for news. Ever hopeful, I'd fancied the power of the Berkoff piece would have sealed the deal. Sadly not the case.

Undeterred I tried again, and spurred on by my belief I had just been unlucky at Mountview, I applied to all the other 'accredited' drama schools in the land: the Bristol Old Vic, Central School of Speech and Drama, Webber Douglas, Drama Centre, Welsh College of Speech and Drama, Drama Studio, LAMDA and the number-one school of them all, the Royal Academy of Dramatic Art (RADA).

I started to recognise familiar faces at auditions: students from Oxford, Cambridge, Durham and Kent, ex-factory workers and people who'd had enough of working in the City (one was Nigel Lindsay, who later went on to star in Chris Morris' film satire *Four Lions*).

At the Bristol Old Vic I had a session with the legendary old Austrian acting coach Rudi Shelly whose reputation preceded him as the best drama teacher in the country. Rudy gave everybody advice, which, we all agreed later, was life-changing. Sometimes he could be very harsh. 'You are beautiful,' he said to one girl (who was indeed beautiful but not pleasant), pointing his finger at her slowly and deliberately, 'but don't think that's going to be enough for the camera to notice. You have to be beautiful inside.' We were shocked. It's what we were thinking but would never dare say. To me he simply asked, 'Are you a big eater?' I admitted I was, to which he replied, 'Don't eat so much. You'll feel so much better.' Later, by the vending machine, as I ploughed angrily through three packets of crisps, I decided that his comments were intrusive and irrelevant.

Rejection after rejection came in almost weekly. Always I got through to the next round and always, despite having learned my lines and feeling the audition had gone very well, I failed to get a place anywhere. It was the A levels all over again – a door was being firmly slammed shut in my face. What was I doing wrong?

Eventually I reached my limit. I'd spent so much money on

train fares to places like Bristol and Cardiff, staying in B&Bs and frittering away my hard-earned cash, I decided I would send a letter to the last place that had rejected me and ask for feedback. This happened to be my fifteenth audition, at the Welsh College of Speech and Drama. It had gone well, particularly the Shakespeare, but unsurprisingly by now, the inevitable rejection came. So I fired off my letter and dared to ask why. Eventually, after two weeks, a report came back:

Dear Mr Djalili

We have looked at the reports from our staff on the day of your audition, and the notes made on your pieces. Technically there were some issues with pitch and diction but nothing a few lessons wouldn't iron out. The feeling was that you are a talented actor but perhaps drama school would not be beneficial for you. You seem very individualistic and are already set in your ways. In many ways you are a finished product. In cases like yours we would advise you to go out and seek work now. I hope you find these comments useful.

We wish you every success in your future endeavours.

Warm regards

It wasn't exactly a balm to my wounds because all I could see from the letter was that I was not a team player. All my life I'd seen myself as a team player. I was a footballer for God's sake, so this was insulting and confusing. I may be individualistic but surely you need a degree of drive and personality in this business? Deeper down, though, something else told me they were actually right. And even deeper down I felt grateful for their candour and their kindness in taking the time to reply to my needy letter. I was more than a little unbridled and I probably would have been a nightmare as a member of any theatrical cast. I had recently attended some self-help self-esteem enhancement courses run by a friend, and the general feedback was that I seemed like someone who felt easier outside of the group. Or to put it their way, I was 'unable to integrate into a team dynamic'.

Whilst realising some important home truths, I still felt sad, because my desire for connection was high, and I yearned to belong.

CHAPTER TWENTY-FIVE

Struggling Actor On The Fringe

'In the course of my life I have often had to eat my words, and I must confess that I have always found it a wholesome diet.'

Winston Churchill

After failing to get into drama school, my heart was heavy. But thanks to sound advice from the Welsh College of Speech and Drama, my resolve to forge ahead regardless had never been more determined.

I decided that doing plays on the London Fringe would give me experience and a modicum of theatre training. 'Those who can, do; those who can't, teach' was a (terribly offensive and unfair) saying going around at the time and it alarmed me enough to want to be part of the 'do' camp. I bought *The Stage* newspaper religiously every Thursday and scoured all the open auditions at the back. I began to lament the fact that I was not a dancer, because there seemed to be so much work for them on cruises. I toyed with ideas to make my Berkoff restaurant monologue accessible to a wider audience. Perhaps it could work as a cabaret piece? I imagined myself doing it as a song and dance number, in homage to the Hollywood movies of the

1940s starring Gene Kelly. I pictured myself dressed in a white-and-blue-striped nautical outfit, singing, dancing, eating and projectile vomiting. Creative as it was, I never took this idea further. Maybe I should have.

At the same time, having seen an advert in *The Stage*, I stumbled across a drama school in Wandsworth. Admittedly it was a non-accredited establishment, and therefore something of a backward step. Nevertheless I applied, probably as a last-ditch attempt to gain some kind of institutional guidance. I auditioned in front of the principal and one other teacher, and inflicted upon them the crazy Berkoffian vomiting that had become my signature audition piece. They offered me a place there and then. I asked if they needed to see a Shakespeare but they insisted I had given them more than enough. I wasn't sure what this meant, but I warmed to their smiley enthusiasm. Unfortunately the ecstatic rush of audition success fizzled pretty quickly. For all I knew they were theatrical pioneers, but it was to be my sixteenth and final drama school audition. I realised my heart had been set on the 'best' drama schools. I became quite depressed by my own snobbery for a while, but decided that there must have been a reason why I had been rejected by luvviedom. Maybe I was just too much of a radical? Maybe I need to be with the *anti*-establishment crowd. This epiphany felt very significant as it coincided with a night where they happened to be showing James Dean in *Rebel Without a Cause* on TV. In a pivotal 'A-ha!' moment I panted heavily at the television, punched the air, deciding I really was going to make it on my own.

I now had a day job delivering office equipment, and it was going well. I worked at a place called ABC Business Machines on Chiltern Street in Marylebone, run by two brothers from Twickenham called Simon and Anthony Leftwich. They were theatregoers and were very supportive of my wish to be an actor. I had a job from 9.30 a.m. to 12.30 p.m. delivering supplies to their regular customers, all dotted around central London. At £95 a week it felt reasonable, as long as I didn't get a parking ticket or, worse, towed away. Delivering a particularly heavy typewriter one hot summer's day I was forced to double-park on Berkeley Square. Lugging this awkward lump of a machine was not only dangerous because of its weight (it was once known to go straight through a floor when dropped by one of my predecessors) but it could also do severe muscle damage to the carrier. Six tight and awkward floors is a long way to carry such a heavy piece of equipment.

After making it to the top, I needed to get my papers signed, but at the crucial moment the client disappeared into the toilet without explanation, leaving me waiting. I called out, 'Are you all right?' as I was anxious about the car. He reassured me that he'd just be a minute. What I didn't know was that the poor man was experiencing the trauma of violent food poisoning. As the seconds ticked by I sprinted back down six flights of stairs to check on the car. It was fine and no wardens were around. I rushed back up, but the poor bloke was still in the toilet. I asked if he needed help. He apologised profusely from behind the door, but sounded under great duress. I doubted his assurance that he would be with me in a mere moment. A minute became three so I rushed back down the stairs. By this time a warden was hovering. Sweating and desperate, I explained the situation to the warden, but he didn't seem sympathetic. I rushed back up again and waited two more minutes. From behind the door the client informed me that it was no good, his personal situation was now irresolvable. He wasn't coming out any time soon, but could I go to the kitchen, and get his medication from the fridge?

I passed him the bottle from behind the door, wondering where on earth his colleagues were, and why couldn't they take care of him, before faking this man's signature (why didn't I think of this earlier?) and racing back downstairs. I was confronted by the image of my car on the back of a tow truck. I chased after it shouting, 'NO! NO! NOOOO!' But to no avail. It cost exactly £95 to retrieve my car. I had to work the rest of the week knowing I was operating at a loss, but consoled myself that this was still not on the same scale as the great Gentle Enterprises crash.

But despite these kind of disasters I had settled into a good routine and was on the whole making decent money. It was shortly after this car towing fiasco that I saw an advert for 'talented actors needed for South American Festival'. This attracted just about every London-based South American actor and quite a few Turkish and Pakistani ones. *Una Dia De Vida* (One Day in Life) was a co-production by a group of North London socialists in conjunction with the Chile Committee for Human Rights. The show was to be a 'festival' of Chilean and South American culture; music, song and dance providing the backdrop to a hard-hitting play about the dictator Augusto Pinochet, during whose regime in the eighties thousands of people had 'disappeared'. I auditioned for the role of 'utility actor', where one actor was given six small parts. Using the film *Scarface* with Al Pacino as my reference and template, I delivered variations on Tony Montana and other generic retrograde Cuban drug dealers. They all said 'que pasa, man?' and 'quaaludes'. The swaggering about worked. I got the part(s).

Thrilled that I was now in a play, I launched into twice-weekly rehearsals with gusto and vigour. The show was to run for four nights, Tuesday to Friday at the Red Rose Club on the Seven Sisters Road. It would have been on Saturday too, but they had complained about a rather stubborn man who was 'being very difficult'. He ran a comedy club at the venue on Saturdays and refused to budge (turns out it was my old comedian friend Ivor Dembina with whom I was to do *The Arab and the Jew* at the 1996 Edinburgh Festival – years later when I brought this up with him, he said in his own inimitable way that he had a vague memory of 'theatre ponces who wanted me to cancel my weekly comedy night for some poxy show. I told them to bugger off').

The cast was as diverse as the project: Spanish, Chilean, Italian, British, Greek and Jewish. The Drama Centre theatre school graduates known for keen adherence to 'the Method' tussled with the more down-to-earth actors who had graduated from the traditional drama schools. There were a few instances where the 'traditionals' kept asking the 'Methods' in a blunt and confrontational manner: 'Why don't you just act?' Another epiphany dawned – the fact that I hadn't gone to drama school meant that I could keep out of the pompous spats about what acting *was* and what it was *not*. It all seemed so tiring and unnecessarily tense.

Interestingly, on the first day, our director took us through some exploratory animal exercises. In other words, to get a better intuitive sense of our characters, we were all assigned an animal to hold in our thoughts. It was generally believed that this would infuse our work with greater depth and understanding. In fact it would even help us absorb our lines rather than laboriously memorise them. I didn't really get it, but certainly enjoyed prowling around like a wolf and howling periodically. Truth to tell I would have preferred to sit quietly with some KitKats and learn my lines on my own, but I didn't dare communicate this, especially as one of the actors, Clive Ramsona, took this exercise very seriously. I remember before our rather tense dress rehearsal Clive went missing. He was later found by one of the 'traditionals' hanging upside-down from a precarious rusty bar on the ceiling of an anteroom two floors above us 'getting into character'. He had chosen a monkey for his animal and much to everyone's chagrin was determined to see the exercise through to its fullest potential.

Fortunately the show, performed in a stiflingly hot venue in mid-July, went down a storm on the first night. My mother and sister had shown up (against my will) and sat in the front row. It seemed fine at first; they laughed in all the right places, clapped along with the songs in time, and with verve. And in the more emotional moments they sobbed uncontrollably. The audience seemed more concerned about their welfare than what was going on during the play. There must have been something about the innocent dancing, the heartfelt songs sung passionately by relatives of the deceased and the general festive mood that made my mother and sister feel they were experiencing something close to their own culture. I was unspeakably embarrassed but couldn't deny their contribution to the night added an extra dimension. Backstage after the show everyone was talking about them: 'Did you see those two women from Chile crying at everything?'

'I know, it was amazing!'

'Apparently they've had family disappear so it was all too much for them!'

Then the director earnestly weighed in: 'Guys, you see the power of what we have on our hands here? Never underestimate what can be achieved over these next few nights. People need to see this play.'

When I emerged post show, I saw my mother and sister were surrounded in the bar. They were being treated with great deference and had geeky-looking students hanging on their every word. My mother was telling them about the plight of the Bahá'ís in Iran and making comparisons with the situation in Chile. I realised that one or two of the crowd were journalists who appeared to be taking rapid notes. People were even giving my mother business cards and asking for interviews next week. There was an excited hubbub but admittedly a great deal of confusion. I watched them from afar and made my exit. Somehow I found it hard that they had made the night all about them. But now as I write, I can't help admire their wish to connect and share in a way that was authentic, albeit outlandish and disruptive.

I hadn't banked on them being such a presence in my artistic life. They followed my every theatrical move. My brother was away living his dream in America and my dad, at that time, seemed rather bewildered by my life choices. A few months after the production of *Una Dia De Vida* I was selected by the producer Joseph Schneider to perform at another Chile Committee for Human Rights rally at St James's Church on Piccadilly. It was going to be a star-studded evening of dramatic scenes, music and poetry readings. The big names in attendance were to include Julie Christie, Peggy Mount and Ben Kingsley (this was before his knighthood). I was to bring the programme to a climax with a rousing speech from *Danton's Death* by Georg Büchner.

I'd seen Gérard Depardieu in a French cinematic version of the story called *Danton* and decided to mimic his subtle intensity for this role. I practised in the mirror at home, imagining I was on trial myself. (This mirror work was becoming an integral part of my own 'Method'.) I prepared the speech, carefully plotting an emotional journey that reached a crescendo in the last words before Danton is guillotined. I was actually modelling this on Al Pacino as the lawyer in . . . *And Justice for All*. In my head I had plans to bring the house down, similar to the moment when he is dragged away and out of the courtroom. I had visions of myself being led away in handcuffs from St James's Church, but realised I was taking things too far and blurring boundaries of reality, even in my imagination.

When the night came, I got to the venue quite late. The place was filling up, and the backstage area was crammed with nervous actors preparing their speeches. It was a frosty December night, close to Christmas, and 450 people were squeezed into this church. The whole place seemed to be crackling with goodwill, energy and expectation. The Christmas candles flickered and the festive vibe added a sparkling ethereal quality to the night: truly magical. People looked on as Julie Christie, a sixties cinema icon, took her place in the front row next to Ben Kingsley and Peggy Mount. From behind a pillar I could see Annabel. I'd mentioned to her that I had seen her in her place of work so maybe she should come one night to watch me, too. To my horror she did! She had taken her seat with a friend in the top-left corner of the balcony, reasonably far away. From this distance she seemed to be twinkling even brighter than the Christmas lights.

All the stars read beautifully. The poetry was well delivered, the actors were restrained and respectful and the audience receptive. Everything was appropriate. But the evening lacked dramatic punch; and this is exactly what Joseph had intended. The night was waiting for my Danton piece: a speech about human rights with modern-day reverberations that highlighted twentieth-century human rights abuses. I solemnly took my place, standing barefoot in the middle of the stage wearing my puffy white shirt and knee-length 'prisonnier français' trousers (no wonder Ivor Dembina thought we were all theatrical ponces). For the first time I didn't clock where my mother and sister were, and felt free from their potential interjections. I began the speech powerfully, confidently even. All those auditions had given me an ease in unfamiliar places and now here, in front of a large crowd, I felt totally at home. I wondered if Ben Kingsley would notice me, and I ramped up the energy. I even managed to induce a couple of supportive laughs. I hadn't expected this, but Joseph had predicted that due to this particular crowd being so *au fait* with the subject, there might well be moments where they'd pick up on a line and react to it spontaneously. In this eventuality I was told to 'just roll with it'. I savoured this moment of oneness with the crowd and paused. I found myself relishing the prospect that afterwards Annabel would tell me she'd enjoyed that bit in particular.

'Which bit?'

'The bit where everyone laughed. It was funny.'

'Really? I mean, it wasn't really meant to be.'

'Well, you're probably just so naturally funny.'

'Really? Well, I just feel happy to be involved in such an important project. That's all that matters really, I'm not interested in praise.'

'That's amazing . . .'

I started imagining us going for a light lunch on the Strand the next day to analyse the minutiae of my performance. Then maybe we would walk down Shaftsbury Avenue and she'd talk about how impressed she was by my confidence, and how struck she'd been by the sheer attack I had given the text and the guts it must have taken to hold such long dramatic pauses. I'd react in a throwaway modest manner, creating the impression that I didn't wish to dwell too long on egotistic conversations about my talent.

I realised I'd been looking up at Annabel in the balcony for quite a long time. She really was shining with an almost shimmering golden aura. Her ethereal twinkliness mesmerised me and I began to shake. Suddenly I realised, to my horror, that it had been about ten seconds since I had said anything, and I was totally lost. The audience were gripped by my pause and you could hear a pin drop. With a sense of encroaching horror I realised it was the Mountview Shakespeare audition all over again – I had totally dried. And this time I couldn't even ask to start again. I began to panic. I moved around with a deliberate casual swagger as if I were ruminating on something profound. By now even Ben Kingsley was probably thinking: 'A pause of over twenty seconds; this young upstart has balls!' Thirty seconds passed. I had nothing. I walked to the side, remembering I had a copy of the script in my bag. Maybe the audience could extend their goodwill to me if I made it seem like part of the scene? But the bag wasn't there. I walked back centre stage as if recalling an important afterthought. I shut my eyes while the audience held its breath. My mind finally found a line, I clutched at it in desperation, and spewed it out – if only to say something, anything – and, like that grotesque Mountview audition, it happened to be the last paragraph of the speech. I shouted it furiously because that's how we had rehearsed it. And it was all over in a flash. Essentially I had been painfully quiet for about a minute, ambled around point-lessly, shouted briefly and sloped off looking ashamed. The crowd didn't even react and waited a full ten seconds before they realised I had finished. The applause was compassionate due to the audience being made up of caring human-rights types.

Afterwards everyone gathered around. I was utterly trauma-tised and embarrassed. Joseph my director had tears in his eyes and couldn't speak to me. To cap it all, my mother turned up out of nowhere and grabbed Ben Kingsley's arm.

'This my son. He is good?'

'Mum, please, don't.'

Ben looked at me and said, 'He's good,' with an unspoken '. . . but not that good'.

I looked up at the balcony that was now enshrouded in dark-ness. The twinkling had vanished. Annabel had gone and the Christmas lights on Piccadilly seemed vulgar and crass.

CHAPTER TWENTY-SIX

False Starts And Fantasies

'The basis of optimisim is sheer terror.'

Oscar Wilde

All was not lost. Word soon got out that an Iranian actor had recently dried on stage in front of the press and several Hollywood A-listers. The phenomenon that an Iranian actor simply existed perhaps was enough to eclipse the reality of this epic failure on my part. A casting director looking for Iranian actors tracked me down and, as I had no agent, rang the house. My mother, multi-tasking with the phone lodged between chin and shoulder while shelling broad beans, took the call. I heard her speaking in a rather irritated and distracted fashion: 'What . . ? When . . ? Where . . ?' then, 'I don't know if he free,' before passing the phone to me dismissively: *'Migeh rajebeh filmeh, nemeedoonam'* (they say it's about a film, I dunno).

A softly spoken woman introduced herself as the casting director for an exciting new British–American film by Pathé Pictures called *Not Without My Daughter* and invited me to audition. The film was to be based on the popular book by Betty Mahmoody, the story of an American woman who had been living happily in the USA for eight years with her Iranian doctor husband and their daughter, Mahtab. On a visit back to the doctor's homeland, Iran, his veneer of Western liberalism disintegrates and he transforms into a religious fanatic, a misogynist and a bigot. Betty is then forced to change from docile wife to a semi-commando, attempting a near-impossible escape from the country with her daughter in heroic circumstances. The film was to star Sally Field and Alfred Molina, and had a proper Hollywood budget. I nearly dropped the phone from excitement.

After two meetings with director Brian Gilbert, an affable, highly complimentary and bearded Brit, I was given the part of Reza, the brother of the doctor. Reza didn't have much to do apart from behave in a gentle and brotherly way towards Sally Field. It was my dream role. Filming was to start next month in Israel so I began a strict gym regime – for no reason other than I thought that's what Hollywood actors did.

I was beside myself with joy. I couldn't believe this was happening. Who needed drama school when I was going to have scenes with Sally Field? I wondered how I would handle the pressure. I was always told handling pressure is what sorted out men from the boys. I began to thank those drama schools that had rejected me, as I was now in a Hollywood film, and all off my own back! Success had made me magnanimous and I bore no ill will towards anyone.

However, despite being on the verge of a massive break, I couldn't help feeling uncomfortable and began to become familiar with the terrible insecurity and unpredictability of the actor's profession. The possibility of the producers using local Israeli hire instead of me 'to save money' had been flagged up a few days after I'd been given the role, and was growing with each passing day. The wait for their verdict was almost unbearable. Furthermore it was terribly confusing – I was an Iranian who spoke fluent Farsi – so what was the problem? This realisation led me onto further disturbing reflections.

From what I gathered, no one else of Iranian heritage was going to be used in the film. They couldn't film in Iran because of the political climate, and moreover, it was clearly an anti-Iranian story. Tensions between Iran, Britain and the United States were high. But this drove me to want to be in the film even more desperately. I wanted to be some sort of role model and show the world that Iranians were decent people. I saw myself on the red carpet at the Cannes Film Festival describing the gentle, brotherly Reza as a symbolic bridge between East and West. I also imagined bantering with Barry Norman on *Film '90* and explaining earnestly that like all reasonable Iranians, I shared the world's indignation at Betty Mahmoody's plight. I rang the production office almost every day waiting for an answer, offering all kinds of incentives to hire me. In one particularly low moment I even offered my services as a dialect coach for free.

Six weeks later I got a letter thanking me for 'being on standby' for the role of Reza but expressing that sadly they couldn't use me on this occasion. Like all the drama schools they wished me the best for my future acting career.

I didn't get depressed. I don't think I even got indignant. I just realised that it is futile and degrading to hang around waiting for crumbs from other people's projects, especially when it was likely to involve projects where Middle Easterners would be denigrated.

Betty Mahmoody's story may well have resonated amongst Western women who had suffered in Middle Eastern families, and I was completely supportive of highlighting this important issue. I also firmly believed that this wasn't the whole picture. At the age of twenty-four, a new cause dawned within. Suddenly I felt that I was the only person I knew who could stand up and tell the world that not all Iranians were a bunch of Islamic fundamentalists who treated women badly. And certainly not all of us took off our tops and beat our hairy chests with chains until they bled. This latest rejection spawned a new artistic crusade. Not just Iranians, but minorities everywhere were depending on me, I had to get proactive.

I started writing scripts, I sent out photographs of myself to theatres up and down the land, I went to every audition, did numerous play readings and networked in every space I could. I saw everything available on the West End stage and on the Fringe. I went to at least three shows a week, determined to immerse myself in a full-throttle theatrical boot camp experience. I went out of my way to see the greats like Jack Lemmon in Jonathan Miller's famous production of Eugene O'Neill's *Long Day's Journey Into Night* that included an eye-catching performance from the young Kevin Spacey. *The Amen Corner* was another production that brought theatreland to its feet. It starred a black actor I particularly liked called Al Matthews who played Sergeant Apone in James Cameron's *Aliens*. However the show that really bowled me over was a production of Mark Rylance's debut in *Hamlet* at the National Theatre, which I saw in early 1990. I went along hoping to hate him having heard he was a new upstart who had been performing Hamlet in pyjamas. Within seconds after the curtain went down I was declaring to everyone, with all my newly acquired, unashamed luvviness, that I was honoured to have witnessed this performance, and been part of it (Luvvie Code number one: if you're in the audience of something significant, *you are a part of it*).

With this renewed sense of purpose regarding my career, I simply had to get back on track with Annabel. It had taken a while to get over the Claire episode, and indeed my *Danton's* disaster, so it was another few months before I plucked up the courage to ask Annabel on a date again. I felt I had to get her on my own patch. I had to make her feel secure in the big city (where I hoped we would live together one day) so that I could drive her around in my father's Mercedes.

I'd seen a fantastic foreign-language film by the French-Canadian director Denys Arcand called *Jesus of Montreal*, which was all the rage at the time. I'd watched it twice, so greatly was I affected by the performance of the lead actor Lothaire Bluteau. He was an exquisite actor, much fêted by the media. In fact, he was to Canada what Mark Rylance was to London. Bluteau later went on to star in many Hollywood film and TV projects, one of them being the American TV series *24*.

I then happened to find out (by pure chance) that Lothaire Bluteau was doing a play in English at a fringe venue in London – the King's Head on Upper Street, Islington in March 1990. I went along on the last night and was not disappointed; it was earth-shatteringly moving. I cursed my luck that I hadn't seen this with Annabel. The London Fringe is littered with nonsense but one could gain real kudos by discovering a gem. Amazingly, though, I subsequently noticed the play had made a West End transfer to the Vaudeville Theatre on the Strand. I bought tickets for 17 April and felt sure that when Annabel saw this play she would see me in a whole new light and the 'Clairegate' fiasco would be erased. She'd be impressed with my refined tastes and see me for the complex artiste I was.

Buzzing with anticipation I waited for her at Charing Cross Station. I'd parked my car inside the grounds of the station near the taxis, and had bought a bag of plums to munch on while I waited. This was not because I was hungry. It was to show that I was a healthy eater, and hence attractive and vital. I'd planned on spotting her from a distance at 6.20 p.m. and as I waved and moved forward I'd take a last bite of the plum, wipe my face, and then nonchalantly throw the stone away before greeting her. The idea was that I'd look masculine, relaxed and inwardly clean. It was foolproof.

I hadn't banked on a delay and by 7 p.m. there was still no sign of her. With no mobile phones all I could do was wait and keep eating the plums until she arrived. By 7.30 p.m. I was down to my last plum. We'd clearly missed dinner so I was grateful to be reasonably satiated on the seven plums now fermenting in my intestines.

By 8 p.m. I was justifiably worried that I'd been stood up. This was a final humiliation and I began to mutter obscenities under my breath about Claire, who I blamed wholeheartedly. By 8.10 p.m. I ruefully finished the last plum, knowing we'd missed the play. On top of that I was beginning to feel sick and gaseous and crashing downwards from a fructose high. Suddenly, Annabel appeared out of nowhere. My heart leapt. She was incredibly effusive in her apology. She was horrified that I had waited two hours (but hopefully impressed with my steadfastness – in truth I would have waited all night) and explained the train had broken down. I was grateful for her apologies but calculated she could still see Lothaire Bluteau if we hurried. There was still time to be impressed with my zeitgeist theatrical choices. I rushed her down the Strand, rapidly explaining the plot to her, reassuring her that the emotional fireworks at the end would still make sense to her – all the while trying to control the chaos going on in my digestive system.

The theatre was disappointingly only a third full. Annabel put on her glasses to watch. She looked different, very earnest and serious. I found it desperately hard not to stare at her. Every time she looked my way I managed to cover it with a number of diversions like looking at my watch. At one point I asked her if she needed directions to the toilet – she looked rather offended. My mouth was dry and I was running out of options. So I just gave in. I stared at her shamelessly. She looked rather disturbed, whispering, 'What?' It must have seemed like I wanted to tell her something important. I did, of course. But I couldn't.

The actors were clearly having an off night, or perhaps were upset by the low numbers for a Friday night (something I would empathise with when I did *What The Butler Saw* in the same theatre twenty-two years later) and it just wasn't happening. Annabel may also have been put off by my constant staring. She said 'What?' again, perhaps worried about the pained expression on my face; I had nothing to say other than the urgent and desperate request to 'please please marry me'. Plus the strain and the discomfort caused by the plums was killing me.

Time to roll out plan B.

Continuing the theme of 'clean insides' and knowing she was an ardent vegetarian, I sped her to a vegetarian Indian restaurant I knew in Stoke Newington. The food was delicious, and she seemed impressed. But not as impressed as I was when she smiled at the Indian waiter with such genuine radiance that I knew I was having dinner with someone very unusual. I felt overcome with emotion as I knew, intrinsically, that I craved this level of kindliness in my life. Someone who could handle my home life, my craziness, and all without a hint of judgement.

Swept along by my spontaneity I took her for a drive after dinner along the Embankment and Regent's Park's inner circle in my father's Mercedes. To display my sophisticated sense of humour I did some ironic 'showing off' by opening and closing the electric sunroof of the car as we drove along whilst staring at her and moving my eyebrows up and down. This seemed to affect her but not in a good way and made her strangely pensive. I'm aware now that this was bizarre behaviour but my logic was that electric sunroofs were not at all common in those days and my father's car was something of a novelty. Little did I know that Annabel was so uninterested in cars that she was not even aware of the prestige of a Mercedes. Thankfully it didn't have a negative impact on the date. We spent the rest of the night talking and walking around London, me with my hands behind my back emulating Prince Philip on royal walkabouts (I have no idea why, it just felt like the right posture to adopt). The date ended at 6.30 a.m. with breakfast in the Up All Night café on the Fulham Road.

On that unusually mild and balmy April night in 1990 I was convinced she was 'the one'.

I received a call the next morning from the almost-forgotten casting director. Sounding a bit sheepish she asked if I could possibly come 'tomorrow' to dub over the character of Reza in *Not Without My Daughter*. Apparently there had been 'issues' with the Israeli actor and it was felt necessary to dub his voice in both English *and* Farsi. This unravelled as rather a painful exercise when I saw that the character originally meant for me had been almost completely shaved down. When I asked why, the director, also a little sheepish, said they'd cut his storyline out when they realised, admittedly a little too late, that Reza had to be a natural Farsi speaker. Sadly, the Israeli actor didn't speak Farsi. A moment of mind-boggling awkwardness passed between us, but I decided to maintain a detached professional dignity. Without any fuss or 'I told you so's' I dubbed Reza's three lines in English and his four lines in Farsi. As time went on, I was surprised to find that I was actually enjoying myself. I'd never done dubbing before but by all accounts I was a natural. So much so that I was asked to stay behind to make up the numbers with a gaggle of other Iranian 'voice artistes' (none of them actors). My voice is quite prominent in the background and in the crowd sequences as one of several 'authentic Iranian voices'.

However, in *Not Without My Daughter* there is no denying

that my real *tour de force* was discovered when I was asked to provide animal noises. Presumably the film was running out of budget. At one point my character on screen slits a goat's throat in honour of Betty Mahmoody and I skilfully provided both the voice of Reza and the distressed sound effects of a goat being sacrificed. I knew the strangled sounds I had cultivated with all that Berkovian vomiting would pay off. I hoped that this minor triumph would mean that I would see the director again and work on something more meaningful. Unfortunately this was not to be. Looking back I can see that the resilience of youth prevented me from the awareness that I had not been treated very well on this film. But I had found a personal crusade, and I had been paid £150. And that was a lot of money.

So, by way of conclusion, in the two years after leaving university, I did a total of six fringe plays, four play readings, two short films, one poetry recital, one ill-fated solo piece, and one voice-over. But I had still managed to 'work with' Ben Kingsley, Julie Christie and Peggy Mount. And I was 'involved' in a Hollywood film (and thus *nearly* worked with Sally Field and Alfred Molina). Supporting myself through delivery jobs, I had spent a total of £1,500 investing in this peculiar education, and received a total of £150 (although I think there were some train fare expenses on top of that, for a very demanding poetry event in Oldham).

All in all, I had given myself a full training in theatre for £1,350. Had I gone to drama school it would have cost at least £10,000 for those two years. As far as I was concerned I was £8,650 up on the deal. Quids in. Or rather, enough to keep me hopeful.

CHAPTER TWENTY-SEVEN

Revolutions

'Why do you stay in prison when the door is wide open?'

Rumi

While I was immersed in theatre and forging ahead with plans to conquer the London Fringe, news was filtering in of seismic events in Eastern Europe. The end of Communism was sudden, unexpected and greeted with great enthusiasm. Revolution was taking place in Poland, East Germany, Czechoslovakia and Romania. We saw shocking footage from Bucharest of their leader Nicolae Ceauşescu and his wife Elena being executed. This came after a ninety-minute 'show trial' where they were accused by a makeshift prosecutor of 'suppressing the soul of the nation'. I saw how outraged the people of Romania were, and how far their patience had been stretched. TV screens juxtaposed images of the deceased Ceauşescu with scenes of people celebrating in the streets. One by one, countries achieved their independence as the former Soviet Union broke up into pieces. Eastern European borders, closed to the West for forty years, were all opened up. History was being made. I've always been fascinated by the concept of revolution – probably because the Iranian revolution was such a prominent backdrop to my adolescence. The revolutions in Eastern Europe were a huge feature of my young adulthood.

In December 1989, immediately after my St James's Church play disgrace, four of us — Sean Hinton, Inder Manocha, Jon Crook and me — had taken my red Renault 5 and driven for twelve hours across northern Europe to Berlin. On Christmas Day in London, feeling rather stuffed and bloated, I had watched Leonard Bernstein conducting Beethoven's 9th Symphony on TV as part of the 'freedom concert' that was taking place in that city. I had been moved to hear that this project involved musicians, children and singers from East and West Germany as well as other international orchestra members. Leonard Bernstein was a great hero of mine. I loved his story of being advised by one of his music teachers to change his name to 'Burns' if he wanted to be a successful conductor. This inspired me years later to stick with Omid Djalili when no one could pronounce my name in comedy clubs. In 1989 Bernstein changed the words of Schiller's 'Ode to Joy' (to which Beethoven's music is set), replacing the word 'joy' with 'freedom' for the purposes of that concert. 'Freedom of speech, freedom of religion, freedom of commerce, freedom of movement' were all proclaimed and celebrated as Western ideals in that concert. I had to be there!

Making our way towards the Brandenburg Gate, the sight of a redundant Checkpoint Charlie was thrilling. We'd seen the jubilant images on BBC News over the last few weeks, and couldn't believe we were actually there viewing it all with our own eyes. Streams of East Germans were coming through the open borders, bemused by the sheer number of West Germans greeting them with resounding applause. In some cases the westerners gave spontaneous shows of emotion, greeting the East Berliners like long-lost brothers and sisters with hugs and tears. I'd never seen so many emotional Teutonics in one place in all my life. Added to this was the presence of musicians dotted about, with the strains of Beethoven string quartets floating into the atmosphere and gathering everyone in a euphoric unity.

To me, the East Germans seemed markedly different from the West Germans; unsullied by Western materialism they dressed plainly with basic brown and blue clothes and, to my over-romanticised mind, looked like they were emerging from a post-WW2 austerity time warp. The phalanx of tourists and West Germans simply looked on, some weeping. They were witnessing people who had lived their entire lives in a small, cut-off part of their city, hidden from the rest of the world, suddenly walking free. Beethoven's String Quartet No. 14 swelled and I felt honoured to witness all this and be a part of it. (Remember the Luvvie Code: 'If you're in a country witnessing world events and revolutions unfold before your eyes, then *you are a part of it*.')

But I *was* definitely part of it! I was mingling with activists and conversing directly with East Germans who were excited to practise their English with native speakers for the first time. Encouraging their enthusiasm, we covered subjects like 'a new dawn' and 'a new human consciousness'. I even brought up Jürgen Sparwasser's goal for East Germany versus West Germany at the World Cup in 1974. This delighted them no end (football really does have a way of connecting people). I went to gatherings discussing the future of a united Germany. At one point my renegade nature took over and I began knocking down bits of the Berlin Wall (along with the many others). I noticed some unscrupulous types selling large chunks of the wall to American tourists for 5 DMs (about £3.50). I actually carried a bit of graffiti-encrusted Berlin Wall back to London and decided I would cherish it forever – especially as it might be worth millions in the future. I still have it somewhere.

At night we wandered into the centre of West Berlin, which was brimming with characters in flamboyant clothing, brandishing cigarette holders. Exhileratingly, Gershwin's 'Rhapsody in Blue' was blaring out. The country was unified for the first time in forty years and the atmosphere was electric. East Berliners discovered for themselves historic landmarks and buildings they had heard about but had never seen. Like me, they were thrilled to find themselves in cafés that had been frequented by the Berliner Ensemble. I was overcome with emotion as I sat drinking coffee and fondly imagined I was sitting in the chair Bertolt Brecht used as he plotted changing the face of German theatre with Kurt Weill.

As the clock drew close to midnight on 31 December 1989, we gathered by the Brandenburg Gate, the former symbol of Communist oppression. It seemed the whole city had the same idea. It was a cold crisp night and sky was dark and clear. On the eve of a new decade, fireworks started blasting off five minutes before the clock struck twelve. As it chimed midnight the night sky filled with what seemed like a million fireworks, let off on both sides of the border. The noise was deafening and the crowd roared its delight as every single patch of the dark sky was now gloriously covered with every exploding colour imaginable. I remember two surges of people going through the Brandenburg Gate, one from the east side coming into West Berlin, the other from the west going into East Berlin; a sea of humanity was revelling in the fact that no one could stop them. Some people were dancing defiantly on the wall by the checkpoint, watching the thousands surge back and forth at a spot where hundreds had been killed doing the same over the last forty years.

During my trip to Berlin reports had been coming in that Czechoslovakia had been experiencing similar unrest. The press were now hyping that the country 'was about to go'.

After a series of demonstrations the civil unrest was quashed in Wenceslas Square and sadly a student was killed. The killing was covered on Czech TV as 'an accident' but it was reported very differently on Austrian TV. People picking up both channels could see the inconsistencies and this tipped the people over the edge. Czechoslovakia thus ended forty-one years of Communist rule with the 'Velvet' or 'Gentle' revolution. I had loved spending time in Berlin so much that later that year, after my *Not Without My Daughter* voice-over job, I decided Czechoslovakia was to be my next destination.

I flew to Vienna and got the bus to Bratislava. Seeing the excitement of the Czechoslovaks and the reciprocity towards Brits and people from Western Europe, I decided to take the plunge and move there for six months. My acting career had hit a bit of a plateau and my relationship with Annabel had also run into some difficulties. Strangely, she did not share my view that three dates was enough of a basis upon which to build an enduring marriage. In fact, she had told me I was being too pushy and overpowering. On top of that she expressed concern that I didn't seem to have clear goals in my life. I had replied with shock that my clearest goal was to marry her! How much clearer did she want me to be?! I was ready for blood tests there and then. After a long emotional talk I understood she 'needed space'. I was left feeling I had a lot to prove. So relocating to Eastern Europe for a while was about demonstrating detachment and dynamism and on top of that a pioneering spirit.

On reflection I did need a break from the world of Fringe plays and constant stressing about whether there would be five or eight people in the audience that night (those extra three always made such a difference).

I made applications for a work visa and was accepted. I decided to teach English as a foreign language and, in a very bizarre twist, I was asked to give lectures (in English) at drama schools on 'traditions in British theatre' (me, a drama school reject, *teaching drama!*).

As cultural exchanges go, this was a good deal. While I was being asked to share whatever it was I knew, I was also sure that they would welcome a teacher who was armed with gusto and a fast-developing international approach to humour which sometimes involved mime, mimicry and standing on a table dancing. I soon discovered that Czechs and Slovaks were inherently intellectual and almost immediately I began to feel like a bit of a buffoon.

My landlord Pan (Mr) Zatko was a football referee who often asked me what I read. He'd never heard of Asterix or Charlie Brown so asked if I knew any Kafka. I said of course and cited *Metamorphosis* (I hadn't read it, just seen a Berkoff production at the Mermaid Theatre in London with Tim Roth in 1987) but I did mention that I'd read Milan Kundera. He was immensely impressed that I had read *The Unbearable Lightness of Being* (again, I'd actually just seen the film with Lena Olin and Daniel Day-Lewis). Delighted, he exclaimed '*Posnas Czeschoslovensky literatura?!*' (you know Czech literature?) and I answered rather shamelessly, '*Samosrjeme*' (of course).

Pan Zatko told me that he'd learned all about English literature at school during Communism. He certainly remembered it well and gave me an energetic version of *Richard III* – reciting what I presumed to be 'now is the winter of our discontent/ made glorious summer by this sun of York' in Slovak. He even had Czech translations of Yeats and Keats in his personal library that contained over 1,000 books, none of which he removed when renting his place to me. I liked being surrounded by books and it felt good to know a lot of them were translations of British authors. This sheer volume of literature was representative of most households I visited there.

I became friends with the popular Slovak playwright Julius

Gajdoš who lived in a more gentrified area of Bratislava called Devínska Nová Ves with his wife Hannah Gajdošova, an English translator. They introduced me to a whole array of artistic types in the city – sculptors, writers, poets and actors, all of them funny, expressive and interested in everything. We spent a magical Christmas together singing Slovak songs ('*Tota Helpa*'), and eating traditional Slovak food (*Brindzova Haloušky*). I declared that it was an honour to be amongst them. They hugged me and said if I really cared I'd stay longer than six months. The gauntlet was well and truly thrown down, and it didn't take me long to decide.

Julius and I agreed to work together. He said he wasn't much of an actor but he was well connected and could 'make things happen'. We started small and modest, with a quickly devised English language show '*pre deti*' (for children) at the *Bibiana* (children's culture house), which proved tremendously popular. We performed it every Saturday morning at 9 a.m., and then toured the show to the big theatres situated in what they called a *Dom Kultury* (house of culture), a multi-purpose building that could accommodate theatre pieces and classical concerts. This basic children's show was presented numerous times to audiences in excess of 1,500.

On one unfortunate day, due to my general haplessness, I arrived at the Dom Kultury in Dúbravka ten minutes before curtain up at 9 a.m. Julius was beside himself with anxiety and let off considerable steam regarding my lack of professionalism. I apologised but tried to reassure him that we'd done the show twenty times already and it would be fine. He replied (quite rightly, I may add with greater wisdom and maturity): 'That is not point! You must show respect to other actors! Respect to technicals [the technical team]! Everybody worry you not come! Everybody not in good mood now!' I stupidly told him to 'chill' and he blew his top. 'This not England!' In a flash I realised that I was an ambassador in his country. Any deep-seated anger against the West could easily leak out if I wasn't up to scratch doing this show. Any laziness was duly noted, and would be blamed on the three lions. I was mortified.

'Now you must act like a god!' he said, striding around the dressing room in his mini pirate outfit with a little dagger swinging by his pocket. Pumped up with a mixture of adrenaline, humiliation, regret and a newfound urgency to protect the good name of St George I went out and proverbially 'smashed the granny out of it'. I took my bow in front of 1,000 screaming Slovak children and smiled at Julius. A moment of understanding passed between us. I would never let him down again.

As our notoriety grew we created IN-THEATRE ('IN for international and IN for cool and hip,' Julius would say in his heavily accented English) and we opened a creative channel that brought over a stream of talented artists from the UK. Edward Hall, son of Sir Peter, came over to direct me in *Decadence* by Berkoff – it was time I dusted off that audition piece and unleashed a full version on an unsuspecting public. The opening at the Slovak Radio Theatre in April of 1991 was a '*velky uspech*' (great success) and Gajdoš was feted as a cultural hero. Directors came over to direct Slovak actors and Julius directed Brits in a frenzy of cultural exchange. It was a heady time. I even did a film for TV called *La Musica* with Slovakia's top actress at the time called Emilia Vašáryova, in which I had a non-speaking role of the barman with whom she became fixated. I have no memory what it was all about (and in fact didn't even understand most of what she said or what was going on) and I didn't do much except try to look smouldering behind a bar while I dried a few pint glasses. It couldn't have been a bad film, though, as Vašáryova won a Telemuse Award as Best TV Actress for the role.

I did plays at several top theatres, including *The Chairs* by

Eugène Ionesco, again directed by Julius. This was significant, as it was the first Ionesco piece performed in Czechoslovakia for over forty-two years. We toured in Denmark, Germany, Austria and even made it to Sweden where the production gained comparisons with the Berliner Ensemble (which obviously I was thrilled about). So much for 'giving up' on my Fringe theatre career, I was now rubbing shoulders with Europe's theatre elite. Who needed the Etcetera Theatre Club in Camden? We even won a Fringe award for Theatre Innovation at the Edinburgh Festival.

On our return to Bratislava I risked humiliation and gave TV and radio interviews in broken Slovak to various Czechoslovakian radio and TV stations. This immediately turned me into a temporary national figure of fun. In the magazines I became known as the first *Lodynčan/Irančan/Bratislavčhan* (Londoner/Iranian/Bratislavian) and featured in several full-page articles in national newspapers. If there's one thing the Eastern Europeans love is a foreigner learning their language, which, by the way, is not an easy one to conquer. Even now when I bump into Slovaks in London who work in coffee shops or motorway service stations and bring out a few words to dazzle them, after an initial shock they all dismiss me and assume I'm someone from Eastern Slovakia, possibly due to my dark gypsy looks. Why would anyone from London up sticks, learn their language or spend so much time in their country? Why indeed . . .

There was no concept of 'celebrity' in Czechoslovakia in those days; during Communism there were no autographs, no pictures; people simply smiled if they recognised someone on the street. I saw this when I was working with a big star like Emilia Vášáryová: all she ever got from fans was just a cursory smile or a discreet wave. The highest compliment you could receive to mark your celebrity was apparently when people began to emulate your looks, quirks and oddities. For example, charismatic politicians in Eastern Europe, the people most visible on TV, were also the most scrutinised. If they wore their ties a certain way, they were suddenly emulated by thousands. Perhaps this explains the Eastern European 'mullet and moustache look' first championed by Lech Walesa, leader of the Polish trade union federation 'Solidarity' that emerged from the Gdansk shipyards in 1980. As Walesa was of the people, this became the adopted look for footballers, shopkeepers, people in the media – the style was all the rage everywhere I went, even in the 1990s. Sadly, the only nod to my slight influence was when groups of children shouted at me in the street, opened their eyes very wide and made a lot of hand gesticulations. It was flattering and humiliating at the same time.

Noticing my car had English number plates, a couple of strapping young men from a touring English rugby club approached Julius and myself in the middle of Prague before a performance of *Decadence* at the Laterna Magika Stage (Divadlo bez Zábradlí), one of the most famous theatre spaces in Prague where English-language productions often play. They seemed excited to see me and asked what I was doing. I mentioned the play and encouraged them to come, as it was not yet sold out. Julius was also anxious because all the top critics were coming to review our new show and the fuller the theatre the better. I explained to the British boys that the play was a wild and outlandish indictment of the British class system. Getting excited (perhaps for the wrong reasons) they said they'd try to make it but couldn't promise. The theatre itself was steeped in tradition, much loved and revered for its experimental approach. The space was a little cavern, 120 seats boxed in with short, raked seating. The front two rows were practically on stage.

The show was to start at 7.30 and I was a little disturbed

that already by 7 p.m. I could hear from my dressing room chants of 'Why are we waiting?' in English. The entire rugby squad (about twenty of them) had shown up, and the two original boys we met in the street had now, in their drunken haze, completely forgotten it was a piece of theatre. Due to the title *Decadence*, the squad were now expecting some sort of insalubrious underground offering, possibly involving stripping. I worried things would get out of hand but trusting desperately that all would be OK if we stayed focused and started the show at 7.25 (starting early is normal in Prague; Czech audiences are usually all in well before curtain up).

As soon as lights went up the rugby team reacted, in unison, to almost everything that happened on stage, rather like a football crowd. It wasn't just 'ooohs' and 'aaahs', they roared their disapproval at the upper classes, mimicked my (affected) accent en masse (with almost perfectly syncopated timing) and cheered with delight when I switched to the cockney character. It was Greek chorus-like, adding nuance and texture to everything being presented on stage. After my initial panic, I had to admit that their presence gave an electric boost to the show. The largely local audience watched on, absolutely thrilled.

Towards the end, one guy in the front row was listening to his Sony Walkman, the tinny noise of which bled audibly into the tight space and distracted actors and audience. As it was a massive black guy attached to the headphones no one asked him to turn it off. My nerves already shredded, I inwardly begged him to keep the headphones on as I knew that a terribly racist speech lampooning upper-class attitudes was coming up. Sadly, as I started the speech, his friends nudged him urgently, whispering loudly: 'Eddie! Listen to this!' Eddie's eyes bulged and he bolted up immediately and tried to jump on to the stage. Thankfully two others restrained him, shouting, 'It's a play, Eddie, it's a show!' Refusing to sit back down Eddie made a point of walking out, shouting 'this show is a disgrace!' and soon others followed.

Moments later a woman yelped and left in haste when one of the rugby boys – after loudly warning his friend next to him 'I'm gonna be sick' – projectile-vomited on to the floor next to her bag. By the end, all that was left from the previously sold-out show were a few random Czech intellectuals who looked thrilled by what they had witnessed, and the rugby team captain who gave me a standing ovation. To be fair to him he apologised for his friends and said to me afterwards it was the best play he'd seen in ages.

Julius translated the headline review from the *Prague Post* the next day with glee: 'Big Hit At Laterna Magika'. There followed a detailed account of how this 'brilliant ensemble' had made a 'timely statement to the Czechs warning of the evils of the West and insidious influence of materialism'. The play was hailed as 'a clear admonishment to all Eastern Europeans of the dangers of materialism and the impending inevitability of a free market economy' and that 'the message that money had ultimately divided British society who once ruled the world with its empire, was painfully and tragically poignant and apt'. The journalist then apologised for not being able to stay to the end because one of the cast members, 'in a moment of dramatic genius', had vomited on her bag 'as a symbol of disdain for the Communist press'. She supported this powerful statement. Julius was hailed as a hero for producing the piece and IN-THEATRE was hailed as a crack team of new theatre pioneers who were 'the ones to watch'. This was it. I'd made it in Europe.

CHAPTER TWENTY-EIGHT

End Of An Era

'Before death takes away what you are given, give away what there is to give.'

Rumi

Feeling worn down by my constant phone calls and letters from Bratislava saying it was cool, there was no pressure, I didn't want her to feel hassled by me signing off 'PS: when are we getting married?', Annabel retreated from me and made it clear she didn't want me in her life. I found this out at a phone box in Vienna, a city that I often visited from Slovakia to get a monthly fix of McDonald's. I was so upset I drove around the Vienna ring road three times coming to terms with this devastating news, weeping and listening to Tracy Chapman 'Talkin' Bout A Revolution' on a loop (I was trying to play 'Baby Can I Hold You' but the tape was stuck).

But never one to give in to failure I made one last-ditch attempt to win her over. I made a 28-hour bus journey back to England and carefully made a case for her to visit Slovakia and possibly collaborate on IN-THEATRE's next project – an experimental piece with musicians based on Kahlil Gibran's *The Prophet*.

Rather wonderfully our relationship was revived and, though she said 'against my better judgement, and I know I'm in for a rough ride', a miracle happened in 1992 and Annabel and I actually did get married. To this day when I look back at my younger self I am still astonished that I pulled this one off and have managed to hang on to her all these years – let alone have three amazing children together. To say that I have not been easy to live with is an understatement. But as far as I'm concerned she continues to make me laugh more than anyone I know, so I congratulate myself that I was, and have been ever since, gloriously right: she really was 'the one'.

It was while we were working in Prague one weekend in Febuary 1995 that I called home, feeling guilty that I hadn't been in touch for a while. My sister and I caught up and then she tentatively informed me that my mother wasn't well and maybe I should come back home as soon as possible. I asked what she meant by 'as soon as possible' and she replied, 'Maybe this week?' My mother had kept her 'illness' a secret from my family for a good two years. She had cancer and had come to the decision that it was now OK for me to know. I was angry that I had not been told earlier but my mother had been adamant that I should know nothing until it was absolutely unavoidable.

I travelled back to London immediately and unsurprisingly found the flat in a sombre mood. My mother was in the newly built Chelsea and Westminster Hospital. I was given instructions to visit a ward on the third floor. Annabel and I walked in, I looked at the six patients, realised that she wasn't there, and walked back out again. I went to the reception desk to check I had the correct ward and told them that my mother wasn't there and there must be some mistake. In fact, I had not recognised my own mother. In the bed by the window a tiny woman lay asleep. This figure bore no resemblance to my funny, colourful mother. Annabel looked at me with eyes filled with tears: 'That's your mum, Omid.'

I stood motionless, aghast. She had literally shrunk to half the size. This was a different woman. My larger-than-life lioness of a mother was now a tiny shadow of her former self. I stared at her while she slept. I couldn't bear to wake her up to tell her I was there. Perhaps if she got some good sleep now she would regain her strength? Perhaps the doctors had got it all wrong and she just needed a rest? The pain of seeing my mother who had lived her life in such an unflagging, fearless and powerful manner just lie there alone in this strange ward was almost too much to bear.

She eventually woke up and seemed genuinely happy to see me and as she spoke I began to recognise her again. She told me not to worry and that she was 'fine with everything'. I asked what she meant by that and she said bluntly *'marrg'* (death). I told her not to say such foolish things. My mother elaborated on the subject in a later conversation, when we were alone in an ambulance being transferred from Chelsea and Westminster to Charing Cross Hospital on the Fulham Palace Road.

'I'm dying.'

'No, you're not.'

'I don't want you to be upset. I know it and I'm all right with it. I had a dream the other night that I was entering the next world and my father said, "What are you doing here? It's too carly," and I said, "I'm ready now," and he said, "But it's not your time." I replied: "I know, but there's no point hanging around. I might as well come now," and he said, 'All right, come on then. But don't rush. You're always rushing."'

She seemed calm about it. I told her that at sixty-three years old she was too young to die.

'No, it's not. I've lived my life. It's time to go.'

I was floored by her bluntness, but she was very open about

her impending demise. She even made jokes, right up to the end. Her favourites were some Jewish jokes she'd always loved, jokes that always started typically with something like: 'Jacob was on his death bed with his family gathered around him . . .' Strange as it may sound, we did all laugh, and they were genuinely funny jokes. Continuing the habit of a lifetime, my mother always felt obliged to become hilariously upbeat when more than three people were gathered. When I asked: 'Why haven't you told me these jokes before?' she smiled and said, 'Thought I'd leave the best to last.'

Looking back, I am astonished at the number of visitors who came to see her in hospital. In many ways it was difficult for my family, as we wanted to have her to ourselves. But she was so popular that it would have been churlish to prevent people from coming to pay their respects. Often there were people in the hospital my mother didn't even like but she never made them feel unwelcome.

One night, I awoke at 1.30 a.m. and I had a faint but distinct feeling that my mother wanted to see me. I immediately got out of bed, drove to the hospital and there she was in bed, but awake, as if waiting. She seemed very happy I had come.

'Are you allowed to be here?'

'Don't care. I wanted to see you.'

She was delighted by my spontaneity. She had a 'I've taught him well' look on her face as I smiled back at her. In that one hour we said everything we needed to say to each other.

My mother declared that I had always been good and she had never regarded me as a problem. She recalled how she used to let me play on my own and I was happy, sometimes for hours, just looking out the window and playing with my cars. In all of this there was a slight subtext that perhaps my mother had been concerned I might have not been quite 'all there' but she told me that her life had been so stressful after

I was born that she thanked God for giving her a child who made such little fuss. She remembered that I never grumbled. 'I should have played with you more. I'm so sorry. Please forgive me . . .'

At this point she started crying, overcome with regret. I told her the truth that I was happy playing alone. At least I didn't have to worry about other children taking my toys away, I hated that. And besides, she seemed to have no idea how much I enjoyed my rich fantasy world. I was grateful to have been left to my own devices and always felt sorry for children whose parents hovered around them.

My mother was on a roll and reminded me of a fortune-teller who had once stayed in our home. Apparently she had told my mother that her third child was going to do something unusual and spectacular. She was surprised because she always thought the third one (me) was a bit dim and had the least potential. I was quite shocked to hear this and wanted to ask more, but my mother was crying, telling me: 'I'm so sad I won't be able to see it. So sad . . . you have no idea . . .'

I was touched by her belief in me and I held her hand. She told me that I was her Omid, her Hope. I told her she was a wonderful mother. I apologised if I'd done anything to hurt or disappoint her and she said there was nothing to forgive. She said with enormous conviction that she would be looking out for me in the next world. I felt a peace come over me. I made a vow in my head to dedicate every show, every live performance, every appearance anywhere, to her, and to ask continuously for her assistance. I knew this moment of spontaneity of going to see her was highly significant. Later I realised that it was to be the longest time we ever had alone together in my adult life.

Days after that visit my mother deteriorated with alarming rapidity. She fell into a coma and couldn't speak. We played her *'Dastam Begir 'Abdu'l-Bahá'* ('Hold My Hand 'Abdu'l Bahá'), a beautiful Bahá'í-inspired ballad on a little stereo by her bedside.

When she finally passed away I was at home. A call came from my father. He was at the hospital but wasn't making any sense on the phone. I rushed there and saw him looking forlorn by the elevators. *'Tamoom shod'* (it's over), he said.

The famous funeral director Barry Albin helped our family to give my mother a proper send-off. Five hundred people from all walks of life showed up at the funeral at New Southgate Cemetery and an equal number at the memorial at the Kensington Hilton on Holland Park Avenue. One line in her handwritten will and testament summed her up: '. . . If I did anything to offend or upset anyone, please know I didn't mean it. I am very sorry.'

That was my mother: a simple girl who wanted to have fun and had the courage to be herself to the very end. She was acutely aware that her exuberant ways might have offended some. And she cared enough to apologise sincerely to those few.

What I learned most from my mother, which in a sense is at the heart of a comedian's spirit, was her immense capacity to burst the balloon of self-importance. I don't know if she did this consciously or not but it's definitely rubbed off on me throughout my career. As a result I've always tried not to take myself too seriously. Some actors need ninety minutes of visualisations or a session of complicated breathing exercises before they take to the stage, as if it is some kind of sacred act. This is all well and good but frankly I can't think of much art these days that merits that kind of grandiose introspection.

This attitude of my mother's was neatly summed up in 1989 at the Etcetera Theatre Club in Camden, when the 'coconuts' incident from my childhood was revisited in an awful echo of that day. I was appearing in a two-hander called *The Zoo Story* by Edward Albee. The director was a very dynamic and consci-entious guy called Michael French. He had boosted me up, saying I was the best dramatic actor he had ever seen and our working relationship was his most fruitful collaboration.

On the opening night I was pumped with nerves and hung on Michael's every word as he gave me his last pep talk: 'Stay truthful, stay in the moment. And most importantly, enjoy it!'

The opening scene of the play, set entirely in Central Park, involved me walking on, casing the joint and noticing someone seated on a bench. I had to approach this character, then, having second thoughts, back away and leave the stage. After a beat I was told to re-appear, and with renewed vigour, start up a conversation with the man on the bench. In other words, follow basic stage directions for less than a minute, with a view to building an atmosphere of unspoken tension. Or to put it even more simply: come on stage, look at the bench, walk off, come back on again.

To my horror, as I walked on there seemed to be a rather crackling and dangerous atmosphere, punctuated by odd murmurs. As I approached the park bench the crowd fell silent. As I had second thoughts and edged away, there were titters. As I backed towards the exit, the laughs were building, so I stopped. This only served as an unintentional dramatic pause; when I left the stage a huge guffaw erupted. I stood backstage literally shaking, not understanding the root of this unsolicited hysteria. I waited for the laughs to die down and then made my re-entrance. An ironic cheer of 'hooray!' went up at my re-appearance. This set the tone for the rest of the evening, and sadly, every moment where poignancy was intended was met with gales of laughter.

At the end of the story, my character gets stabbed and dies. Surely this would stop everyone laughing? Michael had instructed us not to take a curtain call but instead, as the lights fade, I was told to stay frozen in my final 'dead' position. The idea was that after the applause, the crowd would be confronted by the image of me rigid on stage, and they would have to file awkwardly past this tableau to exit.

When the moment of my stabbing actually arrived, the audience roared their appreciation, apparently having had much more fun than they had expected. But instead of making their way out, shaken and respectful, they all remained in their seats, as if waiting for a punchline. By this point no one was sure what was going on. This was actually our intended reaction, as the director was seeking to milk the delicious beat of awkwardness before the audience leaves. Powerful stuff. It was all about liberating us actors as well as the audience members from the 'tyranny of the proscenium arch'.

However, Michael had not banked on my mother being in the crowd. She had been sitting supportively in the front row, but was clearly uncomfortable that people did not seem to have clear instructions. She was also concerned that I might have been hurt, and her gasps and shrieks during the various fight scenes had been very distracting to say the least. Bearing all this in mind, she decided to get up and approach me on stage, tottering on ludicrously high heels with her fur coat floating around her shoulders (it was summer and we were in a cramped Fringe venue).

With a powerful hand gesture she indicated 'hang on a minute' to the crowd. Everyone was gripped and now convinced that the play had not indeed finished. Was it possible this genius maverick director had constructed an explosive new ending to Edward Albee's masterpiece? In the thick silence my mother's voice was painfully audible as she whispered in my ear: 'Are you really dead?'

Inevitably, this was turning into a comedy gold situation,

and she got a huge laugh. I was forced to reply just so she would leave me alone with my art. I had no choice but to hiss back: 'No, just go. Please. Go.'

My mother turned triumphantly to the crowd, proclaiming: 'It's OK, everybody. He is not dead! We can go! Come on . . .'

Naturally this sparked a final round of whoops and cheers, as people followed her lead and started making their way out. Loyal to Michael I remained frozen on stage and endured several audience members confiding 'so funny' and 'hilarious, mate' in my ear, as they filed out.

During the post-show analysis, the director was flummoxed. 'I don't know what happened there,' he confessed. In one fell swoop my career as the Iranian Al Pacino was over. As was my collaboration with Michael, as he seemed to think I was a jinx.

My mother's actions on that day, and ever since have provided me with an acute awareness regarding the perils of voluntarily placing oneself under public scrutiny and expecting to be taken seriously.

CHAPTER TWENTY-NINE

Inside The Ethnic Bit-Part Actor's Studio

'I know you're tired, but come. This is the way.'

Rumi

It is very important here to mention my gratitude to the much-loved casting director Joyce Gallie, who was dragged to see me in a show at the Riverside Studios in the summer of 1995 by her son Luke and his older half-brother Jason Phipps (who was in my class at Holland Park school). Apparently she 'absolutely loved' what she saw and, hearing I had no agent, recommended one for me and made some important calls to her friends in the business. The fact that one of these friends happened to be Melanie Coupland, at the highly prestigious Talkback agency, felt serendipitous. Talkback belonged to Mel Smith and Griff Rhys Jones. Melanie called me up out the blue and said, 'We're coming to see you in Edinburgh [by this time I was an up-and-coming stand-up comedian with my 'Kebab' show]. I hear you're fabulous. Are you fabulous?' I actually had a terrible festival but the gods of comedy smiled on me the night Melanie came, my one good night of the run. This convinced me it was fate. After all, it was Mel Smith, one of the founders of the agency, who first encouraged me as a fifteen-year-old.

That September of 1995 I wrote to Talkback:

Dear Melanie,

Being aware of my limited talent and experience in this field I think the way forward is to go down the ethnic bit-part route. I'm quite adept at accents: Iranian, Afghani, Turkish and Pakistani. My generic Arab is strong but sounds Egyptian, and the pedant may have issues if I'm cast as someone from Oman or Yemen. Having lived in Eastern Europe, I am familiar with Slavic speech patterns. I could easily play a Russian commandant, Bulgarian gymnast trainer or Slovak border control guard. I can also play French, German and American (Mafia boss). I am good at British regional accents too, e.g. upper-class RP (Oxford-educated Greek diplomat) or East End cockney (bus conductor with Jewish heritage). I think a small part in a Bond film would be great. Failing that a 'villain with a heart' on The Bill. *If I get through the door and into the audition room I will endeavour to be personable and charming. I could also do bits of my act – but only if there are two or more people in the room. I did this once to an audience of one and there were no laughs. I have learned from this experience. Do advise.*

Really looking forward to our collaboration.

Warm regards,

Omid

So now I had an agent and I was ready to rock. My first in a long line of (crucial) ethnic bit parts was in a sitcom called *After The Birth* for Channel 4 where I played 'cabbie number six' from the company Cab-u-Like. My line that day was: 'You order taxi?' – the same line given to all six cabbies who show up simultaneously at the same address. I remember thinking it was going to be my big break so practised the line hundreds of times in my head to make it stand out from the crowd. I sat quietly in the green room waiting to shoot the scene and was thrilled to observe Paula Wilcox from the epic 1970s ITV sitcom *Man About the House* was there too. I made my first stab at having a conversation with a famous person, mainly hoping to reassure her that I understood she might feel uncomfortable sharing a green room with a bunch of cabbie bit-part actors who paid her no attention. I wanted to remind her that she still had admirers from a bygone but not forgotten day: 'You were great in *Man About the House*. What was Richard O'Sullivan like to work with? And how is he, by the way? Like your good self, we don't see him much on the telly these days.'

I was surprised when she got up and left the room. I deduced that it was unlikely she would pass on my best to Richard.

Throughout 1996 I managed to bag a few more bits and pieces, significantly a BBC2 sketch show called *Comedy Nation*, a late-night showcase for up-and-coming talent which included Matt Lucas, David Walliams, Catherine Tate and Ricky Grover. I was surprised my sketches were even filmed. One in particular was of an Arab university professor obsessed with Cliff Richard. His lecture on mathematics quickly descended into an appreciation of 'Sir Cliff', using graphs to chart his 'ageless good looks' against his 'devotion to Jesus'. In one episode the professor was dressed as Heathcliff, with long hair and beard (a homage to Cliff Richard's appearances in the West End production of *Wuthering Heights*). The episode finished with me singing 'Summer Holiday' underneath a multicoloured umbrella while beatboxing in tune to the song as the credits rolled. I think BBC2 received twelve complaints about the show, eight of which were from the Cliff Richard Fan Club who felt the sketch was tantamount to a personal attack.

I had fantasies of a film debut. In a special 'And introducing . . .' role, I saw myself starring as Al Pacino's illegitimate overweight son in a moving saga about connecting with lost relatives. But when my 'big break' came, it was so completely not how I had envisioned it that I didn't even realise it was a 'break'.

On my way to the audition to read for the role of the Warden in *The Mummy* I dismissed the script as the worst few pages of anything I'd ever read. It was my second film audition that week, my first having been for *Notting Hill.* I'd met director Richard Curtis at an audition who gave me a role on the spot. He said he didn't yet know what role I would play, but promised it would be 'significant'. So I rocked up a few weeks later and played a coffee-shop owner who kept giving Hugh Grant's character relationship advice. In the end, after receiving a tactful letter from the producer Duncan Kenworthy I learned that my speaking lines had been cut from the movie. However, I can be clearly glimpsed on screen selling Hugh Grant the orange juice he eventually spills on Julia Roberts as he leaves 'my' café, thus precipitating their relationship. So my part *was* indeed significant. One could say it was pivotal. Unfortunately it caused me some anguish in my leafy suburban neighbourhood as I dropped my kids off at nursery school. Sympathetic middle-class parents would say: 'I saw you in Notting Hill. Do you do *a lot* of extra work?'

So I walked into *The Mummy* audition room with signs outside that said 'Hubbard casting' and the rather intimidating 'Universal Pictures' without too many high expectations. Assuming it was a horror movie I gave them an aggressive reading with grotesque overtones. The director Stephen Sommers, a fresh-faced all-American university jock type, stopped me mid-audition to say he was looking for a character similar to Rifki in the 1978 Oscar-nominated film *Midnight Express,* a larger-than-life Turkish prison warden who commits appalling acts of cruelty and finally gets his gruesome and deserved comeuppance.

'Maybe make him more serious?'

Was he in the same room as me? I felt crushed. And then he said: 'Let's do one more try where you tone down the comedy.'

But the more I read, the more he laughed. I even took long pauses and stared him in the eye threateningly before saying, 'Wallah.' Try as I might, I just couldn't make it sinister enough. An Arab Christopher Lee I was not.

To my amazement the casting director said they had seen sixty-five people for the role and asked me what I was doing between April and September. I said I had a couple of comedy clubs booked in, two nights specifically at the Meccano Club in Islington that I simply couldn't miss. Plus I liked the owner Steve Jameson and I didn't want to let him down. I was told there was no way I could be flown back from Morocco. We were at an impasse. Thankfully Universal Studios made the decision for me and offered to buy me out of the two gigs. I'll always cherish the pay slip highlighting a £120 payment under the heading: *For cancelled comedy appearances at the Steve Jameson Club.*

Here I must pay tribute to a dear friend Phillip O'Brien, an American actor who had lived in London for many years. I found out later he'd had dinner with the Hubbards a few days before the audition, and had mentioned my name. It was in fact Phillip who had made a recommendation that I was 'one to watch'. This personal vouching for me triggered the chain of events that led to me being cast in *The Mummy*. Sadly Phillip lost his battle with cancer several months later, and never saw the film. But his intervention was pivotal and, like Phillip himself, never to be forgotten.

As filming started in 1998 I calculated that I was going to

be with this crowd for fifteen weeks and decided, misguidedly, to consider myself the glue that brought everyone together. I imagined I would be an invaluable catalyst to the social bonding process. Making friends with the locals in the tiny town of Erfoud by joining in spontaneously with a bongo ensemble one night, I was immediately called 'Djaloool' (a simple distortion of Djalili humorously meaning 'the cute one' in their dialect). Through my (A level) French I was able to understand that living on the edge of the Sahara Desert afforded the locals very little opportunity to make money. Therefore any jewellery sold or meals bought by our film crew would go a long way to supporting local families. Fired up to help my new Moroccan friends I took the cast and crew to similar bongo evenings, hosted trips to the local restaurants and encouraged everyone to buy all manner of knick-knacks to take back as gifts. Everywhere I went in town I was greeted with cheers. My name was even upgraded to 'Abu Djaloool' (father of the cute one).

Keen to make an equally good impression with my new actor friends I began to entertain them around the hotel pool with a character called the 'Arab Action Hero'. Subtly trying to impress the producers that they were missing a trick (i.e. I was a ready-made film star and they should be offering me a Jason Bourne-type action hero role), I would sometimes bolt up, usually when people were relaxing, and start chasing myself around the edge of the pool. I would scream in Arabic and fire at imaginary attackers. I even prefaced these actions with 'Cover me!' before going into the pretend fray. These were elaborate action scenarios that rendered everyone dumbstruck. After all, the sight of an overweight man running around in Speedos is impossible to ignore. Akin to a scene in *The St Valentine's Day Massacre*, I would mime being riddled with bullets before dramatically collapsing into the pool and floating as if dead. I did this almost every day and it became a routine for everyone who gathered after filming. It always got a fabulous round of applause and by the end of the week people would plead 'do Arab Action Hero!' and I'd oblige with ever more energy and commitment.

The challenging filming schedule was carried out with minimum fuss and the set was a happy place. Steven Sommer's wide-eyed enthusiasm for life was infectious. I got to know one of the assistant directors called Jim, who I liked enormously because he always brought me extra slices of cake. He was getting married soon to a girl called Kate and everyone was congratulating him. He was kind, good-looking, able to fix things . . . 'Lucky girl,' I thought. Having just finished working on *Hideous Kinky*, also filmed in Morocco, Jim's fiancée was coming to spend a Sunday with us in Erfoud before flying back. Typically, I was the only person wholly unaware that this was Kate Winslet. As she joined us around the pool one Sunday afternoon, we settled down, all fifteen of us, to chat to the couple-to-be. After the briefest pause in the conversation one of the American actors suggested, 'Omid, why don't you do Arab Action Hero for Kate?' There were murmurs of enthusiastic agreement. The Americans were clearly angling for juicy tales from *Titanic* and the Oscars (she had been nominated that year) and wanted me to break the ice. In the right company Kate is known for being tremendously friendly and forthcoming but the ice had not yet been broken and I didn't want to take on the mantle of this pressurising responsibility. Unfortunately, Kate, clearly intrigued said, 'Oh, I'd love to see it.'

Admittedly I buckled quite easily under the pressure. I delivered my usual 'Cover me!' and bolted from the table.

'What's he doing?' said Kate.

'Watch this,' said Jim.

I was off. The intensity of my performance was surprising. Whilst my customary weapon had been an imaginary pistol, I now started experimenting with hand grenades, machine guns and bazookas. I knocked tables over and threw chairs in the pool. The presence of a Hollywood star had convinced me that this was an important turning point in my career. As I reached the diving board I felt inspired to mount a spectacular finale. Dodging imaginary bullets and ducking wildly, I was distracted by the sound of the now-archaic Nokia ring tone. I caught a glimpse of Kate rummaging in her bag and clearly not watching my performance. So I accelerated my efforts, took a flying jump and bounced off the diving board, all the while shouting 'Noooo!' and shaking my body as if sustaining multiple bullet wounds. High on adrenaline mid-air I even had the presence of mind to wonder if the stunt men present were impressed by this acrobatic display.

As I hit the water, I felt my leg muscles suddenly pull at the same time. I'd kicked too hard in the air, like a long jumper, and both my hamstrings had violently snapped on impact with the water. I was now struggling to tread water and called for help. Some of the actors got up and rushed to my assistance, while Kate continued talking on the phone, pacing away with her back to the pool. She was speaking in concerned tones, as if something serious was up (sadly, nothing to do with my predicament). Upon finishing her call, Kate enquired: 'What happened to Arab Action Hero?' At that exact moment she looked over and saw me being ignominiously hauled out of the water by my arms, whereupon I was deposited on to a stretcher and whisked away for immediate medical attention.

As embarrassing moments go, it's right up there . . .

Consequently I missed a week of filming. I couldn't walk and was confined to my room. The director was very annoyed as it meant I had to miss some important scenes. At nights I ruefully looked out of the window and watched everyone cavorting by the pool, happy after a hard day's work, laughing, pushing each other in, performing party pieces I hadn't seen before. Others had taken up the reins of the role of 'life and soul of the party' and seemed positively liberated by my absence. Everyone had come out their shell and didn't need me any more. Perhaps they never did? I had peaked too quickly and felt I was now on the scrap heap. This incident taught me a major life lesson: when you find yourself in work situations with a group of people for an elongated period – pace yourself socially.

CHAPTER THIRTY

A Gladiator Story

'The fault, dear Brutus, is not in our stars, but in ourselves.'
William Shakespeare

The painful memory of my Arab Action Hero 'incident' is the reason why when I arrived in Morocco a year later to play my most high-profile ethnic bit-part role to date in *Gladiator*, I avoided everyone. This wasn't too difficult because unlike the cast of *The Mummy* who were together all the time, the actors in *Gladiator* were never really given the chance to bond due to filming in so many different locations. Oliver Reed was a law unto himself, Djimon Hounsou was intense to the point of muteness, and Russell Crowe was in private accommodation somewhere far away so I never needed to worry about impressing him socially. Though alarmingly, due to some of the same crew being from *The Mummy*, there were rumblings of an Arab Action Hero encore, which I had to nip in the bud from the outset. This was to later come back to bite me in the backside. British film crews are notorious for never letting a joke die.

The actors playing gladiators were a mixed bag, few of them being trained actors. One bloke even had two roles: playing a gladiator who urinates with fear before being killed, and then bizarrely turning up as a senator later on in the film. There was a German strongman called Ralf Möller (who Oliver Reed kept calling 'Kraut') who played 'Hagen' and who kept reminding everyone that he was the 1984 German bodybuilding champion. He often sat smoking a cigar, asking to be told jokes. 'Test me. I am German, I have a sense of humour!' I fired a number of jokes at him and he would laugh, sometimes for a whole ten seconds, before smiling and admitting, 'I don't get it.' Ralf was the most sociable person there, along with Jeff Rudom, a seven-foot ex-basketball player with a great sense of fun, who gets killed off throughout the movie in different guises. His favourite game at meal times was asking Djimon Hounsou advice on how to make his tiny parts bigger. Djimon never got the joke.

'You cannot make a part bigger where there is no room.'

Jeff would pipe up: 'There's got to be a way to get Ridley [Scott] to make me a star. I'm wearing a moose's head in two scenes, for Chrissakes!'

'You must be truthful. The size of role is not relevant.'

'You're always making *your* part bigger!'

'How?'

'You keep saying "not yet". Where the hell is that in the script?!'

'That is in the script.'

'No it's not'

'Yes it is.'

'No it's not.'

Seeing non-British actors discover panto for themselves was one of my secret joys of working on *Gladiator*. Perhaps this kind of discussion would have helped me with my part in *Notting Hill* . . .

Luckily, after *The Mummy*, I felt more psychologically prepared for *Gladiator* and had grasped several of the unsaid rules for the Hollywood ethnic bit-part actor:

1. Don't speak unless you are spoken to.
2. Be spiritually generous as a person and as an actor.
3. Be offended by nothing.
4. If you are not the lead or supporting actor don't demand anything.
5. Don't expect any encouragement.
6. Keep out of harm's way.
7. If you are made fun of by the crew, it's because they like you.
8. If you are scared of an actor keep out of his way.
9. Keep out of Oliver Reed's way.

The crew members who worked with me on *The Mummy* thought it would be great fun to play a trick on me, no doubt as punishment for my refusing to perform Arab Action Hero for them again. Knowing I was scared of Oliver Reed, the writers had kindly reworked the scene where Proximo (Oliver Reed) meets me (Slave Trader). Instead of punching me in the face as originally written, Proximo was to grab my nether regions during our opening dialogue. I wondered about the criteria upon which they based their notions of what scared me, but was determined to take it all in my stride. As we settled down for a rehearsal, Mr Reed respectfully asked me: 'Are you a Method actor?'

'I am.' (I wasn't.)

'Would you mind if I grabbed underneath the tunic rather than on top? Might make it a bit more *realistic*.'

'By all means.' (Thank goodness I was wearing sturdy underwear.)

We rehearsed. All fine. He grabbed me, we said our lines and I even added a tiny nod to a group of Arab extras in the corner of the café to hide the fact that Oliver Reed had my knackers in a vice. Slave traders back in the day had some status in society in AD 180 and the moment made sense (all those years reading Asterix and Obelix finally paid off). Apparently this made the director laugh. 'First time in many years!' as Branko Lustig, the producer, told me later, excitedly.

Usually when the director calls 'Action!' you proceed with the scene until you hear 'Cut!' The actors can then relax for a few moments before re-setting and going for another take. On this occasion, when 'Action!' was called Mr Reed grabbed my testicles, as agreed, and delivered his now-famous lines: 'Those giraffes you sold me, they won't mate. You sold me queer giraffes.' So far so good, but when 'Cut!' was called Mr Reed chose not to relinquish his grip. I assumed this was because he wanted to remain 'in character', as he appeared to be mouthing his lines quietly to himself whilst continuing to squeeze, albeit in a companionable manner. I remained silent and obedient to the school of Method acting. However, by take three he was still holding on and no longer practising his lines.

Keen to cover the awkwardness, some light chit-chat seemed in order. Perhaps he had just forgotten his hands were still gripping my vitals? Or maybe he was lost in his own artistic process? This was delicate as he was a big star and I didn't want to disturb him even though I was now conscious of a dull ache. I figured that by this stage, surely I was entitled to distract him a little? So I asked how he liked the Berber Palace Hotel? He replied monosyllabically that it was fine. I spoke breezily about my love of the food, but my disappointment in the temperature of the pool being so cold and it was perhaps because the water had come from the snowcaps of the nearby mountains and there was no way to warm up the water before it came into the pool. By take four I became slowly and unnervingly aware of a massaging sensation. This was getting ridiculous and I knew I was keeping a very flimsy lid on my mounting panic. In desperation I looked over to the second assistant director Terry Needham and realised that he was crying with silent laughter, whereupon Mr Reed smiled broadly: 'You know this is a wind-up don't you?' A roar of laughter erupted. Rounds and rounds of applause reverberated in my ears after Terry Needham declared me the 'finest sport in all Morocco!' I received the applause modestly, while hastily rearranging my undergarments and wondering if it wasn't too late to return to a career in chauffeuring.

This incident led onto a bizarre sequence of events. Branko (the larger-than-life legendary Israeli producer who has *Schindler's List* among his credits) had developed a habit of laughing when just looking at me, then putting his cigar in his mouth doing a 'jazz hands' gesture while shouting 'be funny' before pushing me on set and retreating behind the camera. After that fateful day with Oliver Reed, I was informed back at the hotel that the director and producers wanted me to join them for 'an important meeting'.

At dinnertime I usually sat alone, preferring a bit of quiet time at the end of the day, especially after a recent disturbing encounter with Omar Sharif (he was shooting another film in the area) who had berated me for putting so much food on my plate. I was rather confused by his assertion that he ate 'like a bird' himself, which was 'why he was Omar Sharif'. After my long hard day leading a caravan in the desert (where I appear in the film as a tiny speck) I had no energy to defend myself and simply pointed out that it was 'an all-you-could-eat buffet' and chances like that didn't come along every day.

The 'important meeting' started with an invitation to join a table with Branko Lustig, Ridley Scott and one of the writers. I felt a bubbling anticipation, and tried to zone out the sight of Omar Sharif staring at me with evident distaste from a neighbouring table.

Branko explained that the production team was having problems with Russell Crowe, because he was lodging alone and didn't socialise with anyone. We were already two weeks into filming and it was not a happy set; tensions were rife and there was a palpable nervousness that, according to Branko, was 'not conducive to a creativity'. He had clearly been angsting rather a lot and had come up with a plan. I was all ears . . .

As I was a comedian from the UK and Russell was a fan of British comedy, maybe I could befriend him? This felt rather full-on, even for me, so I tried to share my hard-earned insights, that perhaps it's as well not to force things? Unfortunately they didn't seem interested in learning more about my 'pacing oneself socially' policy for film sets. I was only there for another two days and it would be really wonderful if I could assist them in this small favour. Naturally, I assumed that this was an elaborate bargaining game that would lead to future film roles and a lifelong collaboration with Ridley Scott, and heartily assented to their requests.

Nevertheless, the enormity of this task dawned on me as I lay in bed that night. I had been asked by the producers of a major Hollywood blockbuster to befriend their leading actor in order to neutralise a highly subjective perspective regarding spurious tensions between people I didn't know.

This was going to be a big movie. Its success depended on the wellbeing of its leading actor. Was I being asked to save this movie? Yes. It would appear I was . . .

I leapt out of bed and started planning my introduction. Start with a joke? Take it easy? I began to feel the same pressure that builds the night before a big comedy gig. I'd done a live recording of a BBC stand-up show a month earlier, and had been advised by my manager to go through my set in the mirror at home – a technique well honed since fringe theatre days. Great. I went immediately to the bathroom.

'Hello, Russell. Hey Russ. How are you? Hey man. Hey dude. Wha' 'appenin'?'

It was useless, there were too many options, possibilities and permutations. I collapsed back into bed sweating and fretting, overwhelmed by sick feelings of pressure and unworthiness.

The following morning, I was driven out to the location, an amazing enclave in the desert, home to the oldest village in the world. Set in caves in the southern Atlas Mountains, this Berber village pre-dates even Fez and Marrakech and is purported to be over 5,000 years old. Nearly all its population was used as extras that day. The small arena where the gladiators fought was built next to the caves and jammed with trainers, fight co-ordinators and stunt men all practising for their scenes in the searing heat. Russell Crowe's assistant had been tipped off by production that I'd arrived to say hello. Apparently she'd been instructed to introduce me to Russell 'casually' in the hope that this would allow a friendship between Russell Crowe and myself to develop free from complications. Ridley Scott and Branko were observing from behind some nearby cameras, as I was taken to Russell, who was sitting on the floor and preparing for his scene. The assistant whispered that Russell was 'getting into character' which sometimes took about an hour and involved a great deal of meditation. Part of me thought 'oh, one of those' but as Maximus was a role of a lifetime I understood. The sun beat down on my neck as introductions were made.

'I'd like you to meet Omid, he's playing the Slave Trader. Your scene with him is tomorrow and we thought you might like to meet first. Omid, Russell; Russell, Omid.'

Russell was obviously in a slight daze but courteously stood up to say, 'How you doing, mate?' I immediately liked his manliness, his no-nonsense Antipodean handshake and his furrowed brow showing genuine interest and respect for a fellow actor. Wow. I replied that I was fine and enquired how filming was going. He replied with a 'you know, ticking over'.

He seemed perfectly happy and was probably just keeping himself to himself. The idea that he needed to hang out with me suddenly seemed ludicrous, but I could feel the oppressive glare, not just of the sun, but of Branko and Ridley Scott in the distance, clearly expecting some kind of result.

I panicked, engulfed by incoherence: 'Russell, hi. Listen, I hear you're all alone in that house doing nothing all day. How about you come over to the hotel and we can hang?'

'Excuse me?'

'There's a pool table, a swimming pool, gym, great food . . . you should come out and play. Plus, I'm a really fun guy . . .'

That was wrong. I should never have said that.

Russell looked uneasy: 'What are you talking about?'

I felt sick. It really was terribly hot . . .

'Nothing, just heard you're all alone and maybe, just maybe we could . . . you know . . .'

Russell looked sharply at his assistant. 'Have they been talking about me?'

I leapt in. 'No, Russell, nooo! I just heard that maybe if you needed a bit of company then I'm your man. We can play table tennis. The guys, we all take our T-shirts off. We can play a bit of pool, hang out, you know, the works.' Unfortunately, when I said 'play pool' I made an action as if holding an imaginary cue and moved my hips in a way that did not make sense, even to me.

Russell seemed to be getting stressed. 'What have they been saying about me? What the hell have they been saying?'

The assistant hastily ushered Russell into the shade. The heat of the desert was pounding in my head and I began to understand the predicament of Meursault in Camus' *L'Étranger.* When asked in court why he shot someone he gave the explanation: '*C'était à cause du soleil.*' (It was because of the sun.) In other words, heat drives one insane. I looked for the cool balm of reassurance from my employers, but both Ridley Scott and Branko had vanished like a mirage, and even though there was no breeze, I could sense the presence of floating tumbleweed.

Somehow I made my way to the lunch tent and spotted Russell and his assistant four tables away. As I ate, I kept my head up on the off-chance that Russell might make eye contact which would allow me to register that I was still available for friendship. He did look at me once but scowled with such hostility that I looked down immediately and soon asked the transport captain if I could be driven back to the hotel straight-away. I had worked myself into a heightened state of anxiety and was positively dreading the next day's filming.

The next morning my nerves were in tatters. I sat alone in the breakfast area feeling once again like an outcast on a film set. Suddenly Russell arrived and walked past me smiling with a very friendly 'how you doing, mate?' His assistant smiled and waved. In fact everyone I saw seemed to be grinning or chuckling at the sight of me. I was mystified.

Thankfully, after breakfast, Russell's assistant approached me and explained that a lot of people mistake Russell's focus for arrogance. It appeared that during our conversation yesterday, Russell had misheard and misunderstood what I'd been struggling to communicate.

What on earth had he misunderstood?

Apparently my nervous physicality with the imaginary snooker cue had sent out some alarming signals. Russell had reacted strongly ('what are they saying about me?') because he had somehow gained the impression that the producers, uncomfortable with him spending so much time alone, had concluded that Russell might be gay and perhaps felt he needed to conceal this part of his identity. Russell had interpreted my appearance as a kind of bizarre gesture of acceptance on the part of the producers.

This had naturally offended Russell on many levels. First and foremost, he needed privacy to prepare for the role of a lifetime. What was strange about that? He meditated in order to get into the nuances of his role. Did this mean he was gay?! And if so, why on earth were they sending the Slave Trader to proposition him?

We shot our scene. All went well, and I flew back home the next day. Unbeknown to me the story ballooned and distorted into an anecdote involving me having taken it upon myself to provide Russell Crowe with romance and companionship during the shoot.

Whatever was said, the tense mood clearly lifted; Russell was on fire, and a happy atmosphere prevailed. Sadly this changed when everyone was rocked by the news of Oliver Reed's tragic passing during the filming in Malta. I felt deeply shocked, and appreciated all the more that I'd had the opportunity of a lifetime to work with this wonderfully wild and generous man.

Looking back, many years later, I believe that my general ineptitude and klutz-like buffoonery created moments that ultimately brought a film production together at a difficult time and helped it on its way to winning the Oscar for best film in 2000. Russell Crowe was great, but frankly I deserve some of the credit. I've kept quiet about this long enough.

CHAPTER THIRTY-ONE

Is There Too Much 'Omid' In 'Comidy'?

'Whoever is calm and sensible is insane.'

Rumi

Like a baby who is initially traumatised when thrown into a swimming pool, then finds itself paddling tentatively before eventually embracing the warm security of the water, so I jumped into the treacherous waters of the comedy industry.

My comfort zone or default setting throughout my childhood and youth had always been to 'dive in'. Fortuitously this was a peculiarly good fit for the mindset required to survive a stand-up comedy career path. Perhaps this was why I felt so comfortable within the conceptual integrity that I found in ITV's *Splash!*, a diving show fronted by Olympic medal winner Tom Daley. There was honesty there, coupled with a craziness that felt downright sensible. I may not be very good at witty banter on panel shows but reckless acts of absurdity? No problem.

Splash! in January 2013, like no other experience to date, brought forth a flurry of epiphanies, all occurring as I hurtled (aged forty-seven, overweight and wearing a spangly onesie that resembled the Sheffield Wednesday home kit from the

1990s) to possible injury and death from a ten-metre diving board on live television.

It was the ultimate act of optimism – flinging myself from a great height and trusting the universe to catch me. It occurred to me during the semi-final that I must possess a specific personality type that best gathers philosophical insights about existence while suspended mid-air. This was my first *Splash!* revelation as I teetered on the edge of the board. Time slowed down, and I felt oddly peaceful, just like the occasion when I nearly fell out the back of a car and on to the Tehran motorway. I also recalled how strangely calm I felt while floating in a pit of excrement in my grandfather's garden. It was a familiar sensation of being outside time, in neither one place nor another. As I fell from the board, learning point number one came to me: I felt, as an established fact in my consciousness, that it's only when you've fallen flat on your face that things start to happen. So you might as well jump, because it doesn't matter if you fall, flat or otherwise. Falling is GOOD. In other words, never be afraid to make a mistake.

Flashes of enlightenment started hitting me like arrows coming from different angles . . . rather like the imaginary bullets I conjured up when I was showing off for *The Mummy*'s cast and crew as the Arab Action Hero.

As the bottom of the pool continued to rush towards me, I was struck by learning point number two: jumping into the void and 'being myself' had, in many ways, been an attempt to connect with mother's example of fearlessness. Perhaps it was part of the grieving process, but the first bit of stand-up I ever did was about my mother's outrageous front to haggle in McDonald's. It's a simple joke based on the tension of feeling embarrassed about the way she ordered our food.

Mum: Two Big Mac, two chip and two Coke please. How much?

Server: That'll be £3.78.

Mum: I give you . . . one pound.

This used to get a fair big laugh back in the day. But it was modified. The truth of what actually happened to inspire the joke was much more dramatic. When my mother was looking to buy a fridge in Barkers of Kensington (now House of Fraser) a shop assistant had grown tired of her constant haggling and, seeking to get rid her, had lost his rag and told her in rather inappropriate terms to 'go away'. My mother, incredulous that a shop assistant would treat her with such discourtesy, continued to haggle a price for the Zanussi fridge freezer. The man simply responded by increasing the velocity and range of his vocabulary, ending with a particularly harsh expletive. My mother, presumably to teach the salesman a lesson, offered him back his words: 'You give me one f***, I give you three f***, two piss and one s***!' She was essentially tipping the haggling process on its head. I was amazed she even knew those words in English.

Learning point three: had my mother lived, she would definitely have ended up in one of my shows and would probably have upstaged me mercilessly.

Learning point number four. I miss my mum. She would have loved *Splash!*

That the British public seem to have accepted me became point number five. I could hear the crowd cheering as I flew off the diving board with arms outstretched and an expression of insane concentration on my face. The newspapers had been very supportive; in fact the *Mirror* had even created the empowering headline 'Pigs CAN Fly'. I have spent most of my career, and indeed my life, trying to figure out who I am in order to make some kind of contribution as a British-born Iranian. I've often felt like an outsider in the various circles I have frequented. And this has less to do with the British public rejecting me and probably more to do with my unusual childhood. I've banged on about being an Iranian in my stand-up, but, to return to football, when David Beckham scored against Greece to send us (look! I said 'us') to the World Cup of 2002 I got light-headed, choked and passed out. I don't think the audience of *Splash!* cared remotely about my ethnic origin. I was a balding and corpulent middle-aged man doing something intrepid. I really hope my audaciousness was as inspirational for others as it was for me. It even gave me the courage to write this book, which I wouldn't have countenanced before *Splash!*

As my head smacked the water, learning point number six hit me with full force: it is all well and good to live the dream, soaring from a great height, but how many times can you expect your nearest and dearest to continue hauling you metaphorically (and literally) out the water? Time to grow up, I thought as my nose narrowly missed scraping the bottom of the pool.

So as I reflect on my life with *Splash!*-ing sagaciousness, a conclusion to this bizarre personal history is beginning to take shape.

Wisdom is often gained in hindsight. You actually learn nothing from falling flat on your face. It's what you do afterwards that counts.

No autobiography is complete without an element of shameless name-dropping, so I will end with my favourite showbiz story to illustrate a point that might become clearer in retrospect:

I, Omid Djalili, from the crazy guesthouse and with my string of failed A levels, spent a brief time with Robert Redford. I'd even tried to be funny with him after we were introduced on the set of the film *Spy Game* (also starring Brad Pitt) by the late and very wonderful director Tony Scott. I was young and eager to make an impression:

'Mr Redford,' I said, 'I'm a big fan. I must say, you were the best thing in *Hawaii 5–0*.'

After a slight pause during which he sized me up with steely blue eyes he replied, 'Why, thank you. You were great in *Dr Zhivago* [starring a young and extremely handsome Omar Sharif] . . . but you've let yourself go.'

Very important learning point number seven – humility. Never mess about with the greats when it comes to being humorous. They're always going to be funnier than you.

But it was on that particular film set where something miraculous occurred. As we finished one day – and I'll never forget those immortal words, 'That's a wrap on Brad, Robert and Omid' – the three of us were led through a marketplace in Casablanca to our waiting cars. It had not gone unnoticed that *The Mummy* was showing several times that week on the local film channel. This was the most popular channel in the country, watched consistently by an audience of two million a day. People in Casablanca were beginning to recognise me, and I must admit this was thrilling, especially as I spent most of my free time roaming the streets (so yes, it happened a lot, I made sure of that).

As we made our way through the market, I walked at a respectful distance behind the two blond bombshell film stars and observed them striding confidently past Moroccan folk who clocked them with a faint glimmer of recognition. With Redford it was 'he looks familiar'; with Brad Pitt, not as famous then as he is now, the Moroccans seemed to be thinking 'that face rings a bell' but still nothing. Suddenly their eyes fell on me and immediately lit up. 'Ya Allahhhh! Mumia! (The Mummy!)' and a crowd surged forwards. There is a photo somewhere of Pitt and Redford looking back to see what the commotion was all about and seeing me surrounded by an eager crowd, hyper-ventilating and signing autographs. Who needed the Mountview Theatre School panel now?

Learning point number eight: never bear grudges. Those

who reject you have their reasons, and better things come along.

Sobering learning point number nine: it's all ephemeral nonsense anyway.

Which leads me to crisis point number one: why have I written this book then?

OK, deep breaths, here's why: I read somewhere about the great landscape painter Turner who never painted scenes that actually existed. Instead he replicated a hedge from there, a stream from somewhere else, a tree, a stray dog, maybe some cattle. And he threw them all together to create a miraculous and healing view, so authentically lovely that art lovers were convinced of its existence and wanted to go there.

Unlike Turner, everything I've said is true and really happened. I hope I have created an emotional landscape that feels familiar to the reader regardless of whether or not they have worked as a medical translator, fallen into an Iranian cesspit, failed a bunch of exams, insulted Russell Crowe, narrowly escaped death by splishsplashsploshing or stumbled unwittingly into stand-up comedy.

As the great Desmond Tutu once said: 'My humanity is bound up in yours, for we can only be human together.'

I've been Omid Djalili and you've been a great audience. In the spirit of my first proper gig that night in Wimbledon where it all went wrong but somehow it was all right:

Can I start again?

EPILOGUE

It All Started In Edinburgh

'Lovers don't finally meet somewhere. They're in each other all along.'

Rumi

On an overcast day in August 1972 we piled into the car, all seven of us. We were going on a trip. Where was not explained. We were going away. That's all I knew.

Two elderly guests, the Rahmanis, travelled with our family. Mr Rahmani liked to entertain me by moving his dentures in and out of his mouth, a party trick he never tired of performing. In those days seven people crammed in a car for nine hours was not uncommon. It wasn't even illegal. Though cramped and uncomfortable, there was security that if we crashed we'd all be together to help each other out of the mangled wreckage.

We were on our way to Edinburgh, to see cousins, but also to see the Tattoo. Someone from my brother's school had gone to the Tattoo the week before, and my brother had been excitedly relaying second-hand descriptions. My parents decided on a whim to indulge him. It was most unlike them.

Edinburgh made little impression on me as a city but the Tattoo was indisputably loud and colourful. Some Japanese people sat near us, and seemed wide-eyed and delighted by the spectacle. Middle England was out in great numbers too; middle-aged people in comfortable shoes and light rainwear were clapping along to military bands and gasping with delight at confusing displays of strength from the various strands of the armed forces. Frankly I couldn't understand why so much energy was put into something that yielded so little. Aged seven I was already dishing out a two-star *Scotsman* review.

The day after the Tattoo, I felt even more disconsolate. We'd spent most of the afternoon in pointless en masse meandering around Edinburgh, ending up in a café at the top of the department store Jenners. Within seconds, a fiery argument broke out between my mother and Mr Rahmani – his dentures trick was pushing her over the edge. I decided to walk away and hide myself in the ladies' clothes that were on display in racks near the cafeteria. At least there I could have a bit of peace and quiet to concentrate on imagining I was somewhere else.

It probably wasn't even an argument, just Iranians speaking loudly in their own language with passion and animation. But this always embarrassed me because it made us the centre of attention. It felt particularly mortifying in Edinburgh where I was conscious that people seemed quieter and more genteel than Londoners.

Suddenly, I noticed a very twinkly little girl sitting at a table with two women who looked like a mother and a grandmother. The women were talking, but the little girl was staring at my noisy family, transfixed and alert, no doubt fascinated by the different language and volume levels of these exotic people. She spotted me lurking in the clothes rack and understood instantly that I was connected to them.

She smiled at me sympathetically, with kind blue eyes, and seemed to feel my anguish. I was grateful and smiled back. Feeling encouraged by this silent communication I pushed my luck and showed her the one and only skill I had mastered in life: moving my eyebrows up and down, not just together but individually. I wasn't sure, but I think this impressed her, because she smiled again and seemed about to laugh. Unfortunately, the next minute, the grandmother took the little girl's hand, and I heard her saying in a strange Scottish-sounding voice that it was time to leave. I sensed that they wanted to whisk her away from this odd little boy making eyebrow shapes.

I always remembered that twinkly little girl. I acknowledge that I am an incurable romantic and prone to elaborate flights of fancy, but I'm fairly convinced that she was the girl I married twenty years later.

Most important learning point of all: truth is stranger than fiction sometimes.

AND . . .

Love at first sight really does exist.

Thank you my beautiful Annabel.

Acknowledgements

It's always hard to write a thank you page, especially as in my view the people who serve as inadvertent anti-role models deserve to be thanked as much as those who have consciously exerted a positive influence. Both aspects have shaped my life.

Luckily, everyone who has helped me specifically with this book has been very generous. There are many names to mention, but I'll whittle things down as best as I can.

Firstly my sincere gratitude goes to the National Spiritual Assembly of the Bahá'ís of the UK.

I'd also like to thank my brother Javid and sister Roxana for not only helping me remember many of the colourful incidents from our childhoods, but also for assisting me with the photos, some of which were retrieved from the bowels of the storage rooms in the block of flats where my father still lives. I'm amazed anyone was able to locate them.

I'm extremely grateful to my father who, as a photographer himself, had the good sense to preserve all his photos, taken over a 65-year span, in fortified albums – not to mention those wrapped in J-cloths and bound with rubber bands.

My dear mother is no longer with us, but writing this book has made me appreciate her enduring influence on me, and I am immensely grateful to and proud of her.

I'd like to thank Paul Stevens at the literary department of Independent Talent who encouraged me sufficiently to think there was a need for this book (I'm still not sure there is – and if there isn't, Paul, it's your fault) and has been hugely supportive throughout the writing process. Profound thanks also to my editor Sarah Emsley at Headline, and my copy-editor Lindsay Davies.

Thanks to my old friend Shahin Sobhani, my self styled 'Chronicler', who started reading the manuscript but stopped, saying he would 'rather just read the book when it came out'. He obviously got bored but was too polite to say.

I also want to thank my dear friends Raymond and Furugh Switzer, as well as Simon Heathcote, who have all provided invaluable help and advice.

The brilliant Professor Bushrui deserves a special thank you. Since the age of seventeen, he has been both a whirlwind, and a silent influence in my life. He has also confirmed from reading extracts that my memory is, as he says, '100 per cent correct'.

I have to thank James and Grahame at the Bearcat comedy club who gave me my first ever five minutes as a stand up comedian all those years ago. After reading my letter asking them for a gig, I imagine you probably invited me down to do five minutes at the club out of sheer curiosity to see 'just who this Kebab plonker is'.

In the same vein I'd like to thank my manager Nigel Klarfeld at Bound & Gagged Comedy for sticking by me all these years (despite the confusion in 1997 when I thought you had been my manager for a year and you told me it was the first you had heard of it). Special thanks too for your immortal words of wisdom during a particularly grim Edinburgh festival, when I only had three people booked to see me one night: 'Omid, there's no business like no business. The show's a failure, we should never have come.'

Appreciations are also due to the vast array of weird and wondrous guests who frequented our family home throughout my childhood. They are an indisputable source of inspiration for this book.

Picture Credits

Section 3, page 1: © Neil Mockford/Getty Images; page 7, top right: Rex/© Universal/Everett; bottom right: © Rex/ITV

Index